# The Beginner's Guide to Investing

# The Beginner's Guide to Investing

## A Practical Guide to Putting Your Money to Work for You

# Richard Croft & Eric Kirzner

HarperBusiness
HarperCollins*PublishersLtd*

http://www.harpercollins.com/canada

First edition

Sample of a stock market page by permission of *The Globe and Mail*, Toronto, Canada

Text reviewed by G.G. Cunningham & Associates, North York, Ontario.

---

Canadian Cataloguing in Publication Data

Croft, Richard, 1952–
    The beginner's guide to investing : a practical guide to putting your money to work for you

"A HarperBusiness book".
Includes index.
ISBN 0-00-638476-5

1. Investments - Canada.   2. Finance, Personal - Canada.
I. Kirzner, Eric, 1945–   II. Title.

HG5152.C76  1997      332.6'78'0971     C96-931893-6

---

97 98 99 ❖ HC 10 9 8 7 6 5 4 3 2 1

Printed and bound in the United States

*To Stanley*
E.K.

*To my wife, Barbara, and my three children: Christopher (14),
Loa (11), and Machaela (4), whose personalities brought
the Nordal family to life.*
R.C.

# Contents

# List of Illustrations

# The Nordal Family Investment Club

My name is Loa Nordal. I'm named after my great grandmother who, I'm told, hailed from Iceland. A tenacious woman, she married, later divorced, and spent most of her adult life working as a nurse to support two daughters. She lived to the ripe old age of 90, and apparently I have many of her characteristics.

I am self-employed. In fact, I run a business, which, given my intense drive, is probably a good thing. I make chocolates—those sinfully delicious gourmet chocolates, individually wrapped with foil. I put in more 16-hour days than I care to remember in order to survive the start-up phase. But survive I did, and the business is on solid footing and growing.

The Nordal Family Investment Club has three members: myself, my older brother Chris, and our younger sister, Machaela. Chris is very conservative, particularly when it comes to investments. He sees a glass half empty, where I see it as half full. Well, that may be too harsh. He sees the risk where I only see the opportunity.

To be fair, Chris has good reason to be cautious. He is a professional, a dentist in fact, and has been at it for more than 10 years. He has a solid practice, earns a six-figure income, and has already set up a regular retirement savings program.

Machaela has been teaching at a high school for just over five years. She is the typical balanced investor, which fits her personality to a tee. Machaela has always been one who could see both sides of the picture. She has a unique ability to separate the wheat from the chaff, and I value her opinion on things because, more often than not, her views fall in between mine and Chris's—the two extremists. But then again, she can afford to approach things from both sides, because in her line of work she is blessed with a DBP—that's defined benefit plan—which for those of us on the outside, means she has a pension plan that vests 2% per year, up to a maximum of 70% of the average of her best five years' earnings. In other words, if over a 60-month span she averages $60,000 a year in earnings, and works the required number of years to qualify for the maximum pension, she would retire with a $42,000 annual pension (35 years of employment × 2% per year in vested earnings = 70% of $60,000—the average annual income) for the rest of her life.

And if that is not enough, the pension is indexed to the cost of living. So whatever standard of living she achieves at retirement is the standard of living she will enjoy for the rest of her life. Her DBP is a platinum retirement plan, as opposed to the gold plans that have no indexing provision. The point is, investing for retirement is not a necessity for her. Neither is the need to put aside enough money to maintain a happy life-style. Her long-term view to investing is much different than mine.

When it comes to my portfolio, I am an aggressive investor. I have to be, because I have no long-term pension plan to draw on. Whatever my retirement portfolio has when I am ready to sell my business is what I will have to live on when I retire. And I intend to retire in comfort.

It's safe to say that the promise of three-day work weeks and hours of leisure time that the economists predicted a decade ago will never come to pass. The reality of life today is that we're all working harder just to keep up with where we were five years ago. We're working harder, so we need to make our money work harder for us, too. Work requires blood, sweat, and tears. Sound investing requires education and information. I like to think that, in the investment game, information is the best offense and education the best defense.

We took the first step down the road to learning about money and investing by enrolling in a workshop taught by Richard Croft and Eric Kirzner who, among other things, were able to explain complex topics in straightforward, easy-to-understand language.

The lessons followed a step-by-step path that took us through the investment maze. Over 12 lessons, we covered many of the important aspects of investing. Those lessons are reproduced here.

*The Beginner's Guide to Investing* explains the real-life rules of the game, using examples. These lessons gave us the confidence to begin an investment program and take control of our destiny. Most importantly, we acquired the tools we need to get the most out of our investment dollars, including the knowledge about what questions to ask.

While *The Beginner's Guide to Investing* gave us an invaluable foundation, it also helped us recognize that there is no classroom setting that can take the place of real-world investing. That's why we started the Nordal Family Investment Club. Not formally, of course. It really started when we took the course. After each lesson, we would sit down over a cup of coffee to discuss what we had learned, what we found confusing, and how each lesson could be applied to our own investment portfolios.

And, looking back, it was those after-class discussions that really added value to our understanding of investment principles and the strategies to use when we began investing our money.

Now, what a course on investing leads to is building a portfolio. Think of a portfolio as a suitcase, full of different items. An investment portfolio is full of different kinds of investments, depending on what you want to—and don't want to—invest in.

Here's how our portfolios look. Terms such as Treasury Bill, cash asset, strip bond, fixed-income asset, money market fund, and Guaranteed Investment Certificate will be explained, as will many more.

## TABLE I.1: LOA'S PORTFOLIO

| Security | Value | Pct |
|---|---|---|
| Treasury Bills | $5,000.00 | |
| **Cash Assets** | **$5,000.00** | 5.00% |
| | | |
| Ontario Strip Bond ($20,000 face value) | $10.000.00 | |
| **Fixed-Income Assets** | **$10,000.00** | 10.00% |
| | | |
| Intel Corp. | $20,000.00 | |
| Microsoft Corp. | 20,000.00 | |
| CIBER Inc. | 5,000.00 | |
| Marathon Equity Fund | 15,000.00 | |
| Saxon Small-Cap Fund | 15,000.00 | |
| Templeton International Stock Fund | $10,000.00 | |
| | **$85,000.00** | 85.00% |
| | | |
| **Total Portfolio** | **$100,000.00** | **100.00%** |

## TABLE I.2: MACHAELA'S PORTFOLIO

| Security | Value | Pct |
|---|---|---|
| Money Market Fund | $5,000.00 | |
| Treasury Bills | 10,000.00 | |
| **Cash Assets** | **$15,000.00** | 15.00% |
| | | |
| Government of Canada Strip Bond ($50,000 face value) | $25,000.00 | |
| **Fixed-Income Assets** | **$25,000.00** | 25.00% |
| | | |
| Altamira Science and Technology Fund | $10,000.00 | |
| TD Greenline U.S. Equity Index Fund | 2,500.00 | |
| CIBER Inc. | 2,500.00 | |
| Saxon Small-Cap Fund | 10,000.00 | |
| Altamira Equity Fund | 12,500.00 | |
| Trimark Canadian Fund | 12,500.00 | |
| Templeton International Stock Fund | 10,000.00 | |
| | **$60,000.00** | 60.00% |
| | | |
| **Total Portfolio** | **$100,000.00** | **100.00%** |

## TABLE I.3: CHRIS'S PORTFOLIO

| Security | Value | |
|---|---|---|
| Guaranteed Investment Certificates | $15,000.00 | |
| Treasury Bills | 10,000.00 | |
| **Cash Assets** | **$25,000.00** | 25.00% |
| | | |
| Royal Bank Preferred Shares | $10,000.00 | |
| Government of Canada Strip Bond ($40,000 face value) | 25,000.00 | |
| **Fixed-Income Assets** | **$35,000.00** | 35.00% |
| | | |
| Standard & Poor Depositary Receipts (SPDRs) | $7,500.00 | |
| Toronto Index Participation Units (TIPs) | 7,500.00 | |
| Royal Bank of Canada | 10,000.00 | |
| Trimark Canadian Fund | 10,000.00 | |
| Templeton International Stock Fund | 5,000.00 | |
| | **$40,000.00** | 40.00% |
| | | |
| **Total Portfolio** | **$100,000.00** | **100.00%** |

*The Beginner's Guide to Investing* provided us with the knowledge, and the after-class cup of coffee gave us the real-world insights. I hope you find it as helpful as we did.

# Who Needs a Financial Plan, Anyway?

"Do I *really* need a financial plan?" Chris groaned in that raise-your-head-roll-your-eyes kind of way. "I mean, a financial plan is nothing more than a tax plan. And what tax breaks are left?" This wasn't a good sign, I thought. Our first class on financial investing was about to begin, and my brother was giving us attitude!

"Well," Machaela interjected, "there are those labor-sponsored funds, and perhaps ..."

"It was a rhetorical question, Machaela!" came Chris's flippant response. "Yeah, there are some unusual tax shelters, where I think you lose as much as you save in taxes. But really, aside from an RRSP, are there any reasonable long-term tax shelters left? Before you answer ... that, too, was a rhetorical question!

"And as far as RRSPs go"—it was clear that Chris was warming up on the subject—"if I hear anyone else telling me to put money into an RRSP, I'm going to start pulling my hair out."

"C'mon, Chris. We all enrolled in this investment program together, and the fact is that a financial plan plays the major role in any long-term investment strategy." I believe that—not that you need to pay someone for a basic financial plan, but that a plan provides the discipline you need to help save money.

A point that Machaela was quick to agree with. "Yes, Loa, a financial plan can help you budget, and that's important if you want to have any money left at the end of the day," she said. "Money, I might add, that you need for investment in the first place."

---

## Class in session ...

*Our teachers, Mr. Croft and Professor Kirzner, introduced themselves and explained they would take turns teaching the lessons. Mr. Croft led off, discussing the need for creating a financial plan.*

There's a lot of talk these days about financial planning. Every week, there are seminars being advertised in the financial press. "How to build a retirement nest egg!" "How to take money out of your RRSP—tax free!" "Ten fail-safe steps to a healthy, wealthy retirement."

If only it were so easy.

The one constant throughout these advertised seminars—and, I might add, the thrust of tonight's discussion—is the fact that we all need a financial plan. It isn't an option. So important is this issue that some companies provide their executives with professional financial-planning assistance—as an employee benefit, no less. The fact is, I cannot imagine a situation where gaining insight into your financial future would not be useful.

We all want to get out of the starting gate and on our way toward the retirement finish line. And most of us make no bones about our objective: we want to get wealthy along the way. Or at least wealthy enough so that we never have to work again. That requires planning. Without a reasonable financial plan, we cannot free up the funds necessary to embark on a successful investment program.

What a financial plan does, or should do, is examine your long- and short-term goals. Where do you want to be five years from now? How about 10 years?

Most of us have to worry about the basic survival issues—paying our rent or mortgage and putting food on the table—as well as educating our children, having adequate life insurance, and the budgeting of day-to-day living expenses. After we take care of those basic issues, what about a plan that provides an income when we're no longer working? If you are lucky, that time will come when you retire. If you are not so lucky, it may come sooner, as the result of corporate downsizing or, if you prefer the current catchphrase, "corporate rightsizing." Indeed, downsizing may be the motivating factor behind corporate financial-planning packages for top executives—a tool to smooth the way along a horizontal career path.

A horizontal career path amounts to a succession of lateral moves along the same pay scale, more days off, and attrition programs marked by incentive packages or edicts from above that keep reminding the workforce about the fear of the unknown. But I digress. The point is, and I hope you all agree, a financial plan is a not an option—it is a necessity.

## Starting an Investment Program

The focus of this class is not on the design or implementation of a financial plan. Professor Kirzner and I are here to show you how to begin an *investment* program. And an investment program is but one part of a financial plan. The goal of this discussion is to share some thoughts about the basics, introduce some of the tools of the trade, and expand on the things you should consider whether you do your own financial plan or do it with the help of a professional.

## Should You Use a Financial Planner?

Speaking of professionals, you've probably noticed a ground swell of financial planners offering financial advice. And the number of ways these planners are compensated only adds to the confusion when you're trying to choose between them.

For the record, planners generally work from one of three basic compensation schemes: commissions generated from products the planner sells, such as insurance products, mutual funds, and so on; a fee-for-service arrangement, where the consumer pays the freight in a fixed fee or hourly rate; or a combination of fees and commissions.

Fee-for-service schemes are relatively straightforward. You pay the planner for advice, you receive a financial blueprint, and in some cases, you go elsewhere to implement the plan.

By far the largest group are financial planners who earn income from commissions. There is nothing wrong with that method. However, some consumers feel that the amount of commission generated by a specific financial product may unduly influence the advisor to recommend that product over another. This is the so-called bias factor. On the other hand, a commission planner will be there to set up the plan, and then help with its implementation. Hand-holding has value, particularly if you are a nervous investor.

I'm not a big fan of financial planners who charge both fees and commissions. In my opinion, it confuses the issue. With this double-dip system, consumers are not always certain what role the financial planner is playing—advisor or salesperson. Paying a fee in return for a lengthy document that sets out a range of proposals, and then provides a list of products that are supposed to help you meet those goals, makes you think that maybe you should have your guard up. The problem is that you're not sure which front to protect.

With that in mind, it is important to set the ground rules at the outset. How much will it cost for what service? If I open an account with you, are you the one I will be dealing with, or will I be directed to an assistant? Does the financial planner offer tax-preparation services, and if so, at what cost? What about tax-planning and estate-planning issues? Can you find all of these services under one roof?

There is one other compensation scheme that offers an alternative approach to financial planning. Think of it as a sort of fee-offset plan, where financial planners charge a flat fee and also earn commission income.

This differs from the double-dip system I spoke of earlier because, in this case, any fees earned from commission income are subtracted from the fixed-fee component. This approach removes the bias from product selection and allows advisors the flexibility of using no-load and load products to meet your financial needs. But let's not get ahead of ourselves. We'll be talking about "loads" in our next lesson.

Finally, there's one thing you should remember at all times. Fees and commissions are negotiable. Don't hesitate to bargain for a better deal.

## The Do-It-Yourself Financial Plan

Now, what about the do-it-yourself approach to financial planning for those people who like to keep their calculators humming and their ink blotters full? For those who prefer to keep their financial affairs a private matter, we have some thoughts.

Most do-it-yourselfers have a long history of such endeavors. They will be the ones cutting their own grass, painting the family home, changing the oil in the car! Clearly, you gain a measure of independence and a sense of accomplishment by doing things for yourself. And for basic needs, that may be the best approach. I'm not sure, however, that trying to manage your own finances is always the right thing to do.

It is really a question of perception. How difficult a job is financial planning? What are the costs and the benefits? A lot of people think that building a financial plan is a lot like cutting grass—it requires more discipline than knowledge.

I'm not so sure. Setting a budget takes discipline, and truth be known, you probably don't need a financial planner standing over your shoulder telling you what percentage of your income should be used to pay for a roof over your head, or to tell you how much you can set aside for entertainment. You may not even want somebody commenting on budget issues.

That being said, there are other issues. Tax planning is also a discipline. But few of us have the wherewithal and knowledge to establish a long-range tax plan. Estate planning falls into the same category. Wills can be drawn up with a guide from your local office supply store, but really, do you feel comfortable drawing up such an important document by yourself, one that has implications for your family long after you're gone?

If you accept that perception differs from reality, then the issue of do-it-yourself or do-it-with-help is a question of degree. You might like to cut the grass, but would you feel comfortable landscaping the front of your house? You might not have a problem painting a room, but would you want to renovate your home? The bottom line with do-it-yourself financial planning is that you get what you pay for.

But I'm not here to judge. If you are set on preparing your own financial plan, here are some issues to consider. At the outset, you need to establish a set of goals. Sounds easy, but few people actually do much planning beyond the next 24 hours.

And you can't plan your future in a vacuum. You need to make some financial assumptions. How much will the cost of living be five, 10, or 20 years from now? What a $50,000 salary allows you to accomplish today will be much different than what a $50,000 salary will allow you to do in the distant future. The point is, any good financial recipe must include a key ingredient—a healthy understanding about the prospects for inflation.

Forecasting, in case you haven't heard, is a challenge in and of itself, especially when you look beyond the next five minutes. With inflation, it is one thing to assume a general increase in prices; it is quite another to forecast price changes for special interests that affect your personal financial plan.

For example, did you know that since 1990 the Canadian consumer price index has been rising, on average, about 3% per year? That would not have a major impact on your long-range forecasts. And on a macro level it gets better. Since the end of 1994, the increase in general consumer prices has been lingering below 2% per annum. "Wrestled to the ground" is, I think, the current party line from the federal government.

But consider this: college costs have risen about 6% a year for private institutions and 10% a year for public institutions. And they are still rising—something to do with a second-generation baby boom on the way. Baby boomers' babies! If you have kids, that's a special interest.

Medical costs have increased by more than 10% annually for most of the 1980s and, so far, well into the 1990s. If you are part of the sandwich generation—children on one side, parents on the other—that, too, is a special interest.

There are no set guidelines to deal with every individual financial plan, just thumbnail sketches you can use. If you are intent on forecasting inflation, figure on about 3% per year through to the turn of the century. After that, it's anyone's guess.

## And Then There Are Pensions ...

Which brings us to another consideration—retirement income. Remember the indexed Canada Pension Plan (CPP) the government promised all Canadians? A minimum retirement income supplement. I like to think of the CPP as a giant Christmas present; if you get it, great, but don't count on it.

There are a lot of problems with the CPP, the most noteworthy being the fact it is not fully funded, although recent changes to the level of payroll contributions is supposed to put CPP back on a solid footing. CPP payments come from the government's general account, which is reasonable, considering that all those CPP contributions that come off our paycheque every two weeks go directly into the general account.

The problem is that politicians were able to find ways of spending all the money in the general account. In fact, they were so good at it, they even found ways to spend money they didn't have.

To finance that high-end spending, we—as in Canadian taxpayers—created a mountain of IOUs, which economists define as the national debt. As opposed, of course, to the deficit we hear finance ministers talk about every year at budget time.

## Debts and Deficits Explained

For the record, the deficit is the difference between the amount of revenue governments take in over the course of a year versus the amount of expenses governments pay out over the year. If we have a federal deficit of, say, $25 billion—give or take $5 billion or so—then we spent $25 billion more than we took in during the year, and to cover that shortfall, the government borrows money, which is then added to the national debt. At last count, the national debt was well over $560 billion.

We've also begun to hear about a new twist in the deficit story. It's called the current account surplus. In recent years, the current account has gained a lot of press, as governments search for any statistic in which the word "surplus" can be prominently displayed.

The current account is essentially the government's operating budget, which looks at income and expenses *before* interest charges. The current account has been operating in a surplus for a some time now.

Without picking on or supporting any political persuasion, suffice it to say that governments at all levels have gotten better at balancing their operating budgets. That being said, they still have a ways to go before we see an overall surplus in any given year.

## A Surplus by Any Other Name

Now, we need to understand the difference between an annual surplus and a current account surplus. The current account only looks at revenue and expenses that are tied to government operations. Those are things like transfer payments to the provinces, salaries for government employees, CPP payments for retirees, health-care costs, defense spending, and so on. In other words, the expenses of running a government.

What the current account does not look at is interest expense. For example, the interest charges related to that $560 billion national debt we spoke of earlier. At last count, those annual interest charges were somewhere between $25 and $35 billion per year. When you include interest charges as a non-operational expense, it quickly turns the current account surplus into an overall deficit.

### Deficit Cutting—At What Cost?

The question, of course, is how much are you willing to contribute to solve this deficit problem. Looking at public opinion polls, it's clear that most Canadians think they are paying too much tax. Assuming you share that point of view, you need a plan to help reduce tax and you need a plan that tells you what after-tax income you can expect.

From a financial-planning perspective, expect to pay anywhere from 30% to 50% tax on your income (including interest income), about 25% less than that on capital gains, and about a third less on dividends.

And, finally, just to wrap up our discussion about inflation, it is safe to count on stocks to provide the best inflation-adjusted return. (That's the return after accounting for inflation. For example, if your investment earns 10% in a year, and consumer prices go up 3% during the year, your inflation-adjusted return is approximately 7%.)

Stocks have, on average, earned double-digit returns since the mid-1920s, about twice what you would expect to get from government bonds. And for the record, stocks are the only financial asset that has consistently beaten inflation over long periods.

## RRSPs—The Last Great Tax Shelter

Having set out some discussion points around a financial plan, we need to gain some insight into your current tax situation. If you can save money by paying less tax, that can be worth more than an investment in a hot new stock.

A financial planner is the person who is generally best equipped to provide information about paying taxes, setting budgets, and laying the bricks and mortar that will support a long-term wealth-building investment program.

Good financial planners should be able to design a long-term financial plan that makes liberal—no political connection intended—use of the limited tax advantages available to individual investors.

A discussion about Registered Retirement Savings Plans (RRSPs) should be one of the key elements in that blueprint and, by itself, could require a couple of pages in the financial plan. There are individual and spousal RRSPs, mutual fund RRSPs, Guaranteed Investment Certificate RRSPs, and self-administered RRSPs—enough types and investment options to frighten even the most sophisticated investor.

In fact, there are so many choices, it is important we spend a couple of minutes discussing some of the basics. Did you know, for example, that the RRSP is one of the few tax-related programs where Canadians are better off than Americans? Hard to believe ... but true!

In the U.S., there is a similar program called an Individual Retirement Account (IRA). U.S. taxpayers can contribute annually to an IRA—within certain prescribed limits—and once the money is inside, it compounds tax free.

But here's the catch: Americans cannot write off a contribution to an IRA! It wasn't always that way, however. In the early 1980s, Americans could get a tax deduction when contributing to an IRA and earn investment income on a tax-free basis with money inside the account.

When the tax deductibility of the contribution was eliminated, many in the financial business thought it spelled the end to IRAs as an investment option. Wrong! After a short period, word got out that the real advantage of any tax-sheltered investment program is the tax-free compounding of assets within the plan. Today, IRAs are still one of the most popular investment options for Americans who are saving for retirement.

So much for our American cousins; now back to the Canadian

advantage. Whether the Canadian government is motivated by the long-term economic benefits of a self-funding retirement program, or by the fear of a political backlash for meddling in the last tax haven, is a moot point. The fact is, we can still write off contributions to an RRSP, which makes investing in one a no-brainer.

Using a conservative tax rate, about half the money going into your RRSP is your own after-tax dollars; the other half is money that, if not contributed, would go to the government. And we haven't even discussed the merits of tax-free compounding inside the RRSP.

Say you own a $10,000 GIC earning 5%. On that GIC, you earn $500 a year in interest. If you earn that interest outside an RRSP, and assuming you are in the top tax bracket, you get to keep about $250. Inside the RRSP, you get to keep all of it.

Now the next year your money is going to earn more interest. Outside the RRSP, you now have $10,250 earning interest, which at 5% yields another $512.50 in annual interest income. Again, you pay half to the government.

Outside the RRSP, then, after the second year, you end up with $10,506.25 ($10,250 + $256.25 = $10,506.25), or about the same amount as you would have had inside an RRSP after only one year. Get the picture? Compute those numbers over a period of years, and the difference, even at 5%, is staggering (see Table 1.1).

## TABLE 1.1: GROWTH OF A GIC YIELDING 5% ANNUALLY

|  | Inside an RRSP | Outside an RRSP* |
| --- | --- | --- |
| **Initial Deposit** | $10,000.00 | $10,000.00 |
| End of Year 1 | 10,500.00 | 10,250.00 |
| End of Year 2 | 11,025.00 | 10,506.25 |
| End of Year 3 | 11,576.25 | 10,768.91 |
| End of Year 4 | 12,155.06 | 11,038.13 |
| End of Year 5 | 12,762.82 | 11,314.08 |
| End of Year 6 | 13,400.96 | 11,596.93 |
| End of Year 7 | 14,071.00 | 11,886.86 |
| End of Year 8 | 14,774.55 | 12,184.03 |
| End of Year 9 | 15,513.28 | 12,488.63 |
| End of Year 10 | 16,288.95 | 12,800.85 |
| End of Year 20 | 26,532.98 | 16,386.16 |
| End of Year 30 | 43,219.42 | 20,975.68 |

* Assumes a 50% personal tax rate.

### *Walking through the RRSP Maze*

RRSPs are not that complicated. Simply stated, an RRSP is nothing more than a safety deposit box, or a savings account if you prefer a bank-friendly comparison. We prefer the safety deposit box analogy, because you can actually put any number of investments into an RRSP (see Figure 1.1)—just as you can with a safety deposit box. You could, for example, hold mutual funds inside an RRSP. You could also hold GICs, stocks and bonds, and even your own mortgage if you structure it properly.

## FIGURE 1.1: RRSP-ELIGIBLE SECURITIES

**Safety Category**
Money market mutual funds
Treasury Bills
Canada Savings Bonds
Term deposits

**Income Category**
Government and corporate bonds
Real estate mortgages
Bond and mortgage mutual funds
Preferred shares
Income and dividend funds
Eurobonds

**Growth Category**
Common shares
Equity mutual funds
Royalty income trusts
Specialty mutual funds

**Other**
Gold bullion
Precious metal mutual funds
Warrants
Convertible bonds

**Foreign Securities (subject to 20%-at-cost rule)**
US$ money market funds
Foreign bonds
US$ preferred shares
Global and international bond mutual funds
Global and international equity mutual funds
Foreign common shares

If you have a GIC-RRSP, one of the types cited above, you can only put GICs into the RRSP safety deposit box. Presumably they will be GICs issued by the same bank that helped you open the RRSP in the first place. Now, an RRSP that only allows you to deposit GICs into it doesn't cost anything to administer. That's much different than a self-directed RRSP, where there is an annual administration fee, generally around $107 (a $100 fee plus $7 GST). So, at first blush, the GIC-RRSP looks attractive.

But is it? Comparing RRSPs on the basis of annual administration costs, I think, misses the point. Think about what the bank is doing with that GIC money. To a bank, the interest you are earning on that GIC is considered an expense. Presumably, the banks are using that GIC interest rate as the basis on which to set interest rates on personal and business loans. Want to know what the interest rate spread is? Just ask what the best loan rate is for a term similar to your GIC.

If, for example, you have a five-year GIC paying 5%, then the bank might be charging 9% for a five-year loan—depending of course, on what the loan is for. A new car loan fully secured by a GIC might only cost 9%, but a business loan might cost 12% or more. If you are able to generate a 9% return with investments that are not GICs, and if you have at least $10,000 inside a self-administered RRSP, then the $100 per year administration plus $7 GST cost is no longer relevant.

## The Self-Directed Advantage

Because of the financial advantages, the trend among baby boomers seems to be towards self-directed RRSPs. In light of the low returns available on GICs, investors have to look beyond traditional investments to meet their long-term goals. And a major part of that strategy means finding tax-sheltered investment vehicles in which to place those assets. Hence the movement toward self-directed RRSPs and self-directed Registered Retirement Income Funds (RRIFs).

Knowing that self-directed RRSPs and RRIFs are nothing more than a tax-sheltered safety deposit box, you realize just how easy it is to buy eligible investments such as stocks and bonds, GICs, equity mutual funds, money market funds, and bond funds. You can even deposit foreign equity funds up to the prescribed limits as defined under Revenue Canada guidelines. Currently, up to 20% of the book value of your assets within either an RRSP or an RRIF can be invested in securities that are domiciled outside Canada.

Even if you are just a GIC investor, there is an advantage to having a self-directed RRSP. One of the attributes of a GIC is the protection accorded by the Canada Deposit Insurance Corporation (CDIC), the government agency that protects your deposits in financial institutions. Some investors maximize CDIC coverage by using several financial institutions. With a self-directed RRSP, you can purchase GICs from several institutions and hold them in one self-directed plan. In terms of comfort, that may by itself be worth the administration fee.

Record keeping is also easier with a self-directed plan. Your records are kept intact under one roof, and your statements show all your GICs. That can be a big help when it comes to renewal time. A phone call to your financial advisor, or more likely a call from your financial advisor during renewals, will provide you with competitive GIC rates. More choice!

Another factor worth noting is that banks will not allow you to purchase GICs in their RRSP programs that mature after you reach the age of 69. The reason is that after age 69, Canadians have to begin taking money out of their RRSPs. The approach used by most Canadians is to turn their RRSP into an RRIF (Registered Retirement Income Fund), where a certain percentage of the assets — the percentages are established by Revenue Canada — must be drawn from the program annually. You can't, therefore, lock up your money for, say, five years in a GIC, if you have to take some of that money out before the end of five years. Hence the rule that forbids you from investing in GICs after age 69.

That, of course, is a drawback for the average holder who does not have a self-directed plan, because it breaks rule number one of GIC investing. The so-called "laddering" rule states that if you are going to hold GICs in your portfolio, then stagger your maturity. For example, have one GIC maturing in one year, another in two years, another in three years — hence the term laddering — and so on, so that you will always have money coming due to invest in new GICs at the prevailing rate of interest. With this strategy you'll be able to avoid having all your money locked into a long-term GIC at a low interest rate.

Then there is the question of fees. Fees are particularly important if you are going to hold mutual funds in your RRSP. Say you dropped into Altamira Investment Services and opened an RRSP. Into that RRSP you could deposit any one of 25 Altamira no-load mutual funds. In essence, that is also a self-directed RRSP, but the administration fee—remember that fee you pay for the self-directed RRSP—might be less than $53.50 per year. So why pay $107 if you can open a self-directed plan and pay less than $50 plus $3.50 GST?

Again, it comes down to an issue of choice. With the Altamira plan, you will only be able to buy Altamira mutual funds. It is just the same as in a GIC-RRSP—you can only buy GICs from that bank. If you want to hold, say, Trimark mutual funds in your RRSP, you need to open another RRSP with Trimark. And now you have two. Over time the pyramiding of your RRSPs can add to your administration costs. Interestingly, since the federal government no longer allows you to write-off the cost of RRSP administration fees, I notice more financial service companies offering no-fee RRSPs. Isn't capitalism wonderful!

But beware of the twists. Generally RRSP/RRIF-eligible mutual funds in Canada have an extra charge assessed for registered plans. But that charge is usually levied against the fund itself rather than the individual, so most investors don't see the charge and tend to ignore the costs. Once again, the alternative is a self-directed plan which holds all the mutual funds under a single trust arrangement. For the record, that's how accounts are administered at many financial-planning and stock brokerage operations.

## Self-Directed RRSP Concerns

Choice also has a cost. It's one thing to avail yourself of new investment vehicles, but it is quite another to understand the implications each investment brings to a portfolio. All too often, individual investors become overwhelmed with choice, and so they usually opt for the course of least resistance. That usually means GICs.

In some cases, you simply forget about monitoring your self-directed plan, because it's too much trouble trying to keep up to date on financial matters. But that can be a problem. Not rebalancing your portfolio over the course of a business cycle can mean missed opportunity, defeating the purpose of the self-directed plan.

Fortunately, this course will help you make informed decisions about investment alternatives, including mutual funds. And there, too, we come back to the important role a financial advisor can play in making sure your personal asset mix is rebalanced periodically, working with a defined set of principles.

## Foreign Content within a Self-Directed Plan

Inside an RRSP/RRIF, investors must invest at least 80% of their assets in securities or funds domiciled in Canada. That means you can hold foreign securities or mutual funds that invest in foreign securities, but they are limited to 20% of the total book value of the assets within your RRSP.

The "book value" concept is critical if you want to avoid paying additional taxes. And the taxes are steep, at 1% per month on the excess value of assets above the foreign content limit.

That book value concept can cause problems when you hold mutual funds in your self-directed plan. Most mutual funds distribute dividends and capital gains on an annual basis, usually at the end of the year. Most investors ask to have those distributions reinvested back into additional units of the fund and, by doing so, that alters the book value of the fund.

For example, suppose you hold $10,000 worth of the XYZ foreign fund, and for simplicity we'll assume the XYZ fund represents 20% of the book value in your self-directed plan. At the end of 1996, XYZ foreign fund declares a 20% distribution, which is reinvested into additional units. By reinvesting in additional units, you are effectively making a new purchase which raises the book value of your XYZ foreign fund to $12,000.

Again, for simplicity, we'll assume the other funds in your self-directed plan—that is, the $40,000 invested in Canadian domiciled assets—paid out a 10% distribution, raising their book value to $44,000. The self-directed plan now has a value of $56,000, which includes $44,000 of Canadian domiciled assets (representing 78.6% of the portfolio), and $12,000 in foreign assets (representing 21.4% of the portfolio). You will owe tax on the 1.4% of your portfolio that is over the 20% foreign content limit.

You and your financial advisor should monitor the foreign content in your self-directed plan to ensure that you don't exceed the limit within your overall portfolio. If foreign content is more than 20% of the book value of your self-directed plan, you have a choice: the excess assets can be sold and transferred to, say, a Canadian money market fund, or you could make an RRSP contribution to bring the foreign content into line. Alternatively, try to keep your foreign content at about 18% to leave a margin for safety.

This leads to yet another advantage of a single self-directed plan. If you hold a number of RRSPs at different institutions, you can only invest up to 20% in foreign content relative to the book value of that specific plan. Suppose you have five RRSPs with total assets of $100,000, and three of them are with mutual fund companies while two are at your local bank. If you have $10,000 in an Altamira RRSP, the most you can invest in one of Altamira's foreign funds would be $2,000. And the same is true for each of the five RRSPs; you could only invest up to a maximum of 20% of a particular RRSP into one of its foreign funds.

By consolidating all RRSP/RRIF investments into one self-directed plan, you could put as much as $20,000 into an Altamira foreign fund, into a Trimark International Fund, or any other foreign holding.

To summarize, self-directed plans offer a cost-effective approach to investment management, flexibility of investments, and the chance to earn superior returns over the long term.

# What Next?

Having established a financial plan, you have presumably calculated how much money you'll need at retirement, the effect inflation will have on your long-range plans, and the amount of insurance that is just right for you, and you have set in motion a reasonable tax plan. What then?

At this point, you have answered "how much," but you have yet to answer "how!" And therein lies the logic that supports the existence of so many professional financial planners and investment advisors.

The broad array of professional help allows you more choice than a delicatessen menu, ranging from financial advisors, financial planners, investment executives, registered representatives, stockbrokers, and investment dealers to mutual fund agents and insurance agents. Confused about who does what?

And then there are the questions. Can you get reliable tax advice from a financial planner? How about an estate plan from an insurance agent? What about portfolio management advice from a stockbroker?

Financial consumers—meaning all you folks with disposable income—are demanding more services from their financial advisors. The message is loud and clear: consumers don't want a financial planner, a banker, a trust agent, an estate lawyer, a stock broker, and an accountant. They would prefer to get all, or most, of the services under one roof. Hence the blurring of the lines between players.

If there is one element of consistency, it is that financial advisors are all attempting to do the same thing—help you invest your disposable income.

And speaking of that, we think one of the first things you should know about financial advisors is how they earn their income. Knowing that helps to level the playing field and helps you to make certain you get the advice you pay for.

## The Banker

Professionals such as lawyers and accountants are generally paid on an hourly, fixed rate. The more hours spent on a case, the more it will cost you. Bankers are paid a salary, and if there is a bonus structure, it is often related to the health and size of their loan portfolio. So a banker, for the most part, is keenly interested in making loans.

If you have enough of that disposable income, you can open a private banking relationship, which is offered by the major Canadian banks. In this case, you will be assigned an account representative who can help you structure your investment portfolio, arrange a line of credit, and provide a credit card.

When we talk about the structure of your investment portfolio, we are really talking about how much of your disposable income should go into stocks, how much into bonds and how much should be kept in short-term GICs or savings accounts. We think of each of those elements as assets within your portfolio, and the percentage of your wealth that is invested in any of the assets determines your asset mix.

## The Stockbroker

The stockbroker is an interesting character on the financial landscape. Stockbrokers earn commissions when you buy and sell stock. As you probably have already guessed, stock brokers promote stock. They will tell you why this one is a good investment or why that one is not a good investment. They also trade bonds, GICs, and mutual funds, not to mention options and futures contracts, something beyond the scope of this course.

In the past 20 years, there has been a change in the mindset of stock-brokers. Now you hear the terms "investment executive," "financial advisor," or "registered representative" to describe a stockbroker. The marketing approach is straightforward—let's broaden the appeal of a stockbroker by including some financial planning. And the fact is, some stockbrokers do provide financial-planning advice. Those that do usually have a Chartered Financial Planner (CFP) designation. Look for that designation, because it is one of the few courses that financial advisors can take to give them some insight into financial-planning issues.

## And Then the Financial Planner ...

Finally, we come to the financial planner, which in the best case is an individual who can provide answers on a broad range of financial, tax, and estate issues. Sometimes, they are simply mutual fund sales agents. Most, although not all, financial planners are only allowed to buy and sell mutual funds and, in some cases, bonds. If you want individual stocks in addition to mutual funds, you need a stockbroker. We've already discussed the various ways that financial planners make their money—commissions, fee-for-service arrangements, or a combination of both.

## Speaking of Stocks, What about Discount Brokers?

One of the questions I am often asked is whether using a discount broker makes sense. Discount stockbrokers, like Toronto Dominion Green Line Investors Services, will buy or sell stocks, bonds, or other securities at a lower commission rate than would be charged by so-called full-service stock brokerage firms. What the discount broker is doing is eliminating the middleman. The middleman in this case is the stockbroker or the registered representative or investment executive.

Whether you should use a discount broker comes down to a very basic question. Do you need advice and help from experts with whom you have a relationship, or do you get your own advice from published sources?

Most investors fall into both camps. A lot of do-it-yourself investors get into trouble because they receive conflicting advice from published sources. Not surprising, really! Getting two economists to agree that the sun will come up tomorrow would mean prefacing the remarks with phrases like "all things being equal." Even investors who receive "expert" advice may hear conflicting stories.

The bottom line is this: if you are comfortable making your own investment decisions and are not willing to pay extra for independent advice, a discount broker will usually be your least expensive option. That being said, even full-service brokers will often negotiate their commission rates if asked.

One final word on the subject from U.S.-based *Worth* magazine: "If you want to consult a professional about what to buy, then you can either work with a fee-only financial planner and have the transactions handled through a discount broker, or you can work with a stockbroker or financial planner and have the higher commissions pay for the advice. In any case, you should not pay a fee or commission simply for the privilege of being sold. Make sure you are getting real value for the money you pay an advisor, no matter what form the payment takes."

The do-it-yourself approach can often work for some people who are prepared to put the time into it. But the research shows that it pays to use professional financial advice.

Now, that wraps up tonight's lesson. Next week we'll talk about assets—what they are and what they mean for building a wealth-creation program.

### *At the coffee shop ...*

Machaela led off the discussion when we'd settled down with tea, coffee, and muffins.

"I always thought RRSPs were an investment. Now I find out they are some sort of holding tank, like a safety deposit box."

"To tell you the truth, until this class, I never really understood what Registered Retirement Savings Plans were all about. I would visit my bank, and quite frankly that experience would leave me more confused than when I went in. For one thing, I always thought that if you wanted to take money out of an RRSP, you had to cash in the whole RRSP. Because of that, I have five different RRSPs at five different financial institutions, and they all have GICs in them."

"Talk about bookkeeping," I replied, sipping my cappuccino. "I have enough problems keeping track of my business bank account. In any event, that is no longer the case, because you can withdraw as much as you want from an RRSP at any time. You will simply pay tax on the amount you withdraw, at your current tax rate. I know—I had to draw money out a few years ago to help me carry the business through a slow period."

"On the other side," Chris intervened, "it doesn't cost you anything to administer an RRSP that only holds GICs. You don't have to fork over an administration fee every year which, by the way, is no longer tax deductible."

"That's a good point," said Machaela, "but it fails to take into account the rather dismal return I am getting on GICs. My return on all GICs averages 6%. I have $50,000 in GICs, and that means my RRSP generates $3,000 a year in income. If I can hold other securities in my RRSP such as a mutual fund or a stock, and I were able to earn, say, 10%, then I would earn an extra $2,000 per year, and only have one RRSP to worry about. A $100 administration fee ..."

"Plus seven dollars for the GST ...," Chris interjected.

"Yes, plus seven dollars for the GST," Machaela continued, "but that still pales in comparison to the extra return I would be able to get on my investments. The trick, of course, is to find investments that will give me that extra return, and to find a financial advisor to help me choose."

"Yeah, that's another big issue," I suggested, "trying to find someone you can work with, who can help you do the things you want."

"From my perspective, the most important issue is tax and estate planning," said Chris. "I have enough to contend with in my dental practice, I need someone who can take control of my finances and who can direct me for the long term."

"It sounds like you need a financial planner, or at least a stockbroker who can offer financial-planning advice. Look for that ... what did he call that? The initials were CFP ...," wondered Machaela.

"You mean the Chartered Financial Planner designation," I replied.

"Yeah, that's it! That's the designation of someone who presumably wants to offer financial-planning advice. There are probably other designations that are just as useful. For example, I remember reading the other day about the Canadian Investment Management program sponsored by the Canadian Securities Institute, which also offers some financial-planning education."

Chris joined in. "But I think that's aimed mostly at stockbrokers. In fact, I think they are mandated to complete that course during their first two years in the business."

"So will all stockbrokers offer financial-planning advice?" I asked.

Chris rejoined, "Not necessarily. It's one thing to take a course, but it's quite another to hang out a shingle that says you specialize in that area. I'm sure most stockbrokers will do what they do best ... sell stock!"

"Makes sense, considering a stockbroker earns commission when you buy a stock and again when you sell the stock," Machaela said.

"So you still have to keep up your guard, even with a stockbroker?" I wondered aloud. "In this case, you needn't be concerned about whether or not the stock the broker is recommending is good, but rather if the broker is encouraging you to buy and sell in order to generate commissions."

"Well, I think you might want to beware of the stock the broker is recommending as well," suggested Chris. "Buying shares of the Fly-by-Night gold mine might not be in your best interest. If I understand the message that was being conveyed in tonight's lesson, it is that all investments should be viewed within the context of where you are now and where you want to get to."

"Well, I suppose the next step is to understand what kinds of investment options are available," Machaela said.

# Understanding the Two Asset Classes—Household and Investment

As I watched Christopher enter the classroom, I observed that he really is a striking character. He has the strong bearing and confident air of someone who gets his teeth into something and won't let go. Boy, I'm sharp tonight. A dental pun without even thinking about it! Anyway, it is evidence, I think, of his disciplined approach to life.

These are personality traits that I've never quite understood. Sure, I too am dedicated to my business. But I'm willing to take risks—maybe because I have to. It's all I know. Chris, on the other hand, doesn't have to take risks. Over time his professional income will give him financial independence. Perhaps his investment personality best fits a person with conservative tastes. Perhaps he is not someone who needs to expand his asset base; it will simply come with time.

His discipline has taught him to ask questions. I envy that. Not because I don't have the same desire to learn, but because I am too stubborn to ask. Don't want to ask the teacher one of those dumb questions. Same as Machaela, really, except she doesn't ask because she is simply too polite to take up the class's time. Fortunately, Chris has enough questions for the three of us, and by the end of every session, we all have a good idea about what is being discussed.

It didn't take Chris long to speculate about our next lesson ...

"I've heard lots of talk about assets. And I've got to tell you, I have no idea what people are talking about. I mean, what is an asset? And what is this talk about asset mix, asset class, asset allocation? The only assets I know about are my BMW, my house, and that friendship ring I got from Millie back in high school."

"You've still got that ring?" Machaela asked. "My God, you haven't seen her for a long time. Didn't she move a couple of years ago?"

Chris and Millie had a thing going in high school. That friendship ring was worth more than $100, a lot of money for a high school student. And he still had it.

After graduating from high school, however, Chris stayed home and attended college in Toronto while Millie went to B.C. to finish her studies at Simon Fraser University. Absence did nothing to make their hearts grow fonder, and when she returned from university, they never rekindled the friendship.

"Yeah, I've still got it, and yes she moved a couple of years ago. What's that got to do with the point at hand?" Chris retorted. "What the heck is an asset?"

I had a feeling that Professor Kirzner was about to tell us as he moved to the front of the class and perched himself comfortably on the edge of the desk.

## *Class in session* ...

Tonight we're going to talk about assets. Now, when I talk about assets, I am talking about things you own that have value. Not the picture of your wedding or of your child's first steps. Those are invaluable pieces of your life, but are not of value to someone else.

In terms of your personal statement of worth, assets must have value to you *and* to someone else. Ideally, your assets should be worth more than your liabilities, which defines what we owe, presumably collateralized by an asset. There are two basic kinds of assets, which we will define as (1) household or consumer assets, and (2) investment assets.

A car is a household asset, and so are your appliances and your furniture. You also own clothes, but we don't normally think of clothing as being a household asset because, aside from the fact your clothes might look good on you, they have very little value to someone else.

We also own assets that have value only in terms of what they are worth to someone else. For example, a five-dollar bill is simply a piece of paper. It has no value as paper, but as we will learn in the next lesson, it is an important attribute of modern-day commerce.

The five-dollar bill does have value as a medium of exchange, which gives it value in terms of what it can buy from someone else. We consider the five-dollar bill as an investment asset. A small investment asset mind you, but an investment asset nonetheless.

For anything we own to be seen as an investment asset, it must satisfy two conditions: (1) the asset must have tangible value in that it can be readily exchanged for something else, and (2) your only motivation for holding this asset is to enhance your wealth.

Using our two-condition model, could a car be considered as an investment asset?

Now, a car certainly has tangible value, but it does not enhance your wealth. It depreciates and is expensive to drive, maintain, and repair.

Having said that, certain cars are collectibles. These are vintage cars which can actually increase in value over time. For example, Jay Leno, host of "The Tonight Show," has a warehouse full of mint-condition vintage cars. Does this mean a car qualifies as an investment asset?

The answer is that while these vehicles may actually increase in value, that by itself does not change the position that cars are a household asset. Classic/vintage car collecting simply does not satisfy our second condition (that the only reason for holding the asset is to enhance your wealth). Most people who collect classic/vintage cars do so because they like classic/vintage cars. That those cars might actually appreciate in value is a secondary issue.

Much of our discussion on cars could also be applied to furniture. Normally, furniture depreciates over time. The exception, of course, is antique furniture which can actually appreciate in value. But like our vintage car example, that fact alone does nothing to change our view that antiques are not investment assets.

## Household Asset Classes

Let's look at how we can classify assets. To construct a personal statement of worth, let's start by building a table that defines various household asset classes (Table 2.1).

### TABLE 2.1: PERSONAL STATEMENT OF WORTH

**Household Asset Classes**
Vehicles
Furniture
Jewelry
Principal Residence

As to owning your principal residence, many people believe that real estate is a sound investment, and there's no question that the family home is the largest single asset for most Canadian families. It's also true that, over time, the family home will normally appreciate in value, leading some financial writers to talk about the family home as an investment, rather than as a place to live. So I recognize that we are drawing a fine line, especially in light of the fact that profits from the sale of your principal residence are tax free.

However, in light of the two-condition model for investment assets, the family home doesn't cut the mustard. The family home simply does not satisfy our second condition, in that the most important reason for owning a principal residence is to have a roof over your head and a place to raise a family. That value exists independently from its ability to create wealth, meaning the family home is a household asset.

### Underlying Possessions

We can extend our definition of household assets to include the actual underlying possession. The Dodge station wagon listed in Table 2.2, for example, is a possession that we classify in our personal statement of worth as a vehicle. If there are two people working in your family, you may own two cars. The BMW sedan is also a possession and is also classified as a vehicle under the household asset category.

The same scheme applies to the diamond necklace, the gold watch, the leather-backed chair—each represents a possession underlying your household asset classes. If we extend our definition of household asset classes to include the underlying possessions, your personal statement of worth might look something like this:

## TABLE 2.2: EXTENDING YOUR PERSONAL STATEMENT OF WORTH

**Household Assets**
**Vehicles**
    Dodge station wagon
    BMW sedan
**Furniture**
    Leather-backed chair
    Appliances (washer/dryer/fridge)
    Queen-size bed
    Coffee table
**Jewelry**
    Diamond necklace
    Gold watch
**Principal Residence**

Now that we have divided your household assets into asset classes and underlying possessions, we have the necessary framework to move to the next step, which is determining the mix of your household assets.

Your household asset mix describes what percentage of your personal statement of worth is tied up in the Dodge station wagon, what percentage in the BMW, the diamond necklace, and so on. We are simply putting a price tag on each of the possessions and then weighting that in terms of the total value of all your household assets.

Let's see now—the Dodge station wagon is worth $2,500, the BMW about $16,000. The diamond necklace is worth $1,000, the gold watch $500. Now, pay attention to the following table.

## TABLE 2.3: DETERMINING YOUR HOUSEHOLD ASSET MIX

**Household Assets**
**Vehicles**

| | | |
|---|---|---|
| Dodge station wagon | 2,500.00 | |
| BMW sedan | 16,000.00 | |
| **Total Vehicle Assets** | **$18,500.00** | **15.18%** |

**Furniture**

| | | |
|---|---|---|
| Leather-backed chair | 250.00 | |
| Appliances (washer/dryer/fridge) | 1,250.00 | |
| Queen-size bed | 350.00 | |
| Coffee table | 50.00 | |
| **Total Furniture Assets** | **$1,900.00** | **1.56%** |

**Jewelry**

| | | |
|---|---|---|
| Diamond necklace | 1,000.00 | |
| Gold watch | 500.00 | |
| **Total Jewelry Assets** | **$1,500.00** | **1.23%** |

| | | |
|---|---|---|
| **Total Household Assets** | **$121,900.00** | |

From Table 2.3, we see that the total value of all the household assets on your personal statement of worth is $121,900. The cars are worth $18,500, which is 15.18% of the total household assets. The furniture accounts for 1.56% of all household assets, and of course the principal residence accounts for 82.03% of the household assets. Table 2.4 describes your current household asset mix.

**TABLE 2.4: YOUR HOUSEHOLD ASSET MIX**

| | |
|---|---|
| Vehicle Assets | 15.18% |
| Furniture Assets | 1.56% |
| Jewelry Assets | 1.23% |
| Principal Residence | 82.03% |
| **Total Household Assets** | **100.00%** |

Now, a question many people ask is, "Do I really need to know what my household asset mix is in order to become reasonably adept at investing?"

Believe it or not, understanding how you allocate money to personal assets can tell you a great deal about your investment personality. For example, the percentage of money you commit to each class within the household asset mix speaks volumes about your life-style. If, for example, your car represented the largest single component of your household asset mix, you would have a very different personality, or be at a different stage in your life cycle, from the person in our example.

## Investment Asset Classes

In essence, the household asset mix illustrates the approach we will take to categorize your investment assets. We have already defined investment assets as having value and whose sole purpose is to enhance your wealth. Investment assets can enhance wealth in one of three ways: (1) interest, dividend, or rental income, (2) capital gains resulting from the sale of the asset for more than you paid for it, or (3) a combination of both capital gains and income.

One long-standing investment metaphor is that of the fruit and the tree. We think of capital as the tree. If the tree produces fruit, we think of that as income—the fruit is analogous to interest or dividends or rent or other such payments.

In many cases, however, the tree will not produce fruit for many years, spending the early years growing in size (effectively enhancing your wealth through capital gains). And, finally, the tree may grow and produce fruit, satisfying our goal of wealth creation from two fronts.

Investment assets can be divided into four broad classifications (see Figure 2.1).

## FIGURE 2.1: INVESTMENT ASSET CLASSES

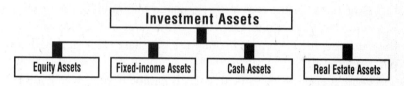

Again, as we did with our household asset classes, we can extend our definition of investment assets to include the underlying securities. Note that we use the term *securities* rather than *possessions* when breaking down the component parts of our investment asset classes.

Canada Savings Bonds, for example, are a type of security that would beclassified as a cash asset. Also considered a cash asset, but with a looser definition, are Guaranteed Investment Certificates (GICs). We will discuss GICs at length in a future lesson. Government and corporate bonds are considered fixed-income assets, because they can provide both income and capital gains. Again, we'll talk more about bonds down the road.

When we talk about real estate as an investment, we are thinking in terms of commercial or investment properties, real estate mutual funds and real estate investment trusts (REITs).

Investment properties might include a triplex that you own and collect rent from, or perhaps a commercial building. If you don't live in the building, then your only motivation for holding the real estate is to earn a profit. The rationale for owning the property is strictly motivated by the potential for wealth creation.

It is the same situation with real estate investment trusts. REITs typically represent ownership in real estate projects or, in some cases, mortgages on commercial or residential properties. REITs trade on an exchange just like the stock of Gerneral Motors, IBM or Bell Canada. REITs are different because, instead of owning part of a company that manufactures automobiles or computers or provides telecommunication services, you own shares of a company that invests in real estate. Profits are distributed to shareholders in the form of dividends. The profits represent the amount of rental income that is in excess of the cost of carrying and maintaining the properties in the trust's portfolio. Of course, if the value of the properties in the trust rise, then it is possible that the per share value of the REITs will rise as well.

The final class of investment assets is equity. If you own shares of General Motors, that would be considered a security classified as an equity asset. So, too, would shares of IBM or a good Canadian mutual fund that invests in stocks.

Now, we'll look at how we extend investment assets.

## FIGURE 2.2: EXTENDING YOUR INVESTMENT ASSETS

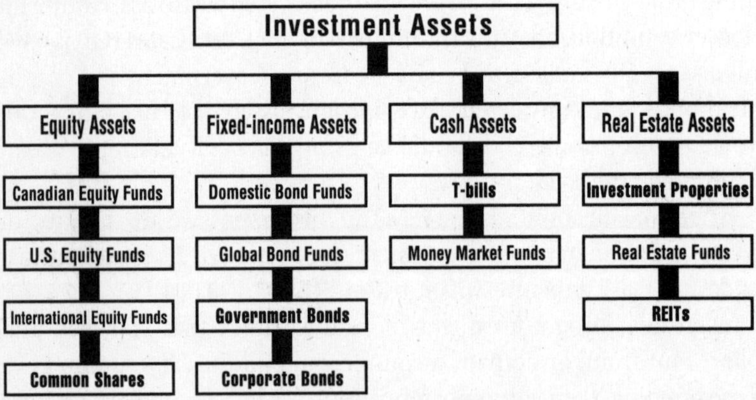

```
                        Investment Assets

   Equity Assets    Fixed-income Assets    Cash Assets    Real Estate Assets

 Canadian Equity Funds  Domestic Bond Funds    T-bills    Investment Properties

  U.S. Equity Funds    Global Bond Funds    Money Market Funds   Real Estate Funds

 International Equity Funds  Government Bonds                      REITs

   Common Shares       Corporate Bonds
```

Returning for a moment to our tree and fruit analogy, we need to understand the total return we attach to each investment security. In point of fact, it is the combination of the tree's fruit (income) and size (growth) that provides us with the total return. The total measure of investment performance, then, reflects all sources of wealth creation—interest income, rental income, dividends, and capital gains—from our investment assets.

To understand total return, consider an investment asset you buy for $10 a unit. You earn 50 cents in interest income, receive a 25-cent dividend, and sell the unit for $11.00. You will have realized a total return of $1.75 (50 cents interest + 25 cents dividend + $1.00 capital gain) or 17.5% before commissions.

There are an infinite number of ways of earning 17.5% on an investment (see Table 2.5). Remember that after tax a dollar of dividend income is worth more than a dollar of interest income. And depending on your tax bracket, a dollar of capital gain is the most tax efficient way to collect income.

## TABLE 2.5: METHODS OF EARNING TOTAL RETURN

| Security | Purchase Price | Interest Income | Dividend Income | Current Price | Total Return |
|---|---|---|---|---|---|
| | ($) | ($) | ($) | ($) | (%) |
| A | 10.00 | 1.75 | nil | 10.00 | 17.5 |
| B | 10.00 | nil | nil | 11.75 | 17.5 |
| C | 10.00 | nil | 1.75 | 10.00 | 17.5 |
| D | 10.00 | 1.00 | nil | 10.75 | 17.5 |
| E | 10.00 | nil | 1.00 | 10.75 | 17.5 |
| F | 10.00 | .50 | .25 | 11.00 | 17.5 |
| etc. | | | | | |

Higher returns also mean higher risks. So it is important to understand that risk and return are two sides of the same coin. Higher return means higher risk. The security market line in Figure 2.3 graphically displays the risk-return trade-off for various types of securities.

## FIGURE 2.3: SECURITY MARKET LINE

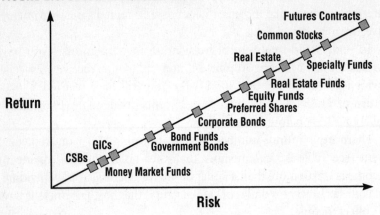

## The Importance of Your Investment Asset Mix

While it might not be necessary for you to break down the components of your household assets, it is in your interest to understand how your investment assets break down. That is, to understand what percentage of your investment assets are in equity, what percentage in fixed income, what percentage in cash, and what percentage in real estate.

Continuing with our personal statement of worth theme, let's examine the investment asset mix of a hypothetical investor. We'll assume, in this case, that our investor has $1,000 in a savings account, $2,500 in CSBs, a government bond worth $2,000, and 100 shares of Consolidated Beltways at $20 per share. The investment asset mix is displayed in Table 2.6.

## TABLE 2.6: INVESTMENT ASSET MIX

### INVESTMENT ASSETS

**Cash Assets**

| | | |
|---|---|---|
| Savings account | $1,000.00 | |
| Canada Savings Bonds | 2,500.00 | |
| **Total Cash Assets** | **$3,500.00** | **46.67%** |

**Fixed-Income Assets**

| | | |
|---|---|---|
| Government bond | $2,000.00 | |
| **Total Fixed-Income Assets** | **$2,000.00** | **26.67%** |

**Equity Assets**

| | | |
|---|---|---|
| Consolidated Beltways | $2,000.00 | |
| **Total Equity Assets** | **$2,000.00** | **26.67%** |

| | | |
|---|---|---|
| **Total Investment Assets** | **$7,500.00** | **100.00%** |

Understanding your investment asset mix is critical for building wealth because that mix has an important bearing on your overall return. Just how important? Studies have shown that 85% (some studies have suggested as much as 90%) of your overall return can be pegged to your asset-mix decision, another 5% to 10% comes from market timing (that is, shifting in and out of investments in response to economic changes), and the remaining 5% to 10% from selecting one specific security over another (for example, buying IBM rather than General Motors, or Microsoft rather than Northern Telecom).

In other words, by determining what percentage of your portfolio is committed to fixed-income assets, what percentage to equity assets, and what percentage to any other asset class, you have laid the basis for controlling 85% of your total return. To make the point, consider a hypothetical two-asset portfolio that includes a portfolio of stocks from around the world, and a portfolio of fixed-income securities.

For the 10-year period between January 1987 and mid-1996, Canadian fixed-income assets returned 8.60% compounded annually. A $10,000 investment in fixed-income assets more than doubled (to $22,819) over that period of time.

Over the same period, a broadly based portfolio of stocks from around the world grew by 10.70% compounded annually. In other words, a $10,000 investment would have been worth $27,636 by mid-1996.

Note what happens when we mix and match these two investment assets in a personal portfolio (Table 2.7). The end value of the investment changes dramatically as the asset mix changes.

## TABLE 2.7: THE IMPACT OF THE ASSET-MIX DECISION

|  | Equity Assets | Fixed-Income Assets | Compound Annual Return | Value of $10,000 Investment after 10 Yrs. |
|---|---|---|---|---|
| Portfolio A | 100% | 0% | 10.70% | $27,636.07 |
| Portfolio B | 80% | 20% | 10.28% | $26,605.26 |
| Portfolio C | 60% | 40% | 9.86% | $25,609.20 |
| Portfolio D | 50% | 50% | 9.65% | $25,123.86 |
| Portfolio E | 40% | 60% | 9.44% | $24,646.82 |
| Portfolio F | 20% | 80% | 9.02% | $23,717.11 |
| Portfolio G | 0% | 100% | 8.60% | $22,819.09 |

Forgetting for the moment that Portfolio G, made up entirely of fixed-income assets, would have provided a decent retirement nest egg over the period in question, look at what happens when we move from Portfolio G to Portfolio D, which is made up of 50% equity assets and 50% fixed-income assets. Portfolio D returned 9.65%—an improvement based entirely on the asset-mix decision, rather than the selection of particular securities. Your $10,000 investment in January 1987 would have been worth $25,123.86 by mid-1996. That one decision, made 10 years ago, was worth an extra $2,304.77 to your pocketbook.

More importantly, incremental returns that are produced through the right asset mix go beyond year-over-year excess returns, because changes in compound return will compound over time. The $10,000 invested in Portfolio D is worth 10.09% more than Portfolio F at the end of the 10-year period.

If we assume the returns from each portfolio continue into the future, at the end of twenty years, Portfolio D would be worth 63,121.08, compared with $52,071.08 for Portfolio G. At the end of 20 years then, Portfolio D would be worth 21.2% more than Portfolio G. That's what I mean when I say the difference in compound returns will also compound over time.

## Reducing Risk through Diversification

Another major issue to consider when thinking about mixing and matching investment assets is the role diversification plays in risk reduction. Take a look at Figure 2.4, a version of the security market line that focuses only on fixed-income and equity assets.

**FIGURE 2.4: SECURITY MARKET LINE**

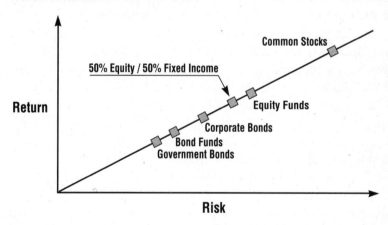

Note the risk associated with common stocks (equity assets) versus the risk associated with bonds (fixed-income assets). If you were to build a portfolio that looked like Portfolio D—50% stocks, 50% bonds—you would reduce the risk associated with having 100% of your money in stocks. The 50/50 split between equity and fixed-income assets would move you down the security market line. Your total return might decline slightly (as seen in Table 2.7), but so too would your risk. Such is the role diversification plays in the management of your portfolio.

Since diversification is such an important aspect of investing, this is probably a good time to introduce mutual funds and the role they play in your portfolio.

## Understanding Diversification and Risk Reduction

In the late 1970s and early 1980s, discussion about diversification inevitably focused on investments in the stock market. The idea that you should not have all your eggs in one basket meant that you should own shares of companies in different industries. Through diversification you could reduce company-specific risk. *Company-specific risk* is a term used to define risks unique to companies. For example, a company's profitability could be affected by poor management decisions, an adverse decision on a lawsuit, or a labor strike.

By purchasing a portfolio of, say, 30 distinct companies in different industries, you could eliminate up to 95% of company-specific risk, which is the principal reason for buying a mutual fund that invests in stock—instant diversification with one purchase.

Note on the security market line how mutual funds in each category are generally less risky than the individual securities. For example, in figure 2.3, an equity fund, which is simply a mutual fund that invests in stocks, is less risky than the individual common stocks.

The stock market crash on October 19, 1987, emphasized the need to revisit preconceived views about diversification. What became apparent in the aftermath of the crash was that even diversified stock portfolios were at risk and that investors could be subjected to substantial bouts of volatility. That revelation led to broader acceptance of a strategy known as asset allocation and a deeper understanding of the role the investment asset mix plays in your investment success. Taking the basket-and-egg theory one step further, the asset-allocation strategy means putting your eggs not only into various stock-market baskets, but also into other asset types.

## Understanding Mutual Funds

What are mutual funds? Well, mutual funds are investment companies that pool the resources of individual investors and use those resources to buy securities. The ownership of the total portfolio is shared proportionally by all investors, on the basis of what they have put into the fund. It's not that different from a condominium, where each apartment dweller owns a piece of the whole building, not just his or her own square footage.

Mutual funds are set up to invest in many types of securities. Some buy shares of stocks (known as equity mutual funds), others invest only in fixed-income securities (known as bond funds), or focus on a specific sector of the economy (as in specialty or sector funds).

Technically, mutual funds both sell shares directly to the investors and buy shares directly from the investors. If you want to sell your shares, the open-ended fund will redeem them at their net asset value per share; that is, what they are valued at, at that particular moment. If you want to buy additional shares, they will be issued by the fund. Again, you will buy them at the net asset value. Net asset values are usually calculated on a daily basis. Mutual funds are open-ended, hence their capitalization is not fixed. New shares can be issued based on the demands of the marketplace.

Mutual funds can provide solutions to many different aspects of the investment decision-making process. In fact, they represent a one-stop approach to investment. A mutual fund can help you make asset-allocation decisions (the percentage of funds to be invested in equity assets versus fixed-income assets), weighting decisions in the stock market (the degree of exposure to the 14 groups that make up the TSE 300—mines, oils, financial companies, and so on), and market-timing decisions (when to be in the market/when to be out), all at once.

The TSE 300 is short for the Toronto Stock Exchange Composite Index of 300 stocks that is used to measure overall stock market performance. We'll explore the stock market later, once we have a grounding in assets and asset allocation.

Now, because mutual funds are professionally managed, they offer the individual investor the benefit of sophisticated decision making, without the trouble of learning the background to that decision-making process.

Mutual funds give you diversification within an asset class. A relatively small amount can be spread around a great deal of investment activity. Funds can also permit you the luxury of being wrong about a single investment or class of investments, because returns are smoothed out over a wider range of possibilities.

## To Load or Not to Load?

Investors are faced with a bewildering array of mutual fund products. One of the more important factors investors must consider are transaction costs. In other words, do you choose a load or no-load mutual fund?

The mutual fund *load* is simply the sales fee you pay when buying a mutual fund. Loads are usually, but not always, charged by mutual funds.

The load is an administrative fee that isn't reflected in the portfolio of the fund. That means you have to recoup the sales charge before you can start making any money. So the up-front expense of the load is a factor to be weighed. In the 1960s and 1970s loads were high at 8% and 9%, so investors who purchased load funds were tied down for years waiting to get their initial investment back.

You're probably wondering why anyone would pay a fee to buy a fund if it is possible to buy a similar fund without a sales charge. The basic reason is that load funds are sold by brokers and mutual fund salespeople who provide an additional level of service and expertise, and many people are willing to pay for that.

In today's competitive environment, there are many good no-load funds, including all of the mutual funds issued by mutual fund dealers at financial institutions. With an open-ended no-load fund, shares are usually bought and sold by the mutual fund company.

There's an old saw that "most load funds are not bought, they are sold." This probably explains why the most popular type of mutual funds sold in Canada are load funds. It is estimated that over 80% of all assets in Canadian mutual funds are held in load funds. While the sales charge varies considerably, the current load is typically 2% to 3% of the initial investment in a fund.

I don't want to come down on either side of the load or no-load debate. Suffice it so say that the longer you hold a fund, the less importance you need attach to the sales commission.

There is another issue that ties in with the load debate. Today, most load funds also charge an annual *trailer fee* based on the assets under administration. The trailer fee is part of the ongoing administration charges of the fund and is included as part of the management-expense ratio (MER). The MER is simply a calculation telling investors what percentage of the fund's assets go towards administration, trading, and management fees. If a fund has $1 million in assets, and the MER is, say, 1.5%, the fund is paying out $15,000 per year in administration, management, and trading costs.

The trailer fee is paid to the financial advisor, theoretically as compensation for managing the day-to-day relationship with the client. In fact, some no-load funds are attractive to financial advisors because the annual trailer fee is higher than it would be if the funds were sold on a load basis. And that brings us to another point in the load/no-load debate. Investors should make certain they understand what percentage of the fund's costs go to the financial advisor in terms of trailer fees, and then assess whether or not that is more cost effective than paying a front-end load with a lower trailer fee. This is not a question as to whether the financial advisor should receive fair compensation; it is simply a matter of what is the most cost-effective way to fund this expense.

Funds should not be selected on the basis of whether they are load or no-load. There are all kinds of well-managed, top-performing funds that charge a commission, and there are plenty that don't. And there are so-so managers running the portfolio at load funds, and there are poor managers running the show at no-load funds.

The real question is, what do you get in return for the money you pay as a commission? At some brokerage firms, about all you get is a salesperson whose job is to convince you to invest as much of your money as possible. More recently, you may have noticed, brokerage firms have begun to train their sales force to deliver some level of financial planning advice. At some of the better financial-planning firms, your commission buys you investment advice and general financial counseling services—a financial plan and an expert to call when you need expertise or advice.

If you're not a do-it-yourselfer, and would like to have an expert find the best funds for your needs, then you might consider paying for this advice through a mutual fund load. You might also consider working with a fee-only financial planner who will recommend both load and no-load funds. At least with fee-only services you eliminate any bias.

## Specialty Funds

Specialty funds are mutual funds that concentrate on specific sectors of the stock market. For example, gold funds are specialty funds because they focus their attention on gold stocks and gold bullion. So too are resource funds which specialize in natural resource stocks, and oil and gas companies. Science and technology funds have become the darling of specialty fund investors in recent years. These, of course, are funds that focus on technology companies.

In general, expect specialty funds to be more volatile than broadly based equity funds, which invest in stocks across many different industries. For example, the Bre-X debacle in the first quarter of 1997 had a dramatic impact on a number of specialty resource funds. Just goes to show you how volatile they can be.

Focusing on one sector of the economy implies, by definition, that a specialty fund will be on the top of the performance parade at any point in time. I also expect the fund at the bottom of the performance tables to be a specialty fund. In recent months, for example, gold funds have been very weak performers, while technology funds have been at the top of the performance parade.

On that high note, we'll close our discussion for tonight. In our next lesson, we'll look at two of our most important possessions (our families aside): time and money.

## At the coffee shop ...

"I suppose we could say that specialty funds are the best of funds and the worst of funds," Chris proclaimed. "Interesting session, and the teacher confirmed what I have been saying for some time—that there are two sides to an investment: risk and return. You have to find some balance if you are to remain invested for the long term."

"Wait a minute," I said, thinking that Chris may have been suffering from tunnel vision. "I don't think a portfolio that includes 100% GICs, and the fact that your discussions in the past focused on risk avoidance, constitute balance. Your idea of balancing risk and return is extending the maturity on your GIC past two years."

"Loa's right," Michaela agreed, in a rare exchange where she came down on my side of the discussion. "There has to be some balance, and I think the focus of this lesson was that higher risk begets higher returns, when viewed over long periods of time."

"And to make that point, the teacher focused on what kinds of risk are associated with different types of investments." I just had to keep this line of discussion moving along. "The security market line, I think, clearly displayed the relationship between risk and return. There is always a trade-off."

"Remember what was at the top of the risk category?" asked Chris. "Does that mean you won't be investing in futures contracts?"

"Exactly."

"From that perspective, then, it was a valuable lesson," Michaela added. "More to the point, we cannot forget the relationship between time and risk. The longer you are willing to hold your investments, the more likely your higher-risk investments will generate higher returns. And to me, that was the most important aspect of the discussion."

"Go on …" Chris and I were really interested in this particular line of reasoning.

Machaela continued. "Well, it seems to me that the concept of assets leads to a discussion on diversification. If, for example, my portfolio was invested 50% in GICs and 50% in stocks, and I was comfortable with the amount that portfolio fluctuated month to month, then I would be more willing to hold that portfolio over a longer term."

"Let me jump in to make sure I understand where you are going with this. If I am holding a portfolio that is 100% invested in higher-risk stocks, I better have the personality to deal with the fluctuations in that portfolio. A stock portfolio will do better over the long term than one invested in 50% GICs and 50% stocks," I said, in an attempt to talk myself through this process. "But then, if the stock portfolio declines by, say, 10% in any given month, it could lead me to sell in a panic. By doing that, I would have effectively removed myself from the role of a long-term investor, and would not be in the game to reap the long-term high returns from that higher-risk portfolio."

"That's exactly my point," exclaimed Machaela reassuring me that I was on the right track. "The trick, of course, is understanding your investment personality, and making sure the portfolio you have is one you can live with over the long term. And that is something a good financial advisor can help you establish, which explains the focus of our first lesson on what roles different financial professionals bring to the table."

# Time, Money, and Value

"'Money is the root of all ... let me see ... root of all evil.' No, that's 'the love of money is the root of all evil.' There's more to it than that." I've always had a very philosophical view of money. "'Money is a good servant but a bad master.' True, but it still doesn't get to the point ..."

"If we can get away from your philosophy for a moment," Machaela said, a voice of reason, "I think we all need to understand a few more things about money—what it can do *for* you, and what it can do *to* you, if you let it."

To which I quickly replied, "Money talks! Yeah, that's more along the lines of how I perceive it. For me, money means independence, opportunity, life-style. Not that I am in love with money, you understand. But, like it or not, in a capitalist system, in order to get ahead, to become financially independent, you need to understand how the free-market economy works, and to do that, you need to understand what roles money and money growth play. It's like Economics 101."

Love it or leave it, "Money makes the world go 'round." And we were about to hear from Mr. Croft just how fast money could spin our world.

## *Class in session ...*

In today's lesson, we are going to talk about money. From all sides. How it is created, how the creation of money affects the economy, how time and interest affect the value of money.

Money is the oil that allows the capitalist engine to run smoothly. It is the foundation on which investments are made. And like the elements, money has been in existence for centuries. Not just in paper form, either.

Historically, many items have served as a medium of exchange. Furs were once used in Upper Canada, tobacco served as a medium of exchange for American colonists, and, of course, gold has always had a place as a medium of exchange.

In essence, then, money is anything that is acceptable as a means of payment. Without some medium of exchange, we would all have to operate under a barter system, which economists refer to as "the double coincidence of wants."

Leave it to an economist to come up with a technical term to explain day-to-day transactions among individuals. Simply stated, a "double coincidence of wants" means that, to buy a loaf of bread, you need to have an item of value that the baker will want in exchange. Both parties *want* something, but both parties must also have what the *other* wants. The fact that two people entering a transaction rarely have what the other wants is where money comes into play. Money provides a medium of exchange so that both parties can get what they want at some point in the future. In summary, money provides a convenient medium of exchange between parties.

But there's more. Money acts as a measuring stick, in that we use it to gauge what things are worth. A loaf of bread probably does not have as much value as, say, a steak. But how many loaves of bread are worth an eight-ounce steak? Money allows us to measure the worth of one item relative to another. Without it, we would spend half our time trying to figure out what a trip to the restaurant is worth in terms of loaves of bread, jelly beans, or the workmanship in your china cabinet.

For money to be effective, you must be able to store it for future use. If our friendly baker doesn't want to buy anything today, tomorrow, or the next day, then he will choose to save money rather than spend it. If you couldn't store money in the form of savings, it would be useless as a medium of exchange. Trade a loaf of bread for a can of soup and you have to consume both in a relatively short period of time. Money, then, must also have a store of value.

It's interesting, when you think about money, to reflect on how we use paper and coins as a form of currency. Paper is particularly interesting, in that it has no value aside from the fact it is widely accepted as a medium of exchange.

Obviously, that wasn't always the case. Not that long ago, in terms of historical significance, gold and silver were the only acceptable forms of money. They shared many of the characteristics of today's paper-based currency, in that gold and silver were in demand, both were easily divisible into smaller units, and both could be stored for future use. In fact, some of the first bankers were goldsmiths.

The problem with any commodity-based system of money, of which gold and silver are the classic examples, is that over time the value of the commodity can be greater as a commodity than as a medium of exchange. And when that happens, you diminish the value of money.

For example, suppose you have a one-ounce gold coin that has a face value of $1,000 (in Canadian dollars). Forgetting for a moment that the coin has value as a collector's item, let's examine what the coin is worth when used as a medium of exchange or as a commodity.

Today, gold is worth approximately $550 an ounce in Canadian dollars. So what we can say, then, is that our gold coin is worth $1,000 as a medium of exchange, or it's worth about $550 if we melt it down and sell it as an ounce of gold. In this case, you would be silly to melt it down, because it has greater value as a medium of exchange.

But what happens when the price of gold rises to, say, $1,250 an ounce? Now the one-ounce gold coin is worth more as a commodity than it is as a medium of exchange. When that happens, people would be inclined to melt down the coin and sell it for a price higher than the face value on the coin. Of course, there are laws that forbid you from defacing money. But the example serves to illustrate the point. For money to be effective as a medium of exchange, it cannot have more value as a commodity than it does as a medium of exchange.

## How Money Is Created

Let's talk about how our banking system creates money. To begin this discussion, let's assume we live on a remote island and we have established our own free-market economy. There are lots of people in our hypothetical economy: bakers, carpenters, painters, dentists, doctors, lawyers—lots of lawyers—and, of course, lots of bankers. In our island economy, there are 10 national banks. There is the First National Bank, the Second National Bank, the Third National Bank … Our island economy is not known for it creativity.

Overseeing the economy is the Central Island Bank, a government organization that guarantees the deposits at the ten national banks and is the only agency allowed to actually print the currency of our Island government, called Island dollars.

Now, the friendly island baker—Mr. Brian Dough—enters the First National Bank and makes a $1,000 deposit—and without so much as a thank you from the teller at the First National Bank. He simply receives a stamped record of the transaction and a wish to "have a nice weekend."

Now, the Central Island Bank requires that all the chartered national banks keep at least 10% of any deposits in reserve. In other words, the bank can only loan out 90% of the overall deposits. We call that the *reserve requirement*.

So now the First National Bank has this $1,000 deposit, and by law, the bank has to keep at least $100 of that deposit in reserve. The other $900 can be put to work in the form of new loans. And the First National Bank will try to loan that money as soon as possible, because until that point, the bank is paying Mr. Dough interest on the $1000 and is not earning anything on it. The money that the First National Bank can actually loan out—$900 in this case—is referred to as "excess reserves."

Ideally, the First National Bank wants to loan out the $900 to other residents or businesses on the island. About that time, a local carpenter—Mr. Mike Hammer—enters the bank and asks to speak with a loans officer, Mr. Tightwad. The conversation goes something like this:

Mr. Tightwad: "Good afternoon, Mr. Hammer, and how can we help you today?"

Mr. Hammer: "I've come to apply for a loan."

Mr. Tightwad: "It's a joke, right?"

Mr. Hammer: "Pardon?"

Mr. Tightwad: "Excuse me, Mr. Hammer. Reflex reaction, I'm afraid. What would you like the loan for?"

Mr. Hammer: "Well, I need to buy some new tools, because I'll be doing some repairs at the doctor's house. The new tools will cost $900, and that's what I need to borrow."

Mr. Tightwad: "I see, Mr. Hammer. If you can spare a few moments, we can fill out a few forms and get you on your way."

Eventually, Mr. Hammer gets his loan. He pledges the tools as collateral for the $900 loan and goes to the local hardware store to make his purchase. From the perspective of the First National Bank, they are making optimum use of their deposits. They now have $1,000 in new deposits, $900 in new loans, and $100 in reserves. The bankers at First National are quite happy with their balance sheet.

So far, we have one bank, one deposit, and one loan. For a bank, the customers' deposits are actually a liability. What is happening is that the bank is borrowing the money from depositors and paying them interest on that money. The balance sheet of the First National Bank is presented in Table 3.1.

## TABLE 3.1: FIRST NATIONAL BANK BALANCE SHEET

### Assets

| | |
|---|---|
| Loans | $900.00 |
| Reserves | $100.00 |
| **Total Assets** | **$1,000.00** |

### Liabilities

| | |
|---|---|
| Customer Deposits | $1,000.00 |
| **Total Liabilities** | **$1,000.00** |

Looking at the First National Bank's balance sheet, we can see why bankers are happy, but there has been no new money created. Over time, the First National Bank will earn a profit on the spread between the interest it charges for the loan and the interest it pays on the customer's deposit. To see where the money is created, we need to carry our example forward.

Ms. Simone Gadget is the owner of the local hardware store, and after the close of business that day, Ms. Gadget deposits the $900 from the sale of tools to Mr. Hammer into the Second National Bank. Now the Second National Bank has $900 in new deposits, $90 of which must be kept in reserve; the remaining $810 can be used to make loans. Which is just about the amount that Barbara Sellwell is interested in borrowing.

Ms. Sellwell is an entrepreneur who wants to start a home-based retail business. Her start-up costs will be $810 for training materials and product. She gets the loan from the Second National Bank, not because they liked her business plan, but because she has $800 in Island Government Savings Bonds that are paying 3% interest. Since the bank has the Island Government Savings Bonds as collateral, they are able to provide Ms. Sellwell with the loan under very favorable terms—10% annual interest compounded monthly.

Now, Ms. Sellwell goes to Sales Corp. for her training and product. Sales Corp. then deposits the $810 into the Third National Bank. It is through these deposit and loan transactions that the banking system adds to the money supply on the Island. Table 3.2 looks at the results of this process through the eyes of our four characters and three banks.

## TABLE 3.2: DEPOSIT AND LOAN TRANSACTIONS

| Bank | Depositor | Borrower | Amount of New Deposits | Amount of New Loans | Total Reserves | Money Supply |
|------|-----------|----------|------------------------|---------------------|----------------|--------------|
| First National Bank | Brian Dough | Mike Hammer | $1,000.00 | $900.00 | $100.00 | $1,000.00 |
| Second National Bank | Simone Gadget | Barbara Sellwell | 900.00 | 810.00 | 90.00 | 900.00 |
| Third National Bank | Sales Corp. | | 810.00 | — | 810.00 | 810.00 |
| **Totals** | | | | | | **$2,710.00** |

From the initial $1,000 deposit, the money supply has increased to $2,710. Over time, if we carried this process through to the ultimate conclusion, and assuming a 10% reserve requirement, the $1,000 initial deposit could grow to as much as $10,000. This potential growth in the money supply is referred to as the *deposit multiplier*.

The deposit multiplier in our island example is 10, which is simply the reciprocal of the reserve requirement as shown:

$$\text{Deposit Multiplier} = \frac{1}{\text{Reserve requirement}} = \frac{1}{.10} = 10$$

The deposit multiplier helps us calculate the maximum increase in the money supply, resulting from one new deposit. That assumes that there are no excess reserves in the banking system and that all money is loaned out and then redeposited.

Table 3.3 takes the process through to the Fifth National Bank, and if that process of depositing and loaning were continued all the way to gain the maximum return on the initial deposit—as seen in "Other

Banks"—we see the end result of $10,000 within the money supply, all stemming from Brian Dough's initial $1,000 deposit.

## TABLE 3.3: DEPOSIT AND LOAN TRANSACTIONS (EXTENDED)

| Bank | Depositor | Borrower | New Deposits | New Loans | New Reserves | Money Supply |
|---|---|---|---|---|---|---|
| First National Bank | Brian Dough | Mike Hammer | $1,000.00 | $900.00 | $100.00 | $1,000.00 |
| Second National Bank | Simone Gadget | Barbara Sellwell | 900.00 | 810.00 | 90.00 | 900.00 |
| Third National Bank | Sales Corp. | Mr. Higgins | 810.00 | 729.00 | 81.00 | 810.00 |
| Fourth National Bank | Mr. Jones | Mrs. Smith | 729.00 | 656.10 | 72.90 | 729.00 |
| Fifth National Bank | Mrs. Sharpe | Mr. Hebert | 656.10 | 590.49 | 65.61 | 656.10 |
| Other Banks | | | 5,904.90 | 5,314.41 | 590.49 | 5,904.90 |
| Totals | | | $10,000.00 | $9,000.00 | $1,000.00 | $10,000.00 |

In the real world, the actual deposit multiplier does not come close to the maximum possible number. With our island economy, the deposit multiplier was 10, but in the real world there would be leaks within the system, so that the actual multiplying effect would be much smaller.

For example, Ms. Gadget, upon receiving a cheque from Mr. Hammer, might not deposit the entire $900 into the Second National Bank. In fact, she may choose to deposit $500 and take the other $400 in cash. Since Ms. Gadget has taken currency, the money remains in circulation, and does not immediately flow into the banking system.

As well, it is rare that a banking system will follow our island example and loan out all of its excess reserves. In point of fact, bankers tend to keep more than the minimum level of reserves at any one time to avoid the embarrassment of having a particularly large number of checks clear through their bank on any given day without sufficient reserves on hand.

With our island example, where the cycle of deposits and loans causes the money supply to expand by a factor of 10, you might be asking yourself, "Isn't it a dangerous situation that banks can be allowed to leverage their deposits by as much as 10 times? Over time, would we not have too many new dollars chasing too few consumer goods? And more to the point, why should banks create money? Why not the government?"

In point of fact, there are checks and balances in the banking system that control the amount of money created. Those checks and balances exist on two fronts: (1) the market itself, and (2) through policies of the central bank.

From the perspective of the market economy, we need to understand what happens when a bank makes a loan. Remember, the bank is in business to make a profit on the spread between what it pays for deposits and what it can charge for loans. A major component of a bank's business plan, then, is to make certain that loans are eventually repaid with interest.

Recall that Mr. Hammer wanted to borrow money to purchase new tools. Presumably, the bank took a lien against those new tools as collateral for the loan. So, in the banking system, there must be sufficient collateral to warrant the loan in the first place, which means that to create new money, there must be an asset supporting it.

The second check in the business of money creation is the role played by the central bank. At the outset, the central bank sets the reserve requirement for the chartered banks. And, as we have seen, the reserve requirement has a dramatic effect on the deposit multiplier.

## The Role of the Central Bank

We know, for example, that when the reserve requirement is at 10%, the money supply could theoretically expand by a factor of 10, the result of any one deposit. If the reserve requirement were set at, say, 25%, then the money supply could expand by no more than a factor of 4:

$$\text{Deposit Multiplier} = \frac{1}{\text{Reserve Requirement}} = \frac{1}{.25} = 4$$

In the real world, the Bank of Canada is Canada's central bank. The Bank of Canada came into being under the Bank of Canada Act of 1935. Prior to 1935, the minister of finance conducted monetary policy through the Bank of Montreal, which acted as the government's bank.

Interestingly, Canada was one of the last countries to have a central bank. The U.S. Federal Reserve system has been in place since 1913, and Europe had central banks as early as the 17th century. But those early European central banks were essentially put in place to solve problems for the monarchs, a far different role than the one played by central banks today.

The Bank of Canada is structured to have three distinct levels of authority:

- The governor, who is appointed by the Government of Canada for a seven-year term. The current governor of the Bank of Canada is Gordon Thiessen, who was appointed in 1994.
- The Board of Directors, which includes the governor, the senior deputy governor, the deputy finance minister, plus 11 men and women from across the country. The board meets about 12 times a year, and the minutes of those meetings are reported in the Bank of Canada's *Monthly Review*. These minutes are particularly important pieces of information to the financial community, because they provide economists and financial analysts with some basis to help them determine the current direction of the economy. Because the board has representatives from all regions of Canada, any policy changes can be viewed from a number of different perspectives.
- Senior staff, who play a role in formulating and carrying out the policies of the Bank of Canada. The senior staff includes a lot of senior economists, most with national and international experience in financial matters. It's their job to take the pulse of the economy on a regular basis.

The role of the Bank of Canada has changed over the years. Originally created as an independent central bank, that role changed when in 1967 the Bank of Canada Act was revised. The 1967 revision redefined the role of the Bank of Canada, making it a servant of the Ministry of Finance in monetary policy matters. That means, when there is a serious disagreement between the Bank of Canada and the Government of Canada on monetary matters, the Ministry of Finance will win every time.

Now that we have a basic understanding of the ground rules, let's see what tools the Bank of Canada can use to influence the money-creating ability of the banking system. One of the most watched signals is the *bank rate.* That's the interest rate a chartered bank would pay to borrow money from the Bank of Canada in order to prop up its reserves. If a chartered bank loaned out more of its total deposits than allowed by the reserve requirement, it can borrow sufficient money from the Bank of Canada to bring up its total reserves to the appropriate level. The cost of that short-term loan is referred to as the bank rate.

But as I said, chartered banks don't normally loan all of their reserves and, if anything, most chartered banks maintain excess reserves.

The bank rate acts as a signal, indicating the direction the Bank of Canada would like to see short-term interest rates going. The bank rate is set every Tuesday, based on the interest rate on three-month Government of Canada Treasury Bills. Listen to any financial commentator and you will hear what the bank rate setting is on any given week.

Generally speaking, when the bank rate rises, it is an indication that the Bank of Canada is seeking a tighter monetary policy—that is, reduced deposits, fewer loans, and a decreased money supply. The chartered banks look at this as a signal that perhaps they should raise the rates they charge on personal loans and mortgages. This is not to suggest the chartered banks immediately raise rates simply because the bank rate went up one week. Occasionally, the bank rate will rise when the Bank of Canada wants to shore up the Canadian dollar. In those cases, an increase in the bank rate may be temporary and not related at all to any change in monetary policy. We'll expand on this when we discuss the bond market.

The Bank of Canada can also deal in what are referred to as *open-market operations.* These are behind-the-scenes maneuvers in which the Bank of Canada buys and sells government securities.

Remember when we talked in lesson 1 about how the Government of Canada finances its annual deficits? Essentially, the Government of

Canada issues bonds and Treasury bills which we refer to as government securities. Large institutions, pension funds, and individual investors can buy these government securities. So, too, can the Bank of Canada.

When the Bank of Canada buys these government securities, it pays for them with newly printed currency. That new money goes to the government, which in turn pumps it back into the economy, where it eventually gets deposited into the banking system. More deposits into the banking system mean more potential loans, and the money supply increases.

Conversely, when the Bank of Canada sells government securities, money is taken out of the banking system, effectively reducing deposits and slowing down the loaning process. In short, a tighter monetary policy.

Finally, the Bank of Canada can simply alter the reserve requirement. If it increases the reserve requirement, then the deposit multiplier will fall. The chartered banks will have to increase their reserves to meet the new requirements, and money supply growth will slow down.

You may be wondering what all of this has to do with your personal investments. Actually, it has everything to do with investments. It may make more sense if we understand what monetary policy is all about, and what the Bank of Canada aims to do by influencing monetary policy.

Essentially, the Bank of Canada is concerned with how much money circulates in the Canadian economy. Equally important, of course, is the value of that money. The objective of a reasonable monetary policy is to protect and enhance the standard of living. To accomplish this, the Bank of Canada seeks to protect the value of the Canadian dollar, so that it can be used with confidence and so that its value is not eroded by inflation.

And that, class, is the real issue. Inflation robs all Canadians of their standard of living. Particularly hard hit are individuals on a fixed income. A 5% inflation rate means that a fixed pension will lose half its value in just over 14 years. If the Bank of Canada, through its monetary policy, can help ensure price stability, it protects the standard of living of all Canadians.

To that end, the Bank of Canada, together with the minister of finance, articulated in February 1991 a series of specific inflation-control targets. In December 1993, inflation-control targets were defined to the end of 1998. "The target," according to the Bank of Canada *Review*, "is a band of 1% to 3% by the end of 1995, and this same inflation-control range will be maintained out to 1998." After that, the Bank of Canada will define more precisely what price stability means in terms of the rate of increase of the consumer price index into the next century.

In other words, the Bank of Canada and the Ministry of Finance are following a monetary policy intent on keeping the inflation rate between 1% and 3% through to the end of 1998. And inflation is probably the most significant macro-economic issue affecting all investments.

So what we have learned so far is the role of banks in the creation of money and the role the central bank plays in controlling the growth of the economy. At both ends of this scale, consumers and savers play a role, and the key element in each of those roles is *interest*. Consumers pay interest to borrow money and savers earn interest through the banking system on the money they make available to consumers.

With that in mind, it is important to understand what interest can do *for* you, or what interest can do *to* you, over time.

## Compounding Your Returns

Think what you could have done by investing an extra $1,000 five years ago. Figure 3.1 graphically demonstrates the magic of time and interest. Compound interest! Compounded at 8% annually, that $1,000 would be worth $1,470 today. At the end of 35 years, it would be worth $14,790. Take that same $1,000 and compound it at 12% annually, and it's worth would be $1,760 today and $52,800 in 35 years.

## FIGURE 3.1: THE MAGIC OF COMPOUNDING

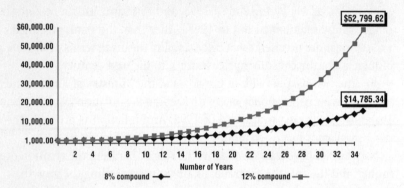

Most individual investors never understand the power of compound interest. It was called "the eighth wonder of the world" by Baron Rothschild. And it is available to all investors who are willing to gain from the experience of the past in order to profit in the future. All it takes is a little foresight, a little common sense, and a lot of discipline. In this section, we will focus on the characteristics of interest—what it does for you, and what it can do to you.

Understanding interest, however, is only one of the issues. Look at the difference a rate makes. Money compounding at 12%, rather than 8%, is worth more than three times as much at the end of 35 years. Having made that point, consider another example.

Suppose you have $5,000 in a savings account at your local bank—safe, secure, and easy to get at. Some might say too easy to get at! Today, that account is probably earning at most 1.5% annually in interest. In fact, usually the interest is only credited on the minimum balance during the month. So, if you withdraw, say, $4,000 in the middle of the month and redeposit it, say, next month, most banks will only pay interest on $1,000 for two months, because that was the minimum monthly balance during each of the two months. Safety and convenience have a price. The price, in this case, is lost opportunity.

There are alternatives to holding money in a savings account. Money market funds, for example, have recently yielded on average about 5% per annum in interest, and that interest is reinvested monthly. Moreover, you can get the money with 24 hours' notice.

Now, you might be saying that the difference between the two rates is not significant enough to justify taking money out of the savings account. But is that really true? Look at how much money you would have at the end of five years by leaving the money in the bank. Remember, the bank is paying 1.5% interest. Assuming that interest is compounded every six months, and assuming that $5,000 is the minimum monthly balance, it would, over five years, grow to $5,387.91.

Now, put that $5,000 into a money market fund, and look what happens if it is left there for five years. Again, assuming a $5,000 initial investment left to compound at an average annual rate of 5% over five years, it would be worth $6,400.42—a difference of $1,012.51 over the savings account.

One more possibility. Let's assume you are comfortable putting money away for five years. Guaranteed Investment Certificates—GICs for short—are another investment alternative. Assuming you were to invest in a five-year GIC compounding at 5.75%, the $5,000 investment would be worth $6,638.48 at the end of the term (see Figure 3.2).

**FIGURE 3.2: $5,000 COMPOUNDED SEMI-ANNUALLY (FIVE YEARS)**

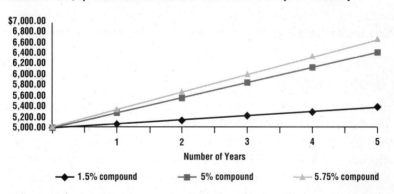

The longer money is left to compound, the more dynamic the results. If your money were left in the bank for 10 years (at 1.5%) it would grow to $5,805.92. In a money market fund—assuming the 5% rate—the initial $5,000 would be worth $8,193.08—a difference of $2,387.16. In the GIC at 5.75%, it would grow to $8,813.88, a difference of $3,007.96 over the savings account.

**FIGURE 3.3: $5,000 COMPOUNDED SEMI-ANNUALLY (TEN YEARS)**

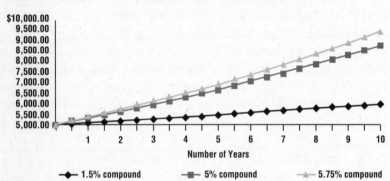

For simply looking beyond traditional savings accounts, you can earn a substantial premium on your initial investment, and the alternative investments are often just as safe, although, in the case of the GIC, not as easy to get at. But in the long run, discipline is its own reward. Most solutions to financial problems are as easy as this. Intelligent investors can apply sound logic, if they understand some basic principles.

## What Is Compound Interest?

The concept of compound interest is not very difficult. Suppose you place money in an investment that pays interest compounded annually. During the first year, you would earn interest on the principal. However, in subsequent years, you would not only earn interest on the original principal, but also on the interest earned in the first year.

For example, assume that $1,000 was invested today, earning 10% interest, compounded annually. At the end of the first year, your investment would have grown to $1,100 ($1,000 × 1.10). This represents the original investment ($1,000) plus $100 ($1,000 × .10) interest earned on the principal. If you reinvested the entire amount for another year, the investment would appreciate to $1,210 ($1,100 × 1.10). During the second year, you have earned $100 interest on the original investment, plus $10 interest on the interest earned in the first year. The amount at the end of two years can be broken down as seen in Table 3.4.

**TABLE 3.4: COMPONENTS OF COMPOUND INTEREST**

| | |
|---|---|
| **Original Investment** | **$1,000.00** |
| First year's interest | 100.00 |
| Second year's interest on original investment | 100.00 |
| Second year's interest on interest ($100 x .10) | 10.00 |
| | |
| **Total Return on Investment** | **$1,210.00** |

Reinvestment for the third year would produce $1,331.00 ($1,210 × 1.10). The third year's interest of $121 consists of $100 on the original $1,000 principal, plus $21 on the interest earned during the first two years.

The interest-on-interest component of the investment is what causes the snowballing effect on the growth of money. To underline the importance of this, assume the original $1,000 investment was left to compound for 50 years. The investment would have grown to $117,390.85. The interest payable on the 50th year would be made up of $100 on the original principal, plus $10,571.89 on the $105,718.96 interest earned during the first 49 years.

## Compound versus Simple Interest

The difference between compound and simple interest is, well, simple. In our previous example, had the interest on the original $1,000 principal been calculated using simple interest, the investment would not have grown to anywhere near to $117,390.85.

When earning simple interest, the investment only earns interest on the original investment. To put this into perspective, our original $1,000 investment would be worth $6,000 ($100 × 50 years + $1,000) at the end of the 50-year period.

---

**Compound interest** is interest on interest. It is calculated not only on the principal investment, but also on the interest that has been generated, which in effect becomes part of the principal.

**Simple interest** is interest calculated on the principal investment only. Any interest earned does not become part of the principal.

---

## Is Compound Interest Important to You?

Money that is not saved will not be available to earn compound interest. To most individuals, that is not a serious consideration, because on the surface, the savings appear trivial. Most individual investors simply miss the big picture. Because of the compounding effect on money, the amount you save is only a small fraction of the potential reward. By saving an extra $100 during the year, you have gained the following:

- $100 in savings
- the interest on that $100 for the remainder of your working life
- plus the interest on the interest for the rest of your working life!

At the end of 35 years, that $100 compounded at 10% will have grown to $2,810.24. The importance of putting money away for yourself cannot be overemphasized! It is important to make certain you don't approach savings with a laissez-faire attitude.

To this point I have been showing you what happens to a one-time investment. Now let's see what compound interest can do for you if you save on a regular basis, and reinvest your earnings.

## The Rate of Investing

While the magic of compounding can do wonders for your financial health, there are other equally important considerations. Let's assume that you don't have a lump sum of money set aside to invest from the outset. That doesn't mean you cannot begin a regular savings program. In many ways, the rate of investment—that is, the amount and frequency of regular deposits—is as important as the rate of return.

When you think about it, you have a substantial pool of assets at your command. Just visualize, for a moment, the vast sums of money that travel through your bank accounts. That's your cash flow.

That cash flow can amount to hundreds of thousands of dollars or more. If you are able to take just a small fraction of that cash flow and convert it into investment capital, it can go a long way toward meeting your investment goals. For most of us, the question of saving for the future is merely a question of discipline. This discipline might take the form of eating one less meal out, delaying a new car purchase for another three months, or cutting Christmas expenditures by 10%.

Let's assume that you work through a family budget with a sharp pencil, and find an additional $100 a month that you can put aside. Put that into a low-risk money market fund compounding at 5% and, in five years, you would have accumulated $6,800.61. If you shopped around and got 7% interest, the $100 per month would grow to $7,159.29. After 10 years at 5%, the portfolio would be worth $15,528.23. At 7%, it would be worth $17,308.48.

Set up a regular savings/contribution program, and most of you will tell me a year from now that it becomes addictive. You need to pay yourself first, and then take care of the incidentals later. The key, of course, is desire and discipline: the desire to increase your wealth by setting up a regular savings/contribution program and the discipline to stick with it. And the most important consideration for maintaining discipline is to set up a savings/contribution program you can live with. The monthly contribution must not be seen as punishment, but rather as a strategy for wealth building.

Just to emphasize just how much of an impact savings and

compounding can have on your net worth, consider what happens if you begin with $100 and save an additional $100 per year. At the end of 35 years, the portfolio is worth $48,446.31 compounded at 12% annually, or $29,912.68 compounded at 10% annually (see Figure 3.4).

**FIGURE 3.4: ANNUAL $100 DEPOSITS COMPOUNDING AT DIFFERENT RATES**

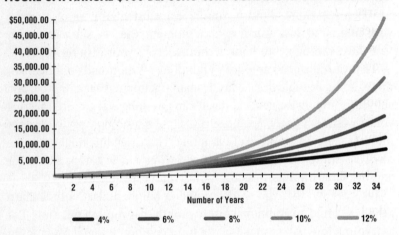

Continuing with the same theme, consider another couple of examples that demonstrate how rates affect your portfolio:

- If you can save $1,000 per year and invest it at 10% compounded annually, in 35 years you will have $298,126.81. If the money is compounding at 12% per year for 35 years, the portfolio will be worth $483,463.12.
- A 40-year-old man plans to work until age 60. Between now and retirement, he wants to save $1,200 per year, which will be deposited into a tax-sheltered vehicle (an RRSP). At 10% interest compounded annually, the value of his retirement nest egg will be $96,838.48

## The Rule of 72

It's one thing to plan for the future, but it is another to understand what it will take to meet those goals. Needless to say, there are a number of tables that can be used to calculate the future value of a lump sum of money put aside today.

But while tables can be useful in determining the value of an investment at some point in the future, they are not a tool that you carry with you to the local bank or trust company. As you probably guessed, there is an easier way to calculate the future value of a fixed investment today. It is known as the "Rule of 72." Simply stated, if you divide the number 72 by the return on a particular investment, it will tell you approximately how many years it will take for your money to double.

For example, if the current rate of return was 9%, your funds would double in about eight years (72 ÷ 9 = 8). If the interest rate is 12%, your original investment would double every six years (72 ÷ 12 = 6).

Now, assuming you invested $10,000 in a bond fund that, historically, has been compounding at 10% a year, how soon will your money double? The answer is about 7.2 years (72 ÷ 10).

How about this? Suppose you have $10,000 you want to double in 10 years to fund your retirement nest egg. What compound rate of return must you earn? Divide 72 by the number of years, and you get 7.2%. To double it in 5 years, you'll have to earn an annual return of 14.4% on your investment—72 divided by 5.

Simplicity at work, yet the Rule of 72 illustrates some powerful investment principles, most notably the magic of compounding. It also drives home the advantages of mutual funds, where dividends and interest can be automatically reinvested into additional shares. Interest makes your investments grow, and compound interest makes it grow faster.

And how about the role 72 plays in assessing the impact of changes in the level of your potential return. Money compounding at 6% annually will take 12 years to double; compounding at 12% it will double in half the time.

The flip side of compounding is the impact inflation can have on your investments. And there, too, the Rule of 72 plays a role. An inflation rate of 3% means that a dollar today will be worth roughly 50 cents in 24 years. A 5% inflation rate means that your cost of living will double every 14.4 years. Tell that to a 40 year old who is just beginning to establish a retirement fund.

## At the coffee shop ...

"Let's bury the banks," declared Machaela. "The banking industry is a license to print money. Loaning money, beyond the reserve requirement—it doesn't cost the bank anything. What's wrong with this picture?"

I hadn't seen this side of my sister for some time. I always knew, seeing that she was a strong believer in the union movement, that behind her facade was a distinct distrust of the corporate elite, of which banks were clearly the elite of the elite.

"I think maybe you are going just a bit overboard with that point of view," Chris replied in a calm tone. And this from someone who is not usually a voice of reason. "If you really believe that banks operate in a business where there is little, if any, risk, then the answer is quite simple—buy bank stocks."

"Well, that might not be a bad investment," I said, offering my two cents' worth in this discussion.

"What I really got from this lesson was the effect the money supply has on all aspects of the economy," offered Chris. "If the Bank of Canada chooses to keep money tight, then the economy will slow down. Even from your perspective, that's bad, because it means lost jobs, higher unemployment, and larger classes in schools as government revenues shrink and the costs for things like welfare and unemployment insurance rise. From an investment perspective, in a slow economy the value of all assets, with the exception of cash, will fall. And sometimes fall sharply."

"The key, I think, is to keep an eye on what the Bank of Canada is doing," I suggested. "If interest rates are falling, at some point that will add to the money supply and the economy will be stronger. In a stronger economy, stocks will rise. Conversely, when the economy slows down, stocks fall in value, which has an impact on a balanced portfolio. The idea, then, is to keep abreast of changes, like inflation for example, that might lead the Bank of Canada to begin tightening the money supply."

# The Business Cycle Roller Coaster

"Boy, what a day I've had," said Chris, as he settled into a chair beside me. "It's one of those days where I don't know if I'm coming or going."

"Chris, it's hard for me to believe that you actually experienced some stress at your job," quipped Machaela.

"All that needs to happen is that a couple of patients get caught in traffic, or their meetings run late, and boom! It blows my schedule to pieces. My routine is gone."

"Sounds like you were on kind of a roller coaster today," I said.

"Lousy segue, Sis. Thought you'd get that one by me, didn't you? Well, I did read the outline for tonight's lecture. I must confess, I don't know if I want to hear about another kind of roller coaster tonight."

"I have a feeling that we're on—that everybody's on—a roller coaster.

I think the trick is going to be to understand when the roller coaster is grinding up the hill, and when it lets loose down the other side. I think it's the difference between making a buck, and losing a buck."

"Okay, Loa, I'll stick it out," said Chris. "It looks like Professor Kirzner's on deck."

## Class in session ...

Economists have an interesting profession. They get to study the economy and then disclose complex pieces of information that, for the average person, are incomprehensible! Issues like marginal propensity to save, adaptive versus rational expectations theory, the elasticity and the deadweight loss due to a tax—these are not party pick-me-ups for the average person.

Economists are also great at bringing to light ideas that work on paper but often fall down in the real world. For example, the idea that we should introduce the GST in the middle of a recession because it will not have a significant impact on economic activity was an interesting case study in this real-world application of theory.

RAESIDE: *The Times-Colonist*, Victoria

At the end of the day, those who study the economy have a very basic goal—to pin down where we are on the business cycle. What is a business cycle, you ask? A business cycle is sort of a state-of-the-economy message, delivered from economic think tanks and government agencies. Both are keenly interested in where we are on the cycle—the think tank so that it can justify its existence and the government agencies so that politicians can decide how much tax you and I can bear.

You would think with so much time and effort going into the study of the business cycle, we would be able to predict when things are about to change. Wrong! Economists have trouble agreeing, even after the fact, about the timing of the peaks and valleys. It's kind of like 20/60 hindsight.

At the same point in time, we can find economists who are bullish, others who are bearish, and still others who would rather sit on the fence. It depends, I suppose, what constituency you are preaching to, and what statistics you are using to make your case. For example, in this game of pin the tail on the business cycle, we often find private economists at odds with government forecasters.

In a sluggish economy, it is hard to determine whether that sluggish economy is an aberration, a slowdown, or a recession. And economists are always trying to seize on bits of information in order to predict the future. In late 1996, for example, we have strong Gross Domestic Product growth, low interest rates, low inflation, and high unemployment.

Gross Domestic Product (GDP) is a measure of the output of all goods and services in Canada. When you pay $10 to get a haircut, that contributes $10 to the GDP. Pick up a birthday cake at the bakery, and that adds $20 to the GDP. Pay a lawyer to draw up a will, and that adds $500 to the GDP. The purchase of a new car adds $20,000 to the GDP. GDP is a measure of the size of the economy in dollars and cents.

The real issue is not so much the size of the GDP, although it is useful information. The real issue is how fast the GDP is growing from one quarter to the next. Statistics Canada measures GDP growth monthly, and translates that number into an annual rate of growth. For example, if GDP grew by 0.25% in September, that works out to a 3% annual growth rate. When the actual GDP number is growing, the economy is expanding; when GDP is shrinking, the economy is contracting.

Of course, the economist looks at where the economy has been, and then proceeds to tell us where it is going. An economic statement is supported by a host of assumptions—it is usually prefaced with the qualifying phrase "All things being equal ..."—and the tone of that statement depends, as I said, on what statistics the economist is focusing on. For example, what will be more important for future growth of the economy—low interest rates, low inflation, or high unemployment?

Looking at historical patterns, you would expect economic growth to bring down the unemployment numbers. We have a set of conflicting signals. Leading up to a federal election, government economists tend to paint a best-case scenario, while private economists—depending on their political persuasion—might be inclined to focus on more troubling issues. It really comes down to how you want to look at the glass—is it half full or half empty?

An economist building a robust economic forecast—that is, the glass is half full—would emphasize the influence that low interest rates will have in the growth of the money supply, leading to business expansion and more jobs.

Someone promoting the half-empty scenario would focus on the unemployment numbers and argue that long-term growth cannot be sustained when 10% of the work force is looking for a job. In support of this scenario, I would expect to see some facts about consumers spending their savings to keep afloat, the high levels of consumer debt, and the poor level of consumer confidence.

## The Four Stages of a Business Cycle

While there are many theories about the cause-and-effect relationship within the business cycle, economists have at least been able to agree that the cycle has four distinct phases: the trough, the expansion phase, the peak, and, finally, the contraction phase (Figure 4.1). The economy moves in distinct waves, but the four parts of the cycle are not as important as the trendline.

Over long periods, a healthy economy must grow, so that each subsequent trough is higher than the previous trough, and each successive peak is higher than the previous peak. Should the fundamental direction—that is, the trendline—of the economy change from positive to negative, all of us are in deep trouble. It would not matter what investment asset you held in a falling economy, because anything of value would lose value. You need look no further than the problems in the Soviet Bloc to understand the implications of an economy on a downward spiral.

Fortunately, real GDP growth—that's GDP growth after accounting for inflation—has historically averaged about 3% year over year. Within that pattern of continuous growth lies the fundamental logic behind equity assets. Over the long haul, stocks grow in value, because stocks are the one asset that benefits from a growing economy. Not to accept the premise that stocks should play a role in every portfolio is to believe that, over the long term, the Canadian economy will not grow. But in a declining economy, I would submit, no investment is safe, including risk-free Treasury Bills.

It is helpful to understand the four distinct stages of the business cycle, because a complete cycle can last anywhere from five to 15 years. And within that period, there will be times when bonds do better than stocks, when real estate outperforms bonds, and, yes, when risk-free

---

[1] Michael Parkin and Robin Bade, for example, define a recession as "a downturn in economic activity in which the GDP falls in two successive quarters." (See *Economics: Canada in the Global Environment*, 2nd ed. (Don Mills, ON: Addison-Wesley, 1991), page 613.)

assets like Treasury bills outperform everything else. The latest example of this performance occurred in 1994, when interest rates were rising and stock prices were falling, and the only assets that produced a positive return were Treasury Bills, GICs and money market funds.

## FIGURE 4.1: THE CANADIAN BUSINESS CYCLE

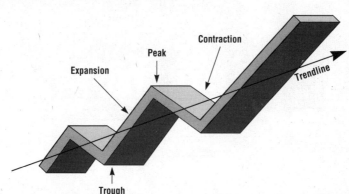

Since World War Two, there have been either eight or nine periods (depending on which economist you consult) of economic slowdown in Canada. Which brings up an interesting issue: what actually constitutes a business slowdown as opposed to a recession?

While views are mixed, most economists agree that to qualify as a recession the domestic economy—as measured by GDP—must decline in real terms (that is, after accounting for inflation) for at least two consecutive quarters.[1] Based on that criteria, there have been eight recessions since 1945. A depression is simply a deeper and longer-lasting version of a recession.

You are unlikely to ever hear the words "recession" or "depression" from the lips of any government in power. Rather, you will hear phrases like "an economic slowdown, temporary in nature," followed, of course, by a rosy forecast for the future.

RÉCESSION

Now, recessions are painful, but necessary, attributes of a market economy. A market economy is a self-correcting model of economic activity. Adam Smith, one of the great economists of the 18th century, coined the phrase "invisible hand" when referring to this self-correcting mechanism. What he was referring to was the invisible hand of supply and demand, influenced by the marketplace. Or, put another way, consumer spending patterns.

Changes in the business cycle occur because of imbalances within the system, most notably an imbalance between supply (production) and demand (consumption). That imbalance may be the result of pricing, where the producer has crossed the dividing line between what the consumer is willing to pay versus what the producer is willing to sell at. It may also be caused by more obscure problems, like a disproportionate amount of savings and investment relative to income spent on goods and services. We are seeing this in the current market as baby boomers invest a disproportionate amount of their disposable income in preparation for retirement.

Given the assumption that the capitalist economy is self-correcting, the business cycle moves from peak to trough and back again, and the invisible hand corrects imbalances in search of a new and more prosperous equilibrium. When prices are too high or wages too low, consumers buy less and the economy slows down. Similarly, when prices are stable and wages are rising, people are feeling good about their jobs, and the economy expands. Sometimes dramatically. Sometimes too dramatically.

In the trough of a typical business cycle, interest rates begin to fall, which in theory encourages businesses to invest in new equipment, and that supports growth. As growth begins to pick up, more jobs are created and labor begins to feel good about itself again. Interest rates have been falling and, as workers begin to gain confidence in their job security, many people will seek loans for big-ticket items like cars or a new home. And the economy continues to gain momentum.

When the economy begins kicking on all cylinders, interest rates will be near the bottom of their cycle. Unemployment should have fallen dramatically, to the point where there may be too few skilled workers for the available jobs. That usually leads to higher salaries, which increases the cost of production, ultimately forcing companies to raise prices in order to maintain their profit margins. Higher prices means inflation, which for the Bank of Canada is public enemy number one. The Bank of Canada will then begin to tighten the money supply by raising interest rates in an attempt to cut inflation off at the pass.

All things being equal—I felt compelled to say that—higher interest rates eventually lead to slower growth and a downturn in economic activity. The economy begins to contract, and since there are fewer people willing to pay the higher price for goods and services, business activity begins to slow down, and that leads to layoffs. Even for workers who are not laid off, there is a fear of being laid off.

Workers, then, are not inclined to buy big-ticket items like cars or homes, and will postpone those purchases until they can feel better about their jobs. And so we have double-digit unemployment, rising interest rates, and inflation. This is the worst of all possible scenarios, and just when all seems lost, the economy begins to once again turn the corner.

Now, what I've described is a typical business cycle, and to be fair, there is no such thing as a typical business cycle. In fact, since the late 1800s, the Canadian economy has gone through eight complete business cycles, enjoying at times sharp upward spurts in economic activity—as measured by the GDP—followed by declines, some of which were intense, others that were merely bumps along the road. Some of those economic contractions have led to recessions and, in at least one case, an all-out depression.

Knowing that the economy ebbs and flows through a series of cycles, however, doesn't make the transition from expansion to contraction any easier. But, if we can gain some insight into what causes the cycle to change, then we have taken a major step towards understanding what drives the performance of various investment assets.

## Some Historical Perspective

The most recent economic contraction occurred in 1990, when the real quarterly GDP declined from a peak of $569 billion to $548 billion by the end of the last quarter 1990—a decline of 3.7% (Figure 4.2). We refer to this as a recession because the economy—as measured by GDP—declined for at least two consecutive quarters.

**FIGURE 4.2: REAL GDP: 1989–1992**

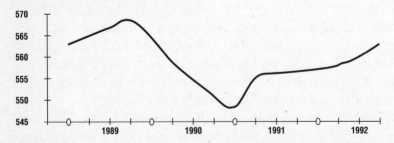

That contraction followed an economic expansion that began in 1982 and peaked during the first quarter of 1990. By the end of 1992, real GDP had yet to reach the previous peak. Mind you, after the first quarter of 1991, Canada was, technically at least, not in a recession, because GDP was actually growing again. But there was nothing in the mindset of Canadians to suggest that the recession had, in fact, passed. Unemployment was, after all, still rising, and peaked at about 11.5% in the middle of 1992.

There were a number of reasons cited for the 1990 recession. The most notable was Bank of Canada Governor John Crow's vendetta against inflation. Policy decisions Mr. Crow had initiated in 1988 were just beginning to take hold by 1990—illustrating the lag between the time the Bank of Canada implements policy to the time it actually has an impact on the economy.

If that were not enough, Canada was implementing the second phase of tariff cuts in January 1990 as part of the North American Free Trade Agreement (NAFTA). As tariffs came tumbling down, multinational corporations doing business on both sides of the border began to rationalize their production capacity, and at the time, that meant lost jobs in Canada. And then, of course, came the slowdown in the U.S., which because of NAFTA put the Canadian economy under even more pressure.

So by 1991, we had high interest rates, a Bank of Canada governor entrenched in a war against inflation, the GST which actually tacked about 1.5% onto the cost of goods and services (that is, more inflation), double-digit unemployment, and a free trade agreement that initially favored employment in the U.S.

If I may borrow from Dickens, 1990 was the worst of times, and 1990 was the best of times. From the perspective of living standards, it was the worst of times. From the perspective of investment opportunity, it was the best of times.

To illustrate, consider what would have happened had you invested in the Canadian stock market at the end of 1990. Your investment would have returned 12.13% compounded annually, so that a $10,000 investment made at the end of 1990 would have been worth $18,774.46 by the end of May 1996.

Similarly, if you had invested in Canadian bonds at the end of 1990, you would have earned 11.72% compounded annually, meaning a $10,000 investment would have been worth $18,398.61 at the end of May 1996. The point is that your greatest investment opportunities come when you least expect them.

## Looking Waaaay Back ...

While the 1990 recession was painful for Canadians, it was nothing compared to the Great Depression, which lasted from 1929 to 1933. The 1929 economic collapse pushed the unemployment rate to 19.3% at a time where there was no unemployment insurance safety net in place to cushion the impact. While inflation and the level of interest rates were not major factors during the Great Depression, the GDP fell 30.1% during that period.

Knowing what we know today about economic cycles, the length of the 1929 depression was an aberration. Normally, economic slow-downs average about 11 months, whereas periods of economic expansion average about five years or better. Periods of expansion begin with a sharp initial recovery, followed by gradual growth. Since the end of World War Two, the average Canadian business cycle, from trough to trough, has lasted about five years. Interestingly, the expansion that started in 1982 was one of the longest since the end of the war.

The 1981–82 recession was also interesting in an atypical fashion, in that it reintroduced *stagflation*. Economists define stagflation as a period during which the economy is moving slowly—as in a recession—but where there is substantial inflation; an inflationary recession, if you will.

## Predicting Changes to the Business Cycle

Unfortunately, there is no one indicator that can predict changes in economic activity—at least not with any accuracy. Therefore, most economists prefer a packaged approach, where they group a number of indicators together and create an index. The most common one is the Index of Leading Economic Indicators. As the name suggests, changes in the level of this index tend to precede changes in economic activity.

Interestingly, one of the components of the Index of Leading Economic Indicators is the stock market. Historically, the performance of the stock market has tended to lead changes in economic activity. This is not surprising when you consider that investors, when they buy stocks, do so in anticipation of future economic gain, and those who sell stocks do so because they may not like the outlook for the economy. So the buyers and the sellers are making bets on the future of the economy with their hard-earned dollars.

Of course, the crowd mindset that drives stock prices cannot predict future economic activity. For example, the October 1987 stock market crash led many economists to conclude that a recession was right around the corner. In point of fact, the recession didn't actually take hold until 1990.

Let's compare, for a moment, the stock market crash of 1929 with the crash of 1987. In both cases, the crash came after a long bull market for stocks. After the 1929 crash, however, the U.S. banking system closed up the vaults. This led to tight money at a time when so many investors had lost fortunes, and it probably did as much as anything to prolong the Great Depression.

Contrast that policy with what took place after the 1987 stock market crash, when the U.S. Federal Reserve opened the vaults and basically told the banking industry to make loans to anyone who needed money. The expansionist monetary policy by the central banks played a central role in delaying the inevitable recession for another four years.

There is also the Index of Coincident Indicators, which tends to mirror current changes in economic activity, and the Index of Lagging Economic Indicators, which usually reflects changes in the business cycle after the fact. These are just the tip of the iceberg. Some economic forecasting agencies use as many as one thousand factors in an attempt to decipher and predict where the economy is going. To understand the factors that influence the business cycle, I want to take a final walk through the business cycle from start to finish.

## 1. The Trough

We'll begin our journey at the bottom. In the trough of the business cycle, consumers and business leaders lack enthusiasm. Indeed, that may be a generous view. There are feelings of despair. Spending on plant and equipment and research and development are put aside until more prosperous times. It's strange, but at a time when management should be aggressive, managers often lack conviction and become what cynics would call "nonproductive fence sitters."

Still, while management may be doing the wrong thing at the wrong time, their reasoning seems sound. The views of business leaders are influenced by the times, and few look beyond the next quarter, let alone past the next turn in the business cycle. Decision makers with that mentality at the top of the corporate food chain find it difficult to justify major expenditures, when prices and sales, particularly of big-ticket items, are falling. If management were to increase production, the new goods would only sit in inventory, which at this stage of the cycle is already bulging at the seams.

That order backlog of just a few months ago has now gone. In fact, there is excess plant capacity, meaning excess workers. The cost of keeping workers has increased dramatically relative to productivity, and that means that cuts have to be made. Unemployment is rising and plants are being closed.

With high unemployment, consumers are feeling the pinch. In an environment where the individual's financial well-being is threatened, there is no motivation to spend, other than on necessities. Especially hard hit are durable goods (such as automobiles, housing, appliances, and furniture) as consumers delay purchasing these goods until times are better.

In the trough, profits have declined to the point where there is an abnormally high number of bankruptcy filings. Liquidity has started to deteriorate as corporations take on more debt or dip into retained earnings to offset the decline in sales.

What's interesting, and what investors should always remain focused on, is the future. Because the value of a company is in its asset base and its ability to generate sales and profits, the price of the company's shares will have declined sharply by the time we reach the bottom of the business cycle. And the price of that company's stock represents the reality of fair market value.

The stock market tends to react positively as the economy rides along the bottom of the business cycle. Share prices stop falling and begin to build a base. Aggressive investors begin buying shares, reasoning that the worst is over. For this reason, share prices tend to lead both positive and negative changes in the business cycle. And as stocks begin to rise, that helps lay the groundwork for a turnaround. That and consumer spending patterns.

Consumption cannot be deferred forever. At some point we will tire of repairing the old car and opt for a new one. Inevitably, we will need new clothes, a new washer and dryer, a new refrigerator. Consumers will eventually have to begin spending.

Prices for big-ticket items are coming down, as are the general rate of inflation and the cost of borrowing money. And because consumers have not been spending, their savings accounts are starting to bulge, and that makes it easier for them to get a loan. When replacement makes more sense than repair, orders for big-ticket items begin to rebound as consumers begin to spend again.

The momentum continues. Business inventories begin to decline, and eventually the shelves have to be restocked. This activity is especially visible in the durable goods sector, where production expands to meet pent-up demand.

Adding more fuel to the fire is cheap labor. In the trough, because unemployment is high, the cost of labor is low relative to productivity. When cheap labor combines with lower costs for raw materials, the stage is set for expanding profit margins.

## 2. Recovery and Expansion

Political rhetoric aside, economists define recovery and expansion as the interval during which the business cycle moves from trough to peak. Many economic indicators must start to turn up before economists, who tend to accentuate the negative, make statements about an economic recovery. Fortunately, because the long-term trend of the economy is positive, the recovery and expansion phase generally lasts longer than the contraction phase.

During the recovery phase, signs of economic expansion abound. Consumer confidence starts to improve, as noted in polls taken by the political parties. You don't want to call an election when consumer confidence is low. Just ask former president George Bush. As confidence improves, so too do retail sales.

That's about the time business leaders begin to notice a change in consumption patterns. With that information firmly in place, management begins to ratchet up production. And just to add further grist for the production mill, Canada's close trading partners, such as the United States, experience the same type of expansion. The trickle-down effect from a giant neighbor demanding more goods and services pushes Canadian manufacturing into high gear.

And the demand-driven revival plays on. Production continues to increase, particularly in the manufacturing sector. Companies like General Motors retool, open up production lines, and add new shifts. Workers who were laid off are rehired, which enhances the collective amount of disposable income that consumers (employees) have.

In the midst of this expansion, profit margins start to improve. And why not? After all, the economic engine is just starting to rev up, so that labor and raw materials are still cheap. Productivity is up, the amount of production per hour of labor begins to improve, and stock prices continue to climb in anticipation of still higher profits, all of which adds to the investor's pocketbook. There's nothing like having some new wealth in your pocket to give you confidence in the economy.

At this stage of the recovery, businesspeople become optimistic because they see that market demand is strengthening, plant capacity is increasing, a backlog of unfilled orders is piling up, sales outlooks are better than they have been for several quarters, and profit margins and the company's stock price continue to improve. New housing construction begins to expand, and durable goods industries, such as automobiles and furniture, beef up their production to meet the anticipated rise in demand.

With sales and profits rising, it is time for business to invest in new plants and equipment. That costs money. Corporations raise that money in one of two ways: (1) borrowing money from the bank or the bond market, or (2) issuing new shares of stock, temporarily diluting shareholders' equity. It is not one choice versus the other. Both are reasonable alternatives at this stage—the former because interest rates are relatively low, and the latter because the stock price is probably close to an all-time high.

Whatever way the corporation chooses to raise the financing, once in place it sets in motion spending plans. New jobs are created in the construction trades, and the higher income from specialty trades reinforces the spending patterns of consumers.

It's at this point we begin to see confidence overload. That's when consumers begin to feel secure about their jobs and believe—foolishly in most cases—that there are plenty of job opportunities. Given this backdrop, they begin to look for ways to enhance their standard of living.

Let's look at buying a new car, for example. Perhaps a car that is just beyond my reach. But why worry? Interest rates are low, the value of my house has gone up, so I'll just borrow a little more. I'm worth it, after all. And what about that vacation we've been putting off for a couple of years? No better time than the present to take that once-in-a-lifetime—actually once-in-a-business-cycle—trip. Maybe it's that dream home that appeals to you, and you decide to buy before home prices rise beyond the point where you could never afford to buy. Who cares that real estate prices have already gone up 20% in the last year? This economic expansion will never end.

Who would dare talk about an impending economic collapse when the economy is picking up speed? We buy that home that is just beyond our reach, expecting a wage increase to eventually bring mortgage costs into line. But we forget that we are borrowing that money when interest rates are low. In fact, many consumers will opt for variable-rate mortgages, hoping to lock in for a longer term when interest rates bottom. Interest rates are, after all, declining, and the politicians are telling us that the best is yet to come. Mind you, the politicians have probably called an election, and that "best-is-yet-to-come" speech really speaks to their hope for reelection.

In time, manufacturing plants approach full capacity. That's the "capacity utilization" number economists like to talk about. It is one of the major statistical figures used by economists to try to pinpoint where we are in the business cycle. For the record, if capacity utilization is 85%, that means that manufacturing plants are operating at 85% of capacity, which in the real world is about as good as it gets. At 85% capacity, any increase in production will likely mean higher end prices, which on a macro scale increases the cost of living. Since it takes time to replace assembly lines, less efficient plants and equipment are brought into production to help fill the backlog of orders.

The cost of raw materials begins to increase at the later stages of the expansion phase. Labor is in demand and shortages in the labor market prevail, especially in the skilled trades. Unionized employees begin to ask for higher wages, but the amount of production per hour of work is stagnant. In that environment, companies have to raise prices at the end of the line in order to maintain their profit margins. And the profit margin is critical at this stage, because stock prices are probably near or at all-time highs because investors are paying premium prices for future earnings.

At this point, price increases are not uniform, and relationships between raw material/wage costs and wholesale/retail prices are distorted. The competitive advantages many Canadian businesses enjoyed when the recovery began are starting to erode. It becomes more difficult to find a foreign market where our goods are priced competitively enough to attract a buyer.

Because consumers continue to borrow to finance their excess spending, the cost of money, reflected by interest rates, starts to rise.

The leading economic indicators start to turn down. Inflation picks up steam, in part because higher interest rates affect the consumer price index. And the cycle continues.

## 3. The Peak

At the peak of the business cycle, there are lots of warning signs about the slowdown to come, but few people are paying attention. It's an old tale—excess breeds excess, until the economy begins to look like a tightly wound spring rather than a fine-tuned Swiss watch.

At this stage in the cycle, management and investment decisions are made without regard to risk. These decisions are driven by an entrepreneurial spirit and the desire to take as much as one can from an economy that seems destined for perpetual expansion. Optimism overshadows prudence.

FRANKLIN: *The Financial Post*

The measures of economic activity are higher than long-term trends suggest they should be. Share prices have'set new records, and trading volumes have increased dramatically. Analysts find new ways of measuring stock market value in order to find new ways to justify current prices and to lend support as to why prices will continue to rise.

Security analysts will suggest—as they did during the second and third quarters of 1987—that share prices relative to per share earnings is no longer a valid tool for measuring value. This makes sense because, at this point, profit margins are being squeezed.

During the mid-to-late-1980s, raiders were buying companies for their breakup value. The component parts of some large multinational companies were worth more than the company as a whole. In 1987, investors were encouraged to focus on how much a company would be worth to someone who could buy it and then sell off its divisions.

At the peak of the cycle, the competitive position of Canadian business erodes even further, and export markets become more selective. Finally, prices increase as inflation kicks in, and the Bank of Canada starts to become concerned and begins to tighten the money supply. That means higher interest rates, and because the cost of borrowing affects the consumer's ability to buy big-ticket items, orders for these items, like cars and appliances, begin to slow.

At first the decline is negligible, probably just an aberration. At least that's what management would like to believe. But commercial banks start to worry, because as output continues to exceed sales, bankers have to finance a growing inventory. Companies start to feel the pinch as receivables become more difficult to collect and the demand for money increases, and that eventually forces the economy into a contraction phase.

## 4. Contraction

The contraction phase is the stage where the business cycle travels from peak to trough. As time passes, the slowdown is of sufficient length that it can no longer be classified as an aberration. The Bank of

Canada is intent on defending the domestic economy against the ravages of inflation. That means a tighter money supply and higher interest rates.

Business confidence deteriorates as labor and material shortages hamper operations. The amount of production per hour of labor continues to decline, and interest rates have reached a point where the cost of carrying short-term debt is higher than the return on equity— that is, the percentage of return a company can expect to earn after accounting for all the costs associated with production and sales. The value of the assets used to collateralize bank loans has declined, which means that companies have become leveraged. That simply means that a larger percentage of the company's balance sheet is made up of debt as opposed to equity. When companies are leveraged, the share price becomes more volatile, and investors become fearful.

In the contraction phase, it costs more to carry a mortgage, which is bad timing for all those homeowners who have a variable-rate mortgage. Indeed, new home buyers are having a more difficult time qualifying for a mortgage as the banks tighten credit restrictions for their commercial borrowers. Interest costs at the corporate level are now dangerously high and, as I said, corporations are now leveraged.

As profits are squeezed, capacity utilization begins to decline, especially since many companies added new production facilities during the expansion phase. Hoping to improve liquidity, and wanting to avoid bankruptcy, companies begin to pay off loans and reduce the hours of work.

That leads to a domino effect because businesses start a program of systematic reduction: work hours are cut, marginal personnel and unskilled labor are laid off, the expansion programs that were in the pipeline are now deferred. New housing construction declines.

The downward spiral gains momentum, leading to the worst of all possible combinations—employees find themselves on an economic teeter-totter as the rate of unemployment rises and job opportunities decline. They shelve any plans to purchase big-ticket items because they no longer can afford them. After all, the value of their assets has declined, as housing prices and the stock market experience a shakeout.

Gradually, however, while staring into the face of despair, inflation finally begins to subside. High interest rates are a boon to investors and a bust to consumers. Over time that pendulum begins to shift, and as the banks begin to ease credit restrictions, interest rates start to decline.

Despite high unemployment, the Bank of Canada and the politicians start to talk about better times ahead. To support that view, governments start spending on capital works projects in the hope of stimulating economic growth. The rate of deterioration slows and eventually stops. As signs of stability return, one full cycle is completed and another begins.

## Summary

A capitalist system is always in transition. You should never make an investment with the expectation that what is will continue to be. We do know, however, that what comes around goes around. Every contraction is followed by another period of expansion. We also know that the average business cycle from trough to trough lasts about five years. And we know that stocks and bonds—the two major investment assets—will rise and fall with the tides of the business cycle. The trick is to keep your eyes fixed firmly on the long term, and to buy when there seems to be no hope. If you must sell, do so when everyone is telling you to buy. Easier said than done, but understanding what drives the business cycle should make it easier to accomplish. An educated investor is usually a long-term investor.

## At the coffee shop ...

"It is starting to come together for me," Chris began. "Last week, we learned how the Bank of Canada influences interest rates and the money supply and, by extension, how those issues affect the economy. This week, we discussed how the business cycle works and learned about its ebb and flow. It gave me a new perspective: when things look the worst, that is the best time to invest. Because at the bottom of the cycle, we are but one step removed from climbing up the other side."

"For me," began Machaela, "it was helpful having someone actually define what the different stages of the business cycle look like. It is another way of understanding the big picture—much like the ocean, where one wave follows another, and over time the tide, like the business cycle, will rise and fall."

Which is where I jumped in. "The key for me was that it laid the foundation from which we can build our investment portfolios. We now understand the macro issues surrounding changes in the economy, we know what to look for at different stages of the business cycle, and we know that an economy in transition will move from trough to trough approximately every five to 10 years. The next step is to understand which investments make the most sense at different stages of the business cycle."

"Well, I wasn't motivated by the lecture to buy and sell different investment assets because of my outlook for the business cycle," came the rebuttal from Chris. "In fact, given the teacher's suggestion that two economists can rarely agree on where we are in the business cycle, or even where we've recently been, leads me to think that I would not have much luck trying to predict the next change. For me, the message is simply that a change will eventually come, and I should stick with my investment philosophy through thick and thin."

"We have a defining moment," declared Machaela. "What the two of you have been talking about are the two different investment philosophies—Chris as a passive investor, looking for some comfort during periods when the storm waters are rising, and Loa, the active investor looking for opportunity from one wave to the next."

"Are we suggesting that one way is better than another?" I asked.

"Of course not," replied Machaela. "I look at it like an abstract painting, where you are never sure which end is the top and which end is the bottom. You're never quite sure which way to hang it, and from my view of it, one way is as good as the other.

"In this case," she continued, "it depends on whether you want to avoid selling in a panic, preferring a passive stance, or whether you enjoy buying in anticipation of a good future, in which case an active stance might better suit your personality."

# Cash in Hand

"I'm glad you were here early, Loa. I'll buy you a coffee next week," Chris promised. "I must've left all my change in my sock at home."

"I know better than that," I retorted. "But I'll hold you to treating me next week."

"I'm glad we're going to be talking about money tonight," Machaela interjected. "I could sure use some advice on saving and earning investment income."

"I think it's going to be a bit more in-depth than that," said Chris. "There are types of investments that you can treat as cash—in other words, get to it in case of an emergency—and other types where your money is locked in. But I wonder if you pay for the flexibility? We'll soon see."

Mr. Croft rounded up the stragglers and started the lesson.

## Class in session ...

This evening, we're going to discuss cash and cash-like securities.

When you reach into your pocket and pull out a $10 bill, you are holding cash. That's a concept that is easy to understand. You know that the $10 bill can be exchanged for something that has a tangible value. It is immediate. However, at the same time, the $10 bill earns no return as long as it sits in your pocket.

Your bank account is also considered cash. You have immediate access to your money and now, with debit cards, you can actually use your bank account in the same way as you use cash in your hand.

The only real difference between having cash in your pocket and cash in a bank account is the fact you can earn interest on money in a bank account.

## Chequing and Savings Accounts

When talking about interest on savings accounts, it is important to understand how that interest is paid. For example, banks may advertise 1.5% interest on savings accounts, but it has little meaning since interest is, under normal conditions, only paid on the minimum monthly balance. Come to think of it, I can't remember the last time I saw a bank advertising the interest rate payable on savings accounts.

In any event, the interest earned in your savings account will only be applied to the minimum monthly balance. If, for example, you had $200 in the account and deposited $3,000 in the middle of the month, you would only earn interest for the month on the $200. The additional money that you deposited would not earn any interest at all.

Normally, chequing and savings accounts are not suitable as investments. However, the increased competition in the financial industry has led to the introduction of some flexible types of savings and chequing accounts. For example, the Bank of Nova Scotia has introduced a "power chequing account." For depositors who keep a minimum monthly balance of $5,000 on deposit at all times, they will get the same rate that is paid on the bank's term deposits. Most of the other banks have similar types of accounts, so it is worth investigating at your particular branch. It's the best of both worlds; your money is flexible and easy to get at, while it earns one of the more favorable rates of interest.

---

### SAVINGS AND CHEQUING ACCOUNTS
- usually pay relatively low rates of interest
- usually pay interest on the minimum monthly balance
- require a minimum balance
- charges, if any, should be reviewed

---

Depositors who have long suffered from the inadequacy of savings accounts are finding that the rate paid on deposits has improved. Competition has pressured many financial institutions into making chequing accounts more flexible. As well, the spin-off effects have benefited savings accounts. Premium rates are available on certain savings accounts if a minimum monthly balance is maintained. The minimum balance is generally less than that required for chequing accounts. A shopping trip to your local bank or trust company would be enlightening.

The point to remember when choosing an account is to look at all the kinds available and to understand whether they do what you want them to. Is the interest compounded daily, monthly, quarterly, semi-annually, or annually? It makes a difference. The more frequently money compounds the more opportunity to earn interest on interest. Remember the effect compounding can make. You should also know how to use the account most effectively. For example, if interest is paid on the minimum monthly balance, be sure that funds are transferred to the account at the beginning of each month, and not in the middle.

Still, no matter how you cut it, bank accounts are not investments. Bank accounts should be a liquid source of funds that can be used to meet your monthly, weekly, and daily obligations. Bank accounts are also a convenient way to accumulate funds for investment purposes.

Cash assets—one of the four broad classifications of investment assets, which we discussed in lesson 2—are an alternative to bank accounts that we can use as cash. To be considered a cash asset, an investment must be short term in nature and present little risk, in the sense that you are guaranteed the return of your principal at maturity and that you will earn a reasonable rate of return during the period you hold the investment.

## Canada Savings Bonds

Canada Savings Bonds (CSBs) are the safest and most liquid investment available in Canada today. They are unconditionally guaranteed by the federal government for payment of all accrued interest and repayment of the principal. CSBs usually pay a rate of interest better than a savings account, and they can be redeemed for cash at any bank, trust company, or credit union.

However, if you are considering cashing them, it is best to wait until the beginning of the month. Regular or simple interest on the bonds accrues to the holder each month. Therefore, if the bonds are cashed in the middle or near the end, you will forfeit all the interest accrued during that month.

The interest on CSBs can be paid by cheque to the holder each year, or can be left to compound. If you elect to let the interest remain, then it would be compounded on an annual basis. Remember the importance of compounding frequency when comparing different rates.

---

### CANADA SAVINGS BONDS
- competitive monthly interest rate
- liquid
- annual compounding
- minimum purchase is $100

---

Should interest rates rise, the government has, in the past, increased the rate of interest payable on all outstanding CSBs. This has been important from the government's point of view, because it doesn't want a large number of CSBs being redeemed at any one time. If bond holders discovered they could get a better rate of return from another investment because interest rates had risen, they might opt to cash the bonds and invest elsewhere.

CSBs can only be purchased in October, during the sales campaign. The sales campaign is usually closed at the end of October. I say "usually" because it depends on the demand for the bonds.

The bonds can be purchased at any bank, trust company, or credit union, or through a brokerage company.

Many companies make CSBs available through a payroll deduction plan. You decide how many bonds you wish to purchase and the money will be deducted from your paycheque each week. At the end of the year, you will receive the bond and it will be paid in full. There are interest charges for financing the purchase through a payroll deduction plan, but the rate is the same as that paid by the bond. It is, therefore, useful as a "forced" savings plan.

The bonds are available in denominations of $100, $300, $500, $1,000, $5,000, and $10,000. The minimum amount you can purchase is $100.

## Treasury Bills

Treasury Bills, or T-bills as they are sometimes called, are used by the federal government to finance short-term cash requirements. They are auctioned on Tuesday of each week by the Bank of Canada, which acts on behalf of the federal government. Brokerage houses, certain banks, and other financial institutions registered as agents with the Bank of Canada submit bids for the amount they wish to purchase, as well as the price they are willing to pay.

The Bank of Canada accepts a range of bids, and distributes the T-bills accordingly. The bank rate is then set 15/100ths of a point above the average rate available at the auction for T-bills. The bank rate is what you hear on the radio, see on TV, or read in the newspapers each week. It is the trendsetting rate that banks follow when structuring their loan costs.

---

### TREASURY BILLS

- liquid
- purchased at a discount
- competitive short-term interest rates
- 91- and 182-day maturities (sometimes a 365-day maturity is available)
- minimum purchase varies, so check with your stockbroker

---

T-bills used to be beyond the reach of the ordinary investor. However, brokerage houses have recently made these very flexible investments available to anyone in almost any denomination. Some firms charge a commission for these purchases, while others use them as a loss leader. What we mean by "loss leader" is that firms do not charge you a commission when you purchase T-bills. The idea is to get you in the door—once you've started to invest your money through the company, the salesperson can then try to sell you other types of investments at a later date. There's nothing wrong with this, and some of the recommendations may be fine. It's just important to realize that nothing is free.

Treasury Bills can be bought for 91-, 182-, and 365-day terms. However, the Bank of Canada does not always offer the longest term at Tuesday's auction.

An excellent secondary market exists for these securities. This means that T-bills can be bought and sold just like stocks. You can sell your T-bills at any time in the secondary market. As well, if you wanted to purchase a T-bill for a term of less than 91 days, your broker would purchase the T-bill in the secondary market. In essence, T-bills are as good as cash, riskless, and available in almost any short-term maturity you could want.

However, buying T-bills in the secondary market does not normally yield as high a return as waiting for the auctions each Tuesday. As well, selling them before they mature will usually result in a yield slightly less than anticipated.

Treasury Bills are bought at a discount. At the end of their term (182 days, for example), they mature for their full face value. For example, suppose you purchased a six-month $10,000 T-bill that yielded 5% annually. In most investments, you would pay $10,000 and, at the end of six months, you would receive $10,000 plus $250 in accrued interest. However, for this Treasury Bill, you would invest approximately $9,750 at the time of purchase and, at the end of the six months, you would receive $10,000.

## Term Deposits

Term deposits are available through banks, trust companies, and credit unions. They are quite safe. Terms are generally for 30, 60, 90, 180, and 365 days. The rates vary depending on current money market rates, but are usually slightly less than the rate available on T-bills.

Term deposits are covered by the Canada Deposit Insurance Corporation (CDIC). This is the arm of the federal government that insures deposits left with banks, trust companies, and most credit unions. The insurance covers individual depositors for $60,000 in principal. More about that later.

These investments are purchased at their full face value (a $10,000 term deposit will cost you $10,000), and when they mature you receive your investment plus accrued interest. However, there may be a penalty for cashing them in early.

Question your banker about any penalties. Usually, since the terms are short, early withdrawal is not one of your major considerations.

> **TERM DEPOSITS**
> - short-term investments
> - competitive rates
> - maturities of 30, 60, 90, 180, and 365 days
> - minimum deposit varies

## Money Market Funds

Another alternative cash investment is a money market fund. A money market fund is a mutual fund. You purchase shares in the fund and the money is pooled with thousands of other investors. The smallest amount that can be offered to purchase a money market fund varies, but often as little as $100 will constitute a minimum investment. A manager invests the money in federal and provincial Treasury Bills, Banker's Acceptances, and other short-term instruments.

The money market fund is a hybrid between a traditional mutual fund and a savings instrument, and is a derived product that was fashioned to meet specific needs. The money market fund has a number of conveniences that are consistent with traditional mutual funds: it is a pooled, professionally managed, diversified product with normally small-dollar entry requirements, dividend reinvestment plans, periodic purchase plans, and no secondary market.

However, unlike traditional mutual funds, Canadian money market funds (with a few exceptions) attempt to maintain a fixed net asset value per share (or NAVPS for short), using various accounting and trading techniques to accomplish this goal. Traditional mutual funds have a floating NAVPS, and calculate the value of their portfolio each day (a process called marking-to-market). For money market funds, instead of a fluctuating NAVPS, it is the interest that fluctuates on a daily basis.

You are entitled to a *pro rata* share of the dividends and interest earned on the fund's portfolio, as well as any capital gains (losses) incurred in the fund's trading of securities before their maturity.

Money market funds only pay interest, so all distributions are likely to be treated as interest income. Normally, income is distributed through additional shares or units rather than through cash payments.

For example, if you bought 100 shares of a money market fund at $10 per share, your total investment would be $1,000. If the yield on the fund was, say, 6%, you would earn approximately 0.5% per month in interest distributions. In most cases you would simply receive ½ a share for each 100 shares held (100 × 0.005 = ½ share). At the end of one month, the net asset value of the mutual fund would still be $10 per share, but you would now own 100.50 shares.

Money market funds are generally no-load funds, which simply means that no commission is charged when you purchase them. However, there is an ongoing fee that is paid to the fund's management. Management fees vary depending on the amount invested and the particular mutual fund company. Because you could purchase most of the investments that the money market fund will purchase for you, the management fees on money market funds are low relative to other funds. The research and analysis required to buy a basket of money market instruments is not intense or expensive. The management fees cover the administration of the fund and help provide services such as cheque-writing privileges. Generally, you should not be charged fees higher than 0.5% of the fund's assets for the administration of the fund. Given that rate, however, we find that money market funds generally yield slightly less than the current T-bill rate. Again, this investment carries very little risk and can be a viable alternative for your cash assets.

---

### MONEY MARKET FUNDS

- liquid (you can access your money, plus any accrued interest, within 24 hours)
- competitive rates of interest
- any term
- management fee is paid from earnings
- minimum purchase varies, but is usually not less than $100

Interest is calculated daily in most funds, and compounded monthly. As well, investors can have the interest mailed to them periodically, depending on their specific circumstances (that is, monthly, semi-annually, or annually).

Virtually every mutual fund dealer sells money market funds. A mutual fund broker can usually show you where to find a good money market fund. Stockbrokers also sell them, and some funds are even sponsored by the brokerage house itself.

## Guaranteed Investment Certificates

These instruments are available through local financial institutions, and are for terms usually between one and five years. The rates for Guaranteed Investment Certificates (GICs) are generally better than T-bills, but your money is tied up for a longer term. Any early withdrawal (if there is that option) will generally result in an interest penalty. This is something you should check into carefully. Money invested in GICs should be excess cash that you do not require any time soon. Nonetheless, you never know when an emergency will happen that requires cash. Always find out if you can cash your GIC early, and if so, what the penalties are.

GICs, like term deposits, are eligible for insurance from the CDIC. Remember that $60,000 is the maximum insurance available for deposits by each individual. Therefore, if you are investing more than that, it would be better to split the investments between more than one family member. For example, if you were depositing $100,000, rather than have $80,000 in your name and $20,000 in your spouse's name, you would be much safer to have $50,000 in each name, although there are tax and legal implications associated with this. Then, both certificates would be fully insured. Bear in mind that the coverage is the amount of principal plus accrued interest, so always deposit less than $60,000 to ensure full coverage.

---

**GUARANTEED INVESTMENT CERTIFICATES**
- one-to five-year maturities
- possible penalties for early withdrawal
- competitive rate of interest
- minimum purchase varies

---

Many banks offer two types of GICs—those that compound and those that pay the interest to the investor periodically. You may choose to have the interest paid monthly, semi-annually, or annually. This is particularly helpful to retirees who want a monthly income. If the interest is left with the financial institution, then it compounds beginning in the second year.

As I've already pointed out, one of the primary attributes of a cash asset is liquidity or, put another way, accessibility. A cash asset, then, is one where the investor can immediately access the funds. This means that a GIC with a five-year term-to-maturity does not fit our definition of cash. In fact, using accessibility as the only criteria means that GICs would have to be viewed as fixed-income assets.

## GICs—Cash or Fixed Income?

As you may have guessed, there is another side to this issue. Indeed, it is a hotly debated issue among investors and financial planners. Should we, when constructing a portfolio, classify Guaranteed Investment Certificates as cash assets or fixed-income assets?

Most investors think of GICs as fixed-income assets because 1) they are not accessible (without a significant penalty) until maturity, and 2) many GICs have rather long term-to-maturities ranging anywhere from one to five, and sometimes seven, years. When you think in terms of how quickly you can "cash" out your investment, GICs don't cut the mustard in the same way as do Canada Savings Bonds, money market funds and even government Treasury Bills.

However, there is another camp of advisors who define GICs as cash assets. Why? Because there is a widespread perception that GICs are risk free, and fixed-income assets, by definition, are not risk free. The price of most fixed-income assets will fluctuate prior to maturity, and as such, you are not guaranteed the return of your principal if you sell your fixed-income asset prior to maturity. Whatever principal you invest in a GIC is guaranteed, and the perception is—assuming you are not forced to pay a penalty for early withdrawl—that the price does not fluctuate prior to maturity.

Investor perception can be a very dangerous thing. In the fall of 1994, after one of my investment planning speeches, a retired lady approached me and asked me what I thought about mortgage funds. For some historical perspective, this was about six months after the U.S. Federal Reserve and the Bank of Canada had begun pushing up interest rates. At this point in the business cycle, the value of most mortgage funds had slipped badly.

In the discussion that followed, I discovered that the only investment she had ever owned was GICs. Her financial advisor had recommended that she roll her maturing GIC portfolio into a mortgage fund, because she could enhance her yield. She was told that the mortgage fund was an alternative to GICs because both were fixed-income investments.

To some extent, that advisor was right. But what she did not understand was that the value of a mortgage fund could fluctuate, something that does not occur in a GIC. Having invested a sizable portion of her portfolio (about $100,000) into this mortgage fund, she was now distraught to learn that the value of her portfolio had declined sharply.

The same holds true for bond funds. In fact, the variability of return in a bond fund is more dramatic than is the case with mortgage funds. And despite that, I have heard of cases where financial advisors will recommend a bond fund as an alternative to a GIC, without explaining that a bond fund can fluctuate. And for a long-term investor, perception is everything.

So we come back to the question at hand: should we classify GICs as a cash asset or a fixed-income asset within the context of your investment portfolio? There is no right or wrong answer. It comes down to perception, to whether you see accessibility or risk as the primary issue when defining the role that GICs play in your portfolio.

---

## At the coffee shop ...

"We've gotten off pretty light tonight," said Chris. "Does anyone mind if I leave? I think I might hit the bowling alley."

"Not to worry, brother dear," said Machaela. "I've got some calls to make and an early night wouldn't be a bad thing at all."

I agreed. I could actually go home, stretch out on the sofa and watch some TV. What a concept! "Okay, all, see you next week. And Chris, remember that you can only throw the ball with one hand."

He just kept walking.

# Bonds—What They Are and How They Work

Chris, Machaela, and I arranged to meet before the class. "Fair warning," I reminded them. "They told us to be well rested for tonight's class. And I'll have that cup of coffee you owe me, Chris."

"I tried to do a little preparation for bonds, but they seem to work in reverse from what I'm used to—you know, earning interest on your savings or a Canada Savings Bond. I don't know if I'll ever get the hang of it!"

Chris has always had a tendency to give up early.

"You're hardly timid about asking questions, Chris," jabbed Machaela. "Just don't leave the rest of us behind."

Mr. Croft looked at the clock. Seven on the dot.

## *Class in session ...*

I have two articles from financial dailies that I'd like all of you to read during the break. The first article talks about something called the "step-up feature" in a recent issue of Canada Savings Bonds. In this particular case, you would receive 3% interest in the first year, and the rate payable steps up each subsequent year to more than 8% interest in the tenth year of the bond. If you held the CSBs for the entire 10-year period, you would earn 6.21% compounded annually.

The second article, which appeared on the following page of *The Globe and Mail*, discusses the direction of Canadian interest rates relative to U.S. interest rates. The reporter talks about 10-year Government of Canada bonds yielding 6.58% compounded annually versus a rate of about 6.71% for 10-year U.S. bonds.

The reporter's point is that it has been a long time since Canadian interest rates were lower than U.S. rates. In this case, 10-year Canadian interest rates were 13 basis points lower than comparable U.S. rates.

A basis point is a tool used within the bond market to describe interest rates. A basis point is equal to $\frac{1}{100}$th of 1%. Stated another way, 1% equals 100 basis points. The difference in the yield on Government of Canada 10-year bonds (6.58%) and U.S. 10-year government bonds (6.71%) is 13 basis points (6.71% – 6.58% = 13 basis points).

For me, what is interesting, and something that is not discussed in either *Globe* article I might add, is the difference between the 10-year compounded annual returns on Canada Savings Bonds versus the 10-year compounded annual return available on Government of Canada bonds.

Here we have two investment alternatives, both issued by the same government with the same guarantees, both called bonds, and yet each having different yields. This example illustrates how the bond market can easily confuse the average investor. Indeed, for an investment whose rules appear to be relatively straightforward— that is, when you buy a bond you receive interest, and at maturity your principal investment is returned—it is astonishing just how much has been written about the subject and how confusing the marketplace can make bonds seem.

Which brings us to the focus of this lesson. Not only will we examine the differences between CSBs and government bonds, but we will also explain some other terms, especially relating to yield, to help you understand the relationship between long-term bonds and interest rates.

## Canada Savings Bonds versus Government of Canada Bonds

Let's begin by clearing up the confusion between Canada Savings Bonds and Government of Canada bonds. In point of fact, Canada Savings Bonds and Government of Canada bonds are really two different animals.

The investment community is using a loose interpretation of the term *bond* when applying it to CSBs. While CSBs mature at a given point in the future, *the interest payable is not fixed.* The rate payable on any CSB issue is adjusted on a needs basis to reflect changes in the rate of interest being paid on savings accounts, one-year GICs, short-term Treasury Bills, and money market funds. In our step-up CSB example, the rate steps up each year through the life of the bond, which resembles some GICs that are currently on the market. In either case, these are investment characteristics that we normally associate with cash assets.

Bonds, on the other hand, are fixed-income instruments that can only be redeemed on the maturity date. The maturity date is fixed when the bond is issued. In some cases, bonds have a clause in their indenture allowing the issuing party—whether it be the federal, provincial, or municipal government or a corporation—to redeem the bonds prior to the maturity date. But again, the date at which the bonds can be redeemed is fixed and clearly spelled out in the bond's indenture.

I think we need to offer some definitions. Specifically, what is a bond?

*Bonds* are financial agreements between a borrower and a lender. The borrowers who issue the bonds in exchange for your money include governments at all levels, as well as major corporations. The lenders are those institutions or individuals who hold the bonds.

The bond's *indenture* is simply the legal terms of the agreement. The issuer of the bond and the buyer of the bond are linked together in an arrangement that is defined for the life of the bond.

The *maturity date* defines a point in the future when the agreement between borrower and lender comes to an end. At that point, the lender will be repaid the principal investment plus any outstanding or accrued interest. And therein lies another term. *Accrued interest* is the amount of interest owed to the bond holder from the time of the last interest payment. More on that in a moment.

## Understanding Fixed Income

The term *fixed income* refers to the interest or coupon rate which, like the maturity date, is fixed for the life of the bond. The *coupon rate* is the rate of interest the bond issuer promises to pay as a percentage of the bond's face or par value. The *face* or *par value* is the amount of principal owed to the lender.

Let's consider a hypothetical example to illustrate these terms. We'll use a $1,000 (that's the bond's face or par value) Government of Canada 8% (8% is the coupon rate, or the rate of interest the bond will pay each year) bond maturing on November 1, 2006.

Assuming we purchase $1,000 face value of this bond, we will receive $80 per year in interest income ($1,000 face value × 8% coupon rate = $80). Just for the record, bonds normally pay interest semi-annually, so that in our example we will receive a $40 interest payment every May 1 and another $40 interest payment every November 1. In an effort to keep this as simple as possible, we'll assume the bond was purchased on November 1, 1996, and the first interest payment will be made on May 1, 1997.

With this Government of Canada bond, we have the right to receive 20 semi-annual interest payments and the return of our principal on November 1, 2006. (See Table 6.1.)

## TABLE 6.1: A BOND'S TOTAL RETURN

| Date | Interest Payment | Principal Repayment |
|------|------------------|---------------------|
| 01-May-97 | $40.00 | |
| 01-Nov-97 | 40.00 | |
| 01-May-98 | 40.00 | |
| 01-Nov-98 | 40.00 | |
| 01-May-99 | 40.00 | |
| 01-Nov-99 | 40.00 | |
| 30-Apr-00 | 40.00 | |
| 31-Oct-00 | 40.00 | |
| 01-May-01 | 40.00 | |
| 01-Nov-01 | 40.00 | |
| 01-May-02 | 40.00 | |
| 01-Nov-02 | 40.00 | |
| 01-May-03 | 40.00 | |
| 01-Nov-03 | 40.00 | |
| 30-Apr-04 | 40.00 | |
| 31-Oct-04 | 40.00 | |
| 01-May-05 | 40.00 | |
| 01-Nov-05 | 40.00 | |
| 01-May-06 | 40.00 | |
| 01-Nov-06 | 40.00 | $1,000.00 |
| **Total Return** | **$800.00** | **$1,000.00** |

*Total interest plus income = $1,800.00*

This bond returns, without reinvesting any of the interest payments, $1,800. If each of the interest payments had been reinvested at 8%, then the bond would have "yielded" the following (See Table 6.2):

**TABLE 6.2: A BOND'S TOTAL RETURN (INCLUDING REINVESTED INCOME)**

| Date | Interest Payment | Principal Repayment | Money for Reinvestment | Total Return on Reinvestment* |
|---|---|---|---|---|
| 01-May-97 | $40.00 | | $40.00 | $44.27 |
| 01-Nov-97 | 40.00 | | 40.00 | 41.03 |
| 01-May-98 | 40.00 | | 40.00 | 37.92 |
| 01-Nov-98 | 40.00 | | 40.00 | 34.92 |
| 01-May-99 | 40.00 | | 40.00 | 32.04 |
| 01-Nov-99 | 40.00 | | 40.00 | 29.27 |
| 30-Apr-00 | 40.00 | | 40.00 | 26.60 |
| 31-Oct-00 | 40.00 | | 40.00 | 24.04 |
| 01-May-01 | 40.00 | | 40.00 | 21.58 |
| 01-Nov-01 | 40.00 | | 40.00 | 19.21 |
| 01-May-02 | 40.00 | | 40.00 | 16.93 |
| 01-Nov-02 | 40.00 | | 40.00 | 14.74 |
| 01-May-03 | 40.00 | | 40.00 | 12.64 |
| 01-Nov-03 | 40.00 | | 40.00 | 10.61 |
| 30-Apr-04 | 40.00 | | 40.00 | 8.67 |
| 31-Oct-04 | 40.00 | | 40.00 | 6.79 |
| 01-May-05 | 40.00 | | 40.00 | 4.99 |
| 01-Nov-05 | 40.00 | | 40.00 | 3.26 |
| 01-May-06 | 40.00 | | 40.00 | 1.60 |
| 01-Nov-06 | 40.00 | $1,000.00 | 40.00 | – |
| **Total Return** | **$800.00** | **$1,000.00** | | **$391.12** |

\* Assumes the interest payments were reinvested at 8%.

As we see from Table 6.3, the combination of semi-annual interest payments ($800) and the interest earned by reinvesting those interest payments ($391.12) is worth more to you than the principal itself. The components that make up the total return for a bond, then, include the return of principal, the semi-annual interest payments, and the return on reinvestment of those semi-annual interest payments.

**TABLE 6.3: COMPONENTS OF A BOND'S TOTAL RETURN**

| | |
|---|---|
| Return of principal | $1,000.00 |
| Semi-annual interest payments | 800.00 |
| Return on reinvestment of interest | 391.12 |
| **Total Return** | **$2,191.12** |

Let's take a moment for a review of the terms in our Government of Canada bond example.

What is the coupon rate?        **Answer:** 8%.

What is the face value of the bond?        **Answer:** $1,000.

What is the maturity date of the bond?        **Answer:** November 1, 2006.

What will happen on the maturity date?        **Answer:** When the bond matures, the bearer will get back the face or par value of the bond and any accrued interest.

This is a good time to talk about accrued interest. Recall from our example that the Government of Canada bond paid interest semi-annually—on May 1 and November 1 of each year—and that we purchased the bond on November 1, 1996, the same date the bond was issued and exactly six months before the first semi-annual interest payment. But what happens if you buy the bond on August 1, 1997, three months after the first interest payment? In that case, you would receive the full semi-annual interest payment in three months (November 1, 1997), and the seller of the bond would have to forgo three months' interest from the last interest payment date.

Now remember, in the bond market, bonds are not being redeemed but rather sold to someone else. If the buyer and seller are executing the deal at some point between two interest payments, then the buyer must pay to the seller any interest that has accrued from the date of the last interest payment. In our current example, the buyer purchased the bond on August 1, halfway between the two semi-annual interest payments. Therefore, in addition to the $1,000 face value of the bond, the buyer is required to pay to the seller $20 in accrued interest (three months' worth).

## Calculating the Yield-to-Maturity

This brings us to a question that many new investors ask. In the second *Globe and Mail* article, Government of Canada bonds maturing in 2006 were quoted as yielding 6.58%. If that is correct, wouldn't that make a bond yielding 8% and maturing in November 2006 a good investment? The answer, of course, is that it would be too good!

With our Government of Canada 8% November 2006 bond, we know the rate is fixed for the life of the bond. We also know that our Government of Canada 8% November 2006 bond should effectively yield the same as other government bonds—approximately 6.58%—maturing at the same time.

So, if the interest rate is fixed, how does a Government of Canada 8% November 2006 fixed coupon bond yield only 6.58% compounded annually? Since we can't change the coupon interest rate, the only alternative is to change the amount that is paid for the bond. And therein lies another significant difference between conventional bonds and CSBs. With CSBs, the price is fixed and you redeem them rather than sell them. With bonds, the rate of interest is fixed, but the price of the bond fluctuates, and if you want to sell the bond prior to maturity, you must sell it to another investor.

To buy $1,000 face value of the Government of Canada 8% November 2006 bond, you will have to pay a premium, or a price higher than the $1,000 face value. Based on my calculations, which I'll explain in a moment, you should expect to pay approximately $1,102.85 for every $1,000 of face value.

Now, if you talk to a professional bond trader and ask her for a price, you will get something back like $110.2, which is a rounded-off price. This is part of that technical bond market language that serves to confuse most investors. Suffice it to say, bond prices are quoted as a percentage of face value. The $110.2 price, then, simply means 110.2% of par or face value.

Even though you pay a premium, this still looks like an attractive investment. After all, you will earn $80 in annual interest. Divide the annual interest by the price of the bond (i.e., $80÷1102.85=7.25%) and the yield is still 7.25%. We refer to that as the bond's *current yield*. In this case, the current yield is still much higher than the 6.58% rate quoted in *The Globe and Mail* article. Confused? Still waiting to buy? Before you do, consider the next step along this path.

If you hold the Government of Canada 8% November 2006 bond to maturity, you will only receive at maturity the $1,000 face value. And there's the rub. Because you paid $1,102.85, your portfolio will suffer a $102.85 capital loss over the next 10 years. That capital loss has to be factored into your total return, which is what bond traders do when they calculate what is called the *yield-to-maturity*.

And while the calculation may be a bit more complicated, the yield-to-maturity is the one measure that allows you to compare bonds with different maturities and different coupon rates. It is the single measure bond traders use when making apples-to-apples comparisons, regardless of maturity, coupon rate, or price.

The yield-to-maturity calculation accounts for all of the facets in the bond's total return, including the semi-annual interest payments as well as the repayment of principal. The yield-to-maturity calculation simply assigns a present-day value to all of the future cash flows, including the principal repayment.

For example, if we purchase our Government of Canada 8% November 2006 bond on November 1, 1996, we will receive our first interest payment—$40 per $1,000 face value—three months later. We also know that similar government bonds maturing in 2006 have a yield-to-maturity of 6.58%, which is the rate we use to discount our payments to their present value.

## The Concept of Present Value

What we already know is that money invested earns a return. If that money is invested in bonds or other fixed-income instruments, the return consists of regular interest payments (usually made every six months) plus the repayment of the principal investment when the bond matures.

If the regular interest payments are not required to finance day-to-day expenses, they can be reinvested. It is the reinvesting of these interest payments that allows the investor to earn interest on interest, a concept we have already defined as compounding. Note that in Table 6.2 we calculated a value for those reinvested interest payments and assumed that we could reinvest each of those interest payments at 8%.

To understand the mathematics of compounding, we need to first understand *present value*. We define present value as the current or beginning value of a quantity subject to compound interest. If you receive $100 today, it is worth $100. You know this because you can spend it immediately, and it will purchase $100 worth of goods and services.

That's different from a promise to pay you $100 two years from now. We refer to this as a future payment, and the $100, then, is the *future value* of the payment. We know that a $100 payment due in two years is clearly not worth $100 today! That's because the $100 you have in your pocket today can be invested immediately, and as such can begin to earn compound interest—which supports the present value definition as a quantity subject to compound interest.

The question, then, is what is the $100 you expect to receive two years from now actually worth today? And the answer depends on what rate of interest the money could be earning over the next two years, assuming it is invested today.

The present value formula calculates the present value of a future payment using a "discount" rate or yield assumption. The *discount rate* or *yield* is simply the compound rate of return you would expect to earn if the money was available to invest today.

These concepts of present value, future value, and discount rate are vital to a solid understanding of how the bond market functions, and are extremely important to retirement planning. The present value formula looks like this:

$$PV = \frac{FV}{(1 + R)^t}$$

where

PV = Present Value
FV = Future Value
R  = Interest (Discount) Rate
t  = Number of periods before the money is received

The FV in the formula represents the amount due at some point in the future. In the example we have been using, the amount due in the future is $100. The number of periods refers to the frequency of compounding. Again, using our $100 payment due two years from now, the number of periods could be two or four, depending on whether the money is compounding annually or semi-annually.

Using the formula, let's calculate how much a $100 payment due in two years is worth today. We'll assume the discount rate is 8%, compounding semi-annually. Note that in the formula, the discount rate is expressed as 4% (or .04), which is the interest earned every six months.

$$PV = \frac{FV}{(1 + R)^t} = \frac{100}{(1+.04)^4} = 85.48$$

Assuming an 8% discount rate compounding semi-annually, a $100 future value payment would be worth $85.48 today. Stated another way, if someone were to pay you $85.48 today, and that money was subjected to an 8% annual interest rate, compounding semi-annually, it would grow to $100 in two years' time.

At first blush, it would appear that the concept of present value becomes even more complicated when we use semi-annual compounding as the basis for the discount. But as we have seen in our previous examples, that's the way it is in the bond market. So why delay the inevitable?

## Present Value Defines What a Bond Is Really Worth

At the heart of a bond's price is the concept of present value. Returning to our previous example—where we purchase $1,000 face value of the Government of Canada 8% bond maturing on November 1, 2006— let's now bring into the discussion the concept of present value and from that calculate the yield-to-maturity.

Remember that a bond is really worth the sum of its parts. Table 6.1 defined this total return concept, in that our Government of Canada bond is really worth the sum of the 20 semi-annual interest payments, plus the principal repayment due in November 2006.

The problem is that we are receiving those interest payments at different stages, and the principal repayment will not occur for another 10 years. And we know that the present value of a dollar in the hand today is greater than the present value of a dollar to be received at some point in the future. Armed with the present value formula, and knowing all of the cash flow components in the bond's total return, we can use a discount rate assumption to ascertain the real value of the bond.

In the case of our hypothetical bond, we are receiving semi-annual interest payments of $40, which equates to the 8% coupon rate. We also know, from our previous discussion supported by the second *Globe and Mail* article, that the yield on 10-year Government of Canada bonds is 6.58%. That 6.58% is the discount rate we must apply to each of the semi-annual interest payments and to the $1,000 principal repayment.

The real value of the bond, then, is simply the present value of each of the interest payments plus the present value of the principal repayment, all discounted at some rate of interest, which for this example is 6.58% (see Table 6.4).

## TABLE 6.4: CALCULATING A BOND'S PRICE (6.58% DISCOUNT RATE)

| Date | Payments | Present Value* |
|------|----------|----------------|
| 01-May-97 | $40.00 | $38.73 |
| 01-Nov-97 | 40.00 | 37.49 |
| 01-May-98 | 40.00 | 36.30 |
| 01-Nov-98 | 40.00 | 35.14 |
| 01-May-99 | 40.00 | 34.02 |
| 01-Nov-99 | 40.00 | 32.94 |
| 30-Apr-00 | 40.00 | 31.89 |
| 31-Oct-00 | 40.00 | 30.87 |
| 01-May-01 | 40.00 | 29.89 |
| 01-Nov-01 | 40.00 | 28.94 |
| 01-May-02 | 40.00 | 28.02 |
| 01-Nov-02 | 40.00 | 27.12 |
| 01-May-03 | 40.00 | 26.26 |
| 01-Nov-03 | 40.00 | 25.42 |
| 30-Apr-04 | 40.00 | 24.61 |
| 31-Oct-04 | 40.00 | 23.83 |
| 01-May-05 | 40.00 | 23.07 |
| 01-Nov-05 | 40.00 | 22.34 |
| 01-May-06 | 40.00 | 21.62 |
| 01-Nov-06 | 40.00 | 20.94 |
| Principal | $1,000.00 | $523.40 |
| **Bond's Price** | | **$1,102.85** |

* Assumes the interest payments were reinvested at 6.58%.

Table 6.4 demonstrates that the bond is merely the sum of its parts. To determine what this bond is really worth, we simply add up the present values in the second column.

Present value of principal repayment      $523.40
Present value of semi-annual interest payments   $579.45

**Total value of bond**          **$1,102.85**

Based on these calculations, the real value of the bond is $1,102.85, which is the price you would pay to buy $1,000 of face value. The bond's price, then, equals 110.3% of par. The discount rate we use to calculate the present value of each semi-annual interest payment and for the repayment of the principal 10 years from now is the basis on which yield-to-maturity is calculated. In Table 6.4, the yield-to-maturity for our bond, assuming we pay 110.3% of par to buy it, is exactly 6.58%.

Here are a couple of points to consider. The yield-to-maturity is more a theoretical concept than a real-world principle. The fact we discounted all the future payments at 6.58% assumes that we will be able to reinvest each of those payments at that rate. In the real world, that is not likely to occur.

However, that does not diminish the importance of the yield-to-maturity concept. The yield-to-maturity is the *best* estimate of your expected realized yield on the bond. Furthermore, understanding yield-to-maturity and the concept of discounting future payments leads us directly into how changes in interest rates impact on the value of a bond.

Suppose, for example, that interest rates for 10-year bonds fall 58 basis points to 6% from the current 6.58%. With the new yield on 10-year bonds at 6%, that now becomes our discount rate. In this case, then, we will go through the same calculations as we did in Table 6.4, only this time we will discount all the semi-annual interest payments and the principal repayment at 6% rather than 6.58% (see Table 6.5).

## TABLE 6.5: CALCULATING A BOND'S PRICE (6% DISCOUNT RATE)

| Date | Payments | Present Value* |
|---|---|---|
| 01-May-97 | $40.00 | $38.83 |
| 01-Nov-97 | 40.00 | 37.70 |
| 01-May-98 | 40.00 | 36.61 |
| 01-Nov-98 | 40.00 | 35.54 |
| 01-May-99 | 40.00 | 34.50 |
| 01-Nov-99 | 40.00 | 33.50 |
| 30-Apr-00 | 40.00 | 32.52 |
| 31-Oct-00 | 40.00 | 31.58 |
| 01-May-01 | 40.00 | 30.66 |
| 01-Nov-01 | 40.00 | 29.76 |
| 01-May-02 | 40.00 | 28.90 |
| 01-Nov-02 | 40.00 | 28.06 |
| 01-May-03 | 40.00 | 27.24 |
| 01-Nov-03 | 40.00 | 26.44 |
| 30-Apr-04 | 40.00 | 25.67 |
| 31-Oct-04 | 40.00 | 24.93 |
| 01-May-05 | 40.00 | 24.20 |
| 01-Nov-05 | 40.00 | 23.50 |
| 01-May-06 | 40.00 | 22.81 |
| 01-Nov-06 | 40.00 | 22.15 |
| Principal | $1,000.00 | $553.68 |
| **Bond's Price** | | **$1,148.77** |

* Assumes the interest payments were reinvested at 6%.

Note how the value of the bond went up when the discount rate assumption went down. In fact, each $1,000 of face value is now worth $1,148.77, or 114.8% of par. Stating this another way, if we pay 114.8% of par to buy our Government of Canada 8% bond maturing in November 2006, our yield-to-maturity will be 6%. The yield-to-maturity approximates—after accounting for the bond's current price—the market rate for similar Government of Canada bonds maturing in 2006.

The yield-to-maturity, then, is the usual measure used by professional bond traders when comparing fixed income assets having similar risk factors and maturities. And remember the distinction between theoretical concept and real-world principles; the yield-to-maturity calculation assumes by default that you are able to reinvest those semi-annual interest payments at the 6% rate (based on the calculations in Table 6.5).

When you think about it, there is no real risk of default with a government bond. Having removed default risk from the discussion, the only factor affecting the price of the bond will be interest rates. And bond prices are inexorably linked to interest rates: when interest rates rise, bond prices fall, and vice versa. It is an inverse relationship that we normally associate with a teeter-totter (see Figure 6.1). This relationship lays the foundation for the remainder of our discussion on bonds.

## FIGURE 6.1: THE TEETER-TOTTER PRINCIPLE

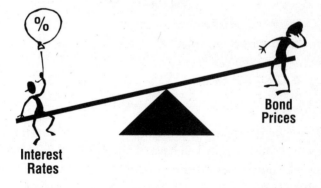

## And Then Comes the Term-to-Maturity ...

When we talk about a bond being long term or short term, we are really talking about the bond's *term-to-maturity*. In our Government of Canada 8% November 2006 example, the bond had a term-to-maturity of 10 years. A bond maturing in November 2021 has a term-to-maturity of 25 years, and one maturing in November 1997 has a term-to-maturity of one year.

The longer the term-to-maturity, the larger a factor the semi-annual interest payments play in the bond's total return. Even with our 10-year bond (from Table 6.4), the present value of the semi-annual interest payments totaled $579.45, which was more than the present value of the $1,000 ($523.40) principal repayment to be received 10 years from now.

If we stretched out the interest payments for 25 years, and used the same discount rate assumption (6.58%), it would have an even more dramatic effect on the importance of the semi-annual income stream versus the present value of the principal repayment 25 years from now.

**Assuming the bond in our example matures November 2021, discounted at 6.58%**

| | |
|---|---|
| Present value of principal repayment | $198.19 |
| Present value of semi-annual interest payments | $974.84 |
| | |
| **Total value of bond** | **$1,173.03** |

What we are doing here is laying a foundation to understand the effect the term-to-maturity will have on the price action of our bond. Watch what happens to the price of our bond maturing in 2021 if we change the discount rate from 6.58% to 6%. The price of the bond (defined as the total value of the bond) rises from 117.3% of par to 125.7% of par. In terms of capital gains, the value of the 25-year bond increased 7.18% because the discount rate fell from 6.58% to 6%.

> **Assuming the bond in our example matures November 2021, discounted at 6%**
>
> | | |
> |---|---|
> | Present value of principal repayment | $228.11 |
> | Present value of semi-annual interest payments | $1,029.19 |
> | | |
> | **Total value of bond** | **$1,257.30** |

Compare that to the change in the value of the 10-year bond from tables 6.4 and 6.5, whose price went from 110.2% of par to 114.8% of par, for a total capital gain of 4.16%. Again, that was the result of changing the discount rate assumption from 6.58% to 6%.

To review, then, we know that bond prices will rise when interest rates fall, and conversely we know that when interest rates rise, bond prices will fall. We also know that the longer the term-to-maturity, the more dramatic the effect a change in interest rates will have on the value of our bond.

## Strip Bonds

In recent years, there has been a lot of talk about strip bonds, particularly when talk focuses on retirement planning. A strip bond, as the name suggests, represents the stripped component parts of a bond's total return. Looking back at Table 6.4, we see 21 component parts of our 10-year bond: 20 semi-annual interest payments and one principal repayment. In that same table, we also calculated the present value of each of the component parts.

If we could strip away, say, the $40 interest payment due November 1, 2001, we could sell it for $28.94. If we simply divide the present value—$28.94—by the face value of the interest payment, the result is .7235, which is the discounting factor that provides a yield-to-maturity of 6.58%. If you were interested, then, in purchasing a $10,000 strip bond—that is, the face value component, without the interest payments—maturing November 1, 2001, it would cost you $7,235 to buy it today, assuming a discount rate of 6.58%.

The value of the strip bond will also rise and fall with a change in the level of interest rates. And like our previous example, the longer the term-to-maturity, the more dramatic the price shift caused by a change in interest rates. For some perspective on just how much impact a change in the discount rate will have on the price of our strip bond, simply look at Table 6.5 and follow it down to the present value for the November 1, 2001, interest payment when discounted at 6%.

The advantage of a strip bond is that it eliminates the reinvestment risk. Remember that the yield-to-maturity is really a theoretical concept, because it assumes that each semi-annual interest payment can be reinvested at the same discount rate. With a strip bond, there is only one payment to contend with, and that is the repayment of the principal at the end of the term. The good news is that since there are no interim interest payments to reinvest, there is no reinvestment risk. The yield-to-maturity for a strip bond is not only a theoretical concept, but a real-world principle. The bad news is that you have to include an amount in income each year equivalent to the implied interest component of the bond. As a result, strips are best suited only for RRSPs and other tax shelters.

## Mortgage-Backed Securities

Another type of bond is NHA (National Housing Act) mortgage-backed securities (MBS). These are essentially a pool of insured residential first mortgages, where the monthly interest and principal payments are guaranteed by the Government of Canada through the Canada Mortgage and Housing Corporation (CMHC).

Mortgage-backed securities are safe, in that there is no default risk to the investor, and they provide monthly payments that include both principal and interest. There are two types of mortgage-backed securities: (1) prepayable or "open" mortgages where the borrowers have the right to make principal prepayments at any time, and (2) non-prepayable or "closed" mortgages, where the borrowers cannot prepay the principal.

For the investor, an open pool means that the monthly payments will fluctuate depending on the amount of principal repayments. In a closed pool, the monthly mortgage payments will remain the same. One of the factors you need to understand is that part of the monthly income is really a return of your original principal. Since you receive part of your principal as part of your monthly income, the amount of principal you receive when the MBS matures will be less than your initial investment.

---

### At the coffee shop ...

"I never realized that bonds were so complicated," I muttered. "I haven't seen so many numbers flying around since the last time I got audited by Revenue Canada."

"When was that, Loa?" Chris looked innocent. "Last year?"

"Aren't we funny," I sneered. "But seriously, didn't you find all the numbers confusing?"

"I'm not sure I'll ever buy a bond," responded Machaela. "To me, it seemed overwhelming."

"Well, I finally have something to offer to the discussion," Chris countered, "because bonds are something I think I have a grip on."

"The floor is all yours," I said with a wave of my hand.

"The first thing you need to do is get away from all the numbers," Chris began. "The teacher was simply using the numbers to lay a foundation for some very basic principles. Principle number one: bond prices move inversely to interest rates. When rates are rising, bond prices will fall; when rates are falling, bond prices will rise."

"The teeter-totter illustration," Machaela interjected.

"A tip of my hat to the sister providing some visual reinforcement," Chris said with a grin, before continuing. "Principle number two: the longer the term-to-maturity, the more volatile the bond's price will be—that is, a change in interest rates will cause a greater fluctuation in the price of a long-term bond. The bottom line is that long-term bonds are riskier than short-term bonds."

Chris was clearly proud of the fact he had grasped something that we were still struggling with. Well, it was time for me to step in and find out if there was something I could use from this lesson besides an understanding of playground metaphors.

"Alright," I asked, "what should I do with the information I learned?"

"Good question, Loa! How about some investment strategies when interest rates are still low?" It looked like Chris was ready to go on one of his long-winded explanations. I sat back, raised my hand, and ordered another cappuccino.

"For one thing, you should avoid getting locked into low rates of return on long-term investments. If you have GICs maturing when rates are low, don't roll them over into long-term GICs.

"You don't want to buy an annuity or whole life insurance, for that matter, when rates are low. If you buy an annuity, the insurance company is simply guaranteeing a regular income stream to you, and the rate of return it uses to guarantee that income is based on current rates. You have to pay more to get the same income when rates are low. Same with whole life insurance, where the cost is affected by the return the insurance company can get on your premium. Since that return is driven by interest rates, you may have to pay a higher premium for the same coverage."

I was impressed with Chris. I didn't know he had so much insight into insurance. But then again, given his dental practice and his need for malpractice insurance, I guess it shouldn't come as a great surprise.

He rolled along. "How about this? If you are planning to borrow for a house, a major appliance, or a car, consider making the move when rates are low. It's better to preserve cash and borrow for expenditures that can't be put off for at least a few years. Take today's rate and run.

"Keeping with the same theme, it would also make sense to lock in your variable-rate mortgages—quickly. Take a fixed-rate longer-term mortgage when rates are low, and laugh all the way to the bank. There will be better uses for your investment capital in the coming years.

"And, finally, if you are about to receive a settlement, whether it is a damage award from an accident or an employment severance cheque, you are better off taking the lump sum today rather than a payment schedule plus interest. The interest-rate assumption will be based on today's rates, and if those rates are low, it is better to have the lump sum now and the flexibility to invest it later, when rates rise."

"That makes sense when rates are low, but what happens when rates are rising?" asked Machaela.

"Well, some of the same things apply. You want to pay off your variable-rate debt, such as personal loans and credit card balances. Even though these rates never went down much when other rates were falling, you can be certain that they will rise along with other rates.

"Given our understanding of the relationship between bond prices and interest rates, you want to sell your longer-term bonds and move into shorter-term bonds when rates are beginning to rise. Mind you, that's easier said than done, because who really knows when interest rates will start to rise."

"Which brings up a thought." I raised my hand, looking for permission to speak. "Maybe the best approach is to ladder your bond portfolio." It was one of those terms I had read in an investment book.

"What do you mean when you say 'ladder'?" asked Chris.

"Well, it's really no different than how you invest in GICs," I answered. "You basically stagger your term, so that a GIC will come due every year. Laddering your bond portfolio is essentially the same thing. Buy a short-term bond, a mid-term bond, and a long-term bond so that something is coming due on a regular basis. At least with this approach you don't have to forecast interest rates, and at the end of the day you will probably do as well as most professional money managers."

# Going to Market— The Stock Market, That Is!

After last week's discussion of bond rates, Chris, Machaela, and I were looking for a little relief. At least tonight's topic was going to be different—stock markets and exchanges. I had images of wealth and luxury, office towers and gold. It sounded exotic, and Professor Kirzner had a captivated audience before he even began.

## Class in session ...

A recent *Globe and Mail* article in the Report on Business section offered the following commentary on the U.S. stock market:

"Yesterday's gain on the Dow Jones Industrial Average—just 17.38 points to 5,711.27—was uninspiring. It did not even compensate for all of Monday's 28.85 point loss."

Now, let's see if I have this right. The U.S. stock market rises 17.38 points, but the previous day it had fallen 28.85 points, so it didn't recover all it had lost the previous day. Thank goodness the *Globe and Mail* is there to point out the obvious—at least, obvious to anyone who knows what the Dow Jones Industrial Average is!

The *Globe* goes on to talk about the Canadian market: "On Bay Street, pipelines—Monday's best performing industry group on the Toronto Stock Exchange—hit the skids, pressuring the TSE 300 Stock Composite Index, which fell 12.82 points to 5,173.88." Again, what is the TSE 300 Composite Index, and what does that have to do with the market?

These are issues we'll get to in a moment. For now, just understand that when the newspapers, the nightly news, or business reports on your local radio station talk about the stock market, the commentators invariably quote the performance of some major stock market index. The most common index—its notoriety the result of having such a long history as a market barometer and such prominence in the prestigious *Wall Street Journal*—is the Dow Jones Industrial Average. The TSE 300 Composite Index is simply Canada's version of an index that measures the performance of a broad cross-section of stocks.

## The Exchanges
## (Understanding How Financial Securities Are Traded)

Before settling into the indexes, let's look at the creation of common shares. When a company decides to raise equity capital through the issue of shares to the public, it engages in an initial public offering (IPO).

When a company "goes public" by issuing shares in return for cash, it usually employs an investment dealer as an underwriter to assist in the placement of the shares. In a *firm* underwriting, the investment dealer buys the shares and resells them to the public. In a *best efforts* under-writing, the investment dealer sells shares subject to a commission but does not take the risk of the issue.

The purchase of these new issues referred to as initial public offerings, or IPOs, is popular with new investors—and for good reason. There is always an interesting story about the company when the stock is first issued. The financial press will usually play up any stories about the company, which helps to create interest among investors. And of course brokers are expected to sell IPOs because the brokerage firm wants to develop an investment banking relationship with the company issuing the shares. However, buying IPOs can be a speculative venture since the company has no public track record. The purchase of IPOs should be left to seasoned investors.

After the IPO the company is said to be publicly traded. If the financial managers want to raise additional equity capital at a later date they will do so through a new issue of shares, a rights offering or a package issue of common shares and warrants.

## RIGHTS OFFERINGS

When a company wants to raise additional equity capital, it may choose to issue rights to shareholders to buy additional shares at a discount to the current market price.

The rights normally have a life of 30 to 60 days, after which they expire. Shareholders can exercise the rights and acquire new shares, or they can sell the rights for cash. (The rights trade on the same exchange as the common shares.) In a typical rights offering, a shareholder receives one rights for each common share owned and can then exercise the rights on the basis of three (sometimes four or five) rights for one new common share at a specified price.

## WARRANTS

A warrant is similar to a right, except it has a longer term to expiration. Companies often issue warrants as a "sweetener" to a bond or stock issue (i.e., to make the issue more attractive).

Next, let's look at how stocks are traded. When most individual investors think about stocks, they think about "exchange-traded stocks." That is, stocks that are listed on a major stock exchange such as the New York Stock Exchange or the Toronto Stock Exchange.

An exchange is really just a central meeting place where buyers and sellers of financial securities—that is, stocks and listed bonds—meet to transact business. Prices that buyers are willing to pay and sellers are willing to take are posted for all participants to see. Financial market regulators like that visibility of prices, because in theory it means stock market dealings are fair. However, much of today's stock exchange business is conducted through electronic trading. Many companies list their stocks "over the counter," or OTC for short. This is another one of those brokerage terms, which essentially means that the stocks are traded between brokers over computer screens. These are referred to as "unlisted" securities.

Most new investors think that unlisted stocks are smaller companies that can't quite cut the mustard, at least not well enough to be listed on a recognized exchange. To a large extent that view is correct. Many unlisted stocks are small capitalized companies who trade over the counter because they can't meet the financial requirements for an exchange listing. On the other hand, some of the world's largest companies trade over the counter, including some large-cap blue-chip companies, like Intel and Microsoft. It is simply cheaper to have stock traded in the unlisted market.

## How Stocks Prices Are Quoted

Having gained some background knowledge of the exchanges and the OTC markets, the next step is to understand how stocks are priced.

Let's assume that a buyer might be willing to pay $10 per share for XYZ stock. The bid on XYZ would then be posted at $10 per share, assuming, of course, that $10 is the highest current bid. A seller might be willing to offer the same stock at, say, $10 ¼ per share. The offered price for XYZ would then be posted as $10 ¼, again assuming that this is the best available sale price offered. So, when you call your stockbroker and ask for the market on XYZ, she would say bid $10, offered at $10 ¼.

Stocks are traded in ⅛ths, or 12.5 cents per share, on many exchanges. It has been that way for decades, although there is now a major move afoot to change the way stocks are priced, in both the U.S. and Canada. The "eighth," by the way, is the heritage of the old "pieces of eight," Spanish silver coins associated with sunken treasures.

In Canada, we have already begun to change the way stocks are traded. The Toronto Stock Exchange recently began trading in decimals, so that you can actually see stock where the bid is $10 and the offered price is $10.05. In the day of the computer, decimal trading makes more sense and, from our perspective, benefits small investors.

Before going too far down this road, let us return for a moment to XYZ stock where the bid is $10 and the offer is $10 ¼. Now, if you were interested in buying XYZ stock and were willing to pay $10 ¼, you would be able to buy the stock instantly. In fact, your stockbroker could probably give you confirmation of the trade while you were still on the phone.

Conversely, if you own XYZ shares, and were willing to sell them at $10 per share, your order would also be filled instantly, assuming, of course, we are talking anywhere from 100 shares to, say, 1,000 shares. Large institutional orders of, say, 100,000 shares at a time may not get filled instantly, but even those orders might be filled quickly if the institution was willing to buy or sell at the quoted prices.

When you are willing to pay the offered price or sell at the bid price, you enter what is called a *market order*, which is simply an order to buy or sell at the current market price.

As a new investor, you may have a price in mind for XYZ. You might, for example, feel that if you could buy XYZ at, say, $10 ⅛, it would be a fair price. And why not?—$10 ⅛ is between the current bid and offered price. Entering an order to buy at $10 ⅛ is referred to as a *limit order*. You have effectively limited what price your stockbroker can, in this case, pay to buy shares of XYZ.

It's not that much different from buying a house, really. I mean, if you like a particular house and you have a price in mind to pay for it, while the vendor has a higher sale price in mind, more often than not you will saw off somewhere between your bid and the vendor's offered price.

Another consideration to bear in mind, one which many new investors are not familiar with, is the standard number of shares you need to buy or sell in a trade. Usually, stocks are traded in 100-share lots—called *round lots*—so in our XYZ example, the bid price would be for a minimum of 100 shares and the offered price would also be for 100 shares.

## Speaking a Language All Their Own (Blue Chip, Large Cap, Growth ...)

There are some other terms you should be familiar with when talking about stocks—terms such as small cap, mid cap, large cap, blue chip, and growth companies.

When stockbrokers and financial commentators talk about small cap, mid cap, or large cap, they are discussing the relative size of the company. In other words, these terms relate to the worth of the company. The term *cap* is short for capitalization.

To use an example, suppose XYZ had one million shares outstanding (shares that are issued and in the hands of the public, i.e., institutional and individual investors). Since we know XYZ is trading at approximately $10 per share, the market capitalization of the company is $10 million, which is simply the price per share multiplied by the number of shares outstanding. In theory, most exchange-listed companies are much larger than our hypothetical XYZ. In fact, XYZ would be considered a micro-cap company, because its market capitalization is below $25 million.

Generally, but not always, a small-cap company is valued between $25 million and $250 million, and in some cases up to $500 million. A mid-cap company is usually valued at $250 to $500 million, and up to $1 billion. Companies whose market capitalization is above $1 billion are referred to as large-cap companies.

The term *blue chip* is simply financial market jargon used to describe the largest, most mature, most profitable companies in which you can invest. General Motors, for example, would be considered a blue-chip company, and so would IBM, BCE Inc. (the parent company of Bell Canada), Microsoft, Intel, Procter & Gamble, Philip Morris, and so on.

IBM was the quintessential blue-chip company of the 1970s and 1980s. In fact, IBM still carries the nickname "Big Blue" which, of course, refers to its blue-chip roots. We generally think of blue-chip companies as those whose share prices will not likely rise or fall as dramatically as smaller companies, when changes are averaged over the course of a business cycle.

Almost invariably, a blue-chip company is a large-cap company, although not all large-cap companies are viewed as being blue chip. Larger-cap blue-chip companies have more capital or access to capital, which allows them, generally speaking, to successfully navigate the ups and downs of the economy. This means they will have a smoother ride through the peaks and troughs of the business cycle.

Blue-chip large-cap companies usually, although again, not always, pay steady quarterly dividends, and those dividends are frequently increased depending on how profitable the company is or is expected to be.

## Speaking of Dividends ...
## (On Being an Owner or a Loaner)

To digress one step further, we should explain what a dividend is. Companies can raise money in one of two ways: they can borrow money, which means the company would issue a bond, or they can sell equity, which simply means selling shares from the treasury. Investors who buy the bonds are loaning money to the company, while investors who buy shares are buying an ownership interest in the company. Hence, as an investor, you have a choice: you can be a "loaner" or an "owner."

When you buy a part of a business, you are taking on a greater risk than if you loaned the business money. At least when you loan money, the borrower promises to pay you interest and to return your principal at some point in the future. Failure to live up to that contract means the company would, technically, be in default. The investor who loans money, then, has prior claims on the assets of the company should it fail to repay the loan or the annual interest payments.

To become an owner, you must buy the common shares of the company, as opposed to preferred shares that some companies issue. You might think, at first blush, that if you are going to buy shares, you should buy preferred rather than common shares. After all, "preferred" infers some sort of advantage—like flying business class versus economy.

The fact is, both classes of shares represent an ownership in the company. However, in most cases, preferred shares only participate in the company's dividends, whereas common shares participate in capital gains and dividends.

Furthermore, preferred shares do not normally empower you to vote at shareholder meetings. Most preferred shareholders only get to vote if the company fails to pay the dividends that were promised in the preferred shareholder agreement.

For example, BCE has a number of different preferred shares outstanding. One class, BCE Preferred Series "P," promises to pay shareholders $1.60 per year in dividends. The dividends must be paid for the Series "P" preferred shares, and all other series of BCE preferred shares, before any dividends can be paid to the common shareholders.

Now, a dividend comes out of the after-tax corporate profits, so a preferred shareholder does not have the same rights as a bond holder. If the company doesn't make a profit, it can't pay a dividend, despite what may appear in the preferred shareholder agreement. What we are saying, then, is that failure to pay a dividend does not, by law, put a company into default.

Of course, most preferred shareholder agreements have contingency plans in place for just such an event. In many cases, if the company fails to pay a dividend to a preferred shareholder, it must make up all of the missed dividend payments before the company can disburse any dividends to common shareholders.

When you look at it from this perspective, preferred shareholders are effectively loaning money to the company in exchange for a fixed or floating[1] dividend payment. However, preferred shareholders cannot force a company into default, as a bond holder can, should the dividend payment not be made. It makes you wonder why anyone would consider owning a preferred share.

The answer is the dividend tax credit. Because dividends are paid from corporate profits, tax has already been paid on this income. As such, dividends receive preferential tax treatment in Canada due to the dividend tax credit. Aside from the tax issue, preferred shareholders stand in line ahead of common shareholders when issuing claims against the assets of a bankrupt company. But that's a small consolation considering that preferred shareholders will stand behind bond holders in the same line.

An owner is someone who buys the common shares of a company, and does so with the intent of earning capital gains as the price of the stock appreciates, or higher dividends because the company's management decides to distribute profits to shareholders. The point is, owners participate in the profits of the company through capital gains and dividends. Owners also share the risks should the company go out of business, and stand at the end of the line for any claim on corporate assets.

At the same time, common shareholders have some control over the company, because they have the right to vote at shareholders' meetings—one share generally equals one vote. Mind you, the right to vote is a perception issue. Owning 100 common shares of General Motors might entitle you to 100 votes, but within a context of more than 750 million shares outstanding, those 100 votes aren't likely to sway much opinion in the company.

Any dividend paid to common shareholders must be declared by the board of directors. Any change in the common shareholder dividend—that is, raising or lowering the dividend—must also be declared by the board of directors. Again, dividends are paid out of after-tax profits

---

[1] Some companies have issued floating rate preferred shares, where the quarterly dividend is based on some percentage of the going rate payable on short-term government Treasury Bills.

and, by definition, represent profits being distributed to shareholders. An owner, then, has greater risk than a loaner. And because of that, owners usually earn higher returns than loaners.

Back to our blue-chip large-cap dividend-paying companies. Dividends are usually paid every three months, or quarterly. If a company's common stock has a high dividend yield, that tells you one of two things: (1) it can be a mature company where most investors believe the prospects for double-digit growth are limited, or (2) it could be a company in trouble, and the high yield is based on previous dividend payments, which many investors don't believe the company can maintain.

BCE Inc. is an example of the former. The company currently pays its common shareholders a quarterly dividend of 68 cents per share, and it has been able to consistently raise that dividend over the years— not always by the same amount, but BCE's record for dividend increases has been impressive.

The dividend yield on BCE Inc. is 4.45%, which is about in line with yields on some of the major bank stocks. We arrive at that yield by dividing the annual dividend (the sum of the four quarterly dividends) by the share price. With BCE Inc. trading at $61.00 per share (at the time of writing), and assuming an annual divided of $2.72 ($0.68 $\times$ 4 = $2.72), the dividend yield is 4.45%. Investors demand high dividends from mature companies like BCE because these companies are not likely to grow at above-average rates into the future. BCE and many of the Canadian bank stocks are so large that to grow at, say, 10% annually would mean an astronomical surge in business.

## Dividend reinvestment plans

Many companies have dividend reinvestment plans (DRIPs). These plans allow you to reinvest your dividends by purchasing new common shares from the company. Normally there are no associated costs. DRIPs are valuable in allowing you to maintain your investment in the company in an efficient manner.

## Growth Companies

Not all blue-chip large-cap companies pay hefty dividends. Just how much of a dividend a company pays depends on how well management views the prospects for increasing sales and profits over the coming years. If management feels it can generate a better return for investors by plowing profits back into the company, they may opt for that strategy. Intel is an example of a company that has a very low dividend—20 cents per share at the time of writing—but Intel's earnings have grown at a double-digit rate for each of the last 10 years. Higher earnings mean higher stock prices, which for investors means capital gains. If potential capital gains resulting from the reinvestment of profits exceeds the benefits of earning a good dividend, few investors would complain.

So the management of growth companies, as the name suggests, works diligently at trying to grow earnings. Which brings us another step down the road to understanding how stocks are priced, specifically to the concept of the price-to-earnings ratio. The per share price of a stock, generally speaking, represents some multiple of current or expected earnings. And the most common tool to measure the price of a stock relative to earnings is the price/earnings ratio—the P/E for short. I'll have more to say on the P/E in a later lesson.

## Industry- and Company-Specific Risk

There are a couple of broadly based risk factors that will affect your financial well-being—even when buying 100 shares of a single, blue-chip, large-cap, dividend-paying stock. Now, there's a mouthful.

The fact is, despite your best intentions to find a good-quality stock, all companies have risks unique to their line of business. Financial analysts define this as *company-specific risk.*

Company-specific risk refers to risks uniquely associated with the company you are buying. For example, suppose you want to buy shares of Air Canada. Now, an airline company, particularly one that in the last few years has been forced to fly without taxpayer support, will have a number of risk factors to consider. The cost of fuel is obviously a consideration. Higher fuel costs will increase the cost to fly, which could dampen demand and weaken profits.

And what about aircraft maintenance? While flying is statistically the safest form of transportation, passenger traffic invariably declines when one of the company jets is involved in a mishap. That, too, is a risk factor for investors.

There is also the union issue. If the mechanics' union or the pilots' union goes on strike, it can have a devastating effect on the profitability of the company, especially if the strike happens to coincide with high traffic volume. Sometimes an airline company never recovers from such a prolonged labor dispute. Remember Eastern Airlines.

Finally, there is the big picture defined as the business cycle, which we talked about in a previous lesson. Suffice it to say that during economic expansion there is more demand for business travel, and that provides the highest profit margin for an airline company. Conversely, when the economy is contracting, business travel often takes a back seat to other forms of communication. Interestingly, this may be a larger risk factor as we enter the 21st century. As companies find more cost-effective ways to communicate with customers and employees—video-conference calling is one example of improvements in communication technology—the need for face-to-face meetings may wane, and that will have a negative impact on the airline industry.

What we are talking about, then, are risks uniquely associated with airline companies and the airline industry. Holding just one airline company in your portfolio will subject you and the value of your portfolio to each of these risk factors.

And that is where diversification can be useful. Professional money managers attempt to offset company- and industry-specific risk by purchasing other companies that would not, in this case since you already are holding Air Canada, be negatively affected by the risks unique to the airline industry. And in some cases, what is bad for an airline company might be good for another type of company in your portfolio.

For example, if you also bought 100 shares of an oil company at the same time you purchased your airline company shares, you could eliminate or at least reduce the potential negative effects that an increase in the price of fuel would have on the airline's profitability. Presumably, in our very basic two-stock portfolio, a rise in fuel prices would have a negative impact on the airline company, but would probably mean increased profits to the oil company, especially if the oil company was able to increase its profit margins as a result of the higher prices. When we talk about profit margin, we are simply referring to the difference between the costs of manufacturing and distributing a product versus the price received at the point of sale.

Of course, the oil company will also be affected by potential labor disruptions; oil company employees are often members of a very strong union. A strike at the oil company will have the same impact on the bottom line as will a strike at the airline company. The only risk-reduction element that can be tied to labor issues is the fact that the airline company and the oil company will not likely be on strike at exactly the same time.

What is interesting about company-specific risk is that it can all but be eliminated with a properly diversified portfolio. In fact, studies tell us that as much as 95% of company-specific risk can be eliminated with a portfolio of 30 different stocks representing a number of different industries. In fact, any additional stocks above the 30-stock benchmark will not result in any measurable benefit in terms of reducing company-specific risk.

Eliminating company-specific risk, however, can present a problem for individual investors. Assuming you are interested in holding a diversified portfolio, and assuming you want to hold at least 30 different stocks in your portfolio, you would need to buy at least 100 shares of 30 different companies at different prices. The commissions to buy and sell—note that stockbrokers charge a commission to buy and another commission to sell—not to mention the spread between the bid and offered price, can add up to a substantial cost when building a portfolio. A properly diversified portfolio of 30 blue-chip stocks—assuming 100-share minimums—could add up to more than $100,000, which is beyond the reach of many small investors.

# Market Risk

But suppose you can afford $100,000 and you set out to invest evenly among 30 blue-chip large-cap Canadian stocks in different industries. You eliminate virtually all risk—right?

Wrong! While you may—assuming the portfolio is properly diversified across most industries—be able to eliminate virtually all company-specific risk, your portfolio is still subject to *market risk*, or as financial analysts would say, the risk of owning a company that publicly trades its stock.

When the stock market rises, so too do most stocks. When the stock market declines, so too do most stocks. That individual stocks follow the general trend in the market is not surprising when you consider that the price changes of individual stocks ultimately dictate whether the market is rising or falling.

If we can get beyond what looks like an exercise in double-talk, allow me to explain. When the financial press talks about the action in the stock market, one of the barometers used is the number of *advances* versus *declines*. That is, the number of advancing stocks versus the number of declining stocks on any given day. And because some stocks don't move during the day, the exchanges also calculate the number of stocks that were unchanged on the day. When the market is rising, you should expect to see more stocks advancing in price than stocks declining in price. Conversely, when the stock market is declining, you should expect to see more stocks decline than advance during that day. Such is the risk associated with investing.

Market risk is not trivial. Going through periods when the stock market is particularly volatile can be unnerving. In some cases, dramatic shifts can incite panic. In October 1987, when the stock market as measured by the Dow Jones Industrial Average declined more than 500 points in one day, over 20% of shareholder value was wiped out. The trick, then, is to build a diversified portfolio that eliminates company-specific risk and minimizes the impact of market risk. I'll have more to say on market risk later.

## Measuring the Market—"The Need to Know"

When we see comments in the financial press like those cited at the beginning of this lesson, we need to understand a few more terms—in this case, terms related to stock market indexes or gauges used to measure the performance of the financial markets.

The most celebrated stock market index is not even an index, but is really an average—the Dow Jones Industrial Average. "The Dow average was originally created by Charles Dow [in 1896] as an index for his *Customers' Afternoon Letter*, the forerunner of *The Wall Street Journal*. The idea was to take a handful of widely held stocks, calculate their average price and change for the day and divide the total by eleven—there were eleven stocks in the original Dow average."[2]

In Mr. Dow's column, forecasts were made about the direction of the stock market, all premised on the movements in the Dow indexes. His views were later expanded to become known as the Dow Theory.

The current Dow Jones Industrial Average includes 30 of the largest blue-chip stocks in corporate America—General Motors, IBM, Philip Morris, General Electric, Procter & Gamble, American Telephone and Telegraph, to name a few. We're talking the elite companies.

In 1922, when the index included 20 issues, the editors were faced with their first major hurdle—a stock split. In this case, American Tobacco was split two for one. In a stock split, the company issues twice as many shares as before, but the shares are valued at half the previous price. Has anything fundamentally changed for investors who hold the stock? I mean, is owning 100 shares of a $10 stock any different than owning 200 shares of a $5 stock? Of course not. In both cases, your portfolio is still worth $1,000.

What a stock split does, however, is change investor perception. The idea is to encourage more individual investors to consider the company's stock when shopping for new investments. After the stock

---

[2] These comments about the history of the Dow are excerpted from a weekly column by the late Jim Yates in his DYR and Associates newsletter. The newsletter, which is still published by his son, provides option research for brokerage firms.

split, it is cheaper to buy 100 shares at $5—the minimum round lot order discussed earlier—than it is to buy 100 shares at $10.

When a press release announces that a company intends to split its stock, occasionally the price of the stock will rise in anticipation of the split. Conventional wisdom, that I'm not sure is correct, suggests that more investors will buy into a company if the per share price is lower. If more investors begin to take an interest in the stock, then as conventional wisdom suggests, a split stock will go higher in price after the split. But that may be more perception than reality. Studies suggest that a stock's price will rise after a split only if there is a major announcement of some other change at the same time as the split. You might see, for example, a company announce a stock split and a dividend increase. That push and pull effect on the stock may be enough to push the price of the shares higher. The fact that the stock split, however, should not alone have any meaningful effect on whether the stock price rises or falls after the fact.

But a stock split can have a major impact on the computation of a price-weighted index, which, by the way, is how the Dow Averages are calculated. For the record there are now four Dow Averages: (1) the Dow Jones Industrial Average, (2) the Dow Jones Transportation Average, (3) the Dow Jones Utility Average, and (4) the Dow Jones Composite Average.

## Price-Weighted Indexes

In a price-weighted index, you simply add up the closing prices of all the stocks and then divide by the index divisor. Assuming you were to calculate the price-weighted average of a two-stock index—where stock A was worth $100 and stock B was worth $50—you would simply add the prices together and divide by 2. The value of our two-stock index, then, is 75 (100 + 50 = 150 divided by 2 = 75).

## TABLE 7.1: TWO-STOCK PRICE-WEIGHTED INDEX CALCULATION

|  | Closing Price | Impact on Index | Pct. Impact on Index |
|---|---|---|---|
| Stock A | $100.00 | 50.00 | 66.67% |
| Stock B | $50.00 | 25.00 | 33.33% |
| Index Divisor | 2.00 | | |
| Index Value | 75.00 | 75.00 | 100.00% |

Analysts have expressed two serious concerns about the Dow Averages. Specifically, these concerns relate to: (1) the mathematical validity of price-weighted averages, and (2) whether the Dow Averages accurately reflect the mood of the market in today's modern economy.

Let's first examine the concerns about the mathematical validity of a price-weighted index. In a price-weighted index, a $1 per share price movement will have the same impact on the index regardless of what the current price of the stock is.

For example, suppose the price of IBM shares—one of the stocks in the Dow Jones Industrial Average—rises by US$1.00. On the same day, the price of General Motors (another Dow component) also rises by US$1.00. In terms of how we calculate the Dow Jones Industrial Average, the impact from the price movement of both stocks is the same. The problem is one of degree.

IBM is trading at about US$100 per share at the time of writing, while General Motors is trading at approximately US$50 per share, or half the value of IBM. In terms of percentage moves, a $1 move in the value of General Motors stock represents a 2% increase in the value of the shares. The same $1 move in the value of IBM represents a 1% increase in the value of IBM shares. Yet the moves have equal impact on the calculated value of the Dow Jones Industrial Average.

How accurate is the Dow Jones Industrial Average as a barometer of the modern financial marketplace? The Dow Jones Industrial Average is an index of 30 stocks out of a list that includes more than 35,000 U.S. publicly traded companies. It may be a blue-chip list of 30 stocks, but how can it hope to be representative of U.S. industry? That so many analysts question its use as a barometer is the reason we now have available so many other indexes that measure everything from the stock market to the consumer price index to the composite of collectibles including art, coins, and probably pop bottles.

## Modern Capitalization-Weighted Indexes

Modern stock market indexes such as the Standard & Poor's 500 Composite Index, the New York Stock Exchange Composite Index, and, of course, the Toronto Stock Exchange 300 Composite Index are capitalization weighted and track the performance of many stocks in many different industries. This provides analysts with a better measure of overall stock market performance.

A capitalization index takes into account the size of the companies that make up the index. By weighting the component stocks by market capitalization, the index gives greater weight to larger companies in the final calculation.

To understand how a market capitalization index is calculated, we will again return to our hypothetical two-stock index. Table 7.2 looks at how the index is calculated at the outset. Normally, all capitalization-weighted indexes begin with a base value of 100. The divisor then brings the market cap of all the stocks in the component index back to a base value of 100. In Table 7.2, we see that while the stock prices vary, both stock A and stock B are, in terms of market capitalization, the same size and as such carry the same weight in the calculation of the index.

**TABLE 7.2: TWO-STOCK CAPITALIZATION-WEIGHTED INDEX CALCULATION**

|  | Closing Price | Number of shares | Market Cap | Impact on Index | Pct. Impact on Index |
|---|---|---|---|---|---|
| Stock A | $100.00 | 10,000 | $1,000,000 | 50.00 | 50.00% |
| Stock B | $50.00 | 20,000 | $1,000,000 | 50.00 | 50.00% |
| Index Divisor |  |  | 20,000 |  |  |
| Index Value |  |  | 100.00 |  |  |

In Table 7.3, we see what happens when the price of the stocks in the index changes. In this case, the price of both stocks increased by $5 a share. However, a capitalization-weighted index takes into account the percentage changes in the component stocks. Stock B in this case increased in value by 10%, while stock A increased in value by only 5%. That is also reflected in the calculation of the index. Note that the $5 price change of stock B had a greater impact on the value of the index than did the $5 change in the price of stock A.

**TABLE 7.3: TWO-STOCK CAPITALIZATION-WEIGHTED INDEX AFTER PRICE CHANGE**

|  | Closing Price | Number of Shares | Market Cap | Impact on Index | Pct. Impact on Index |
|---|---|---|---|---|---|
| Stock A | $105.00 | 10,000 | $1,050,000 | 2.50 | 2.33% |
| Stock B | $55.00 | 20,000 | $1,100,000 | 5.00 | 4.65% |
| Index Divisor |  |  | 20,000 |  |  |
| Index Value |  |  | 107.50 |  |  |

We think that capitalization-weighted indexes provide a better gauge of market performance. At least they take into account the relative size of the companies when doing a random sample of the market. The Toronto Stock Exchange 300 Composite Index is also a capitalization-weighted index, and all of the major indexes are recalculated on a minute-to-minute basis to take into account any intra-day changes in the value of the component stocks.

## The Value Line Composite Index—A Geometric Average

There is one other tool for measuring the performance of the stock market—or at least another tool to provide a different spin on market performance—the Value Line Composite Index.

Value Line is a large U.S.-based investment advisory service that ranks approximately 1,700 stocks on the basis of timeliness and safety. Value Line ranks stocks from 1 (best) to 5 (worst) and, over the years, the company's methodology has gained a serious following in the financial community.

The Value Line Composite Index is a capitalization-weighted index, but what makes the index so different is the way it is calculated. It is, by definition, an equally weighted index in terms of each stock's percentage change. For example, the 30 stocks in the Dow Jones Industrial Average are also components in the Value Line Composite Index, as they are in the S&P 500 Composite Index. But in the S&P index, the 30 Dow stocks would carry greater weight because they are larger companies. The same is not true in the Value Line model. The 30 Dow stocks carry no greater weight in terms of percentage price change than do any other 30 issues in the Value Line Composite Index.

In other words, a 10% change in the price of IBM has the same impact on the index as does a 10% change in the value of Microsoft. What that does is make the Value Line Composite Index more sensitive to price changes in the smaller-cap companies within the index, which is why some market analysts see the Value Line Composite Index as a proxy for the performance of small-cap stocks.

Value Line accomplishes this computational nightmare by geometrically averaging the resulting price changes. Rather than attempting to explain the potential and pitfalls of geometric averaging, consider again our two-stock index. The geometric average is a two-step calculation. For the first step, we would take the price of stock A ($100) and multiply it by the price of stock B ($50), the result being $5,000. In the second step, we would take the square root (because there are only two stocks) of 5,000, which would be our index value (see table 7.4).

**TABLE 7.4: CALCULATION OF A GEOMETRIC AVERAGE (TWO STOCKS)**

|  | Index Components | Closing Price |
|---|---|---|
|  | Price of Stock A | $100.00 |
|  | Price of Stock B | $50.00 |
| Step 1 | Stock A × B | $5,000.00 |
| Step 2 | Index Value (square root of Step 1) | 70.71 |

If there were three stocks in the index, you would again multiply their values and take the cube root of the total. If there were five stocks in the index, you would multiply the value and take the fifth root to arrive at the index value.

The question you probably want to ask is why go to all that effort when calculating an index? Value Line has plenty of computer power at its disposal and the computations are not that difficult. But more importantly, at least to some analysts, is the integrity of the data.

---

To sum up tonight's lesson, to measure is to know. That is precisely why there are indexes to measure the performance of the financial markets. And in this lesson we only discussed a few stock market indexes.

Now, when someone tells you the U.S. market was up 20 points, you know they are probably talking about the Dow Jones Industrial Average. When someone asks you what the market is doing, you can now look them straight in the eye and ask, "Which one?"

### At the coffee shop ...

"Pretty wild stuff," said Chris. "I learned some terms that until now I had no idea about, but I'm not sure where this is all leading."

"Well, as someone whose entire portfolio is tied up in GICs, you should benefit from this lesson more than anyone," Machaela pointed out. "You have the most to gain from an understanding of the financial markets."

"I agree," I said. "No question about that, Chris. Let's face it, today's lesson was a warm-up. It was all about building a foundation. I mean, you are the quintessential GIC investor. No one needs this foundation more than you. If you do not understand the intricacies of the financial markets, you will never invest in stocks. And before you can understand how the markets work, you need to understand the language. To me, this was a language lesson."

"Well, both of you are probably right," Chris admitted. "Maybe I am being too impatient. And I want to learn. I'm not expecting everything to come to me overnight."

"Neither do I," said Machaela. "But with this lesson, I gained some valuable insights into the financial markets. But I do have a basic question. Should small companies that have yet to earn any profits be considered or not as an investment?"

"Well, I don't know," reflected Chris. "I think a dividend history is an important criterion for investment. I would feel more comfortable with a stock that had been paying dividends for, say, the last 10 years. You, on the other hand"—Chris was looking directly at me—"might be willing to accept the kind of risks associated with a small company with promise. Fair enough. But just because I want more security—and that assumes I would consider buying any stock, which at this point, I'm not convinced is the best course of action—does not mean my approach is wrong."

"I think you hit the nail on the head with that comment. He's right, Loa. And I think we will probably see that in one of our future lessons. Any investment, be it stocks, bonds, GICs, or CSBs, must be viewed within the context of your own personality. And when it comes to personality, we all know that you and Chris are at opposite ends of the spectrum. Maybe that's why you get along so well."

# How to Analyze Your Securities

"Now we've really gone back to school," said Chris. "What were we told to expect? Something about analysis and fundamentals and measuring tools. Where are the Bunsen burners and beakers? Remember the wave machine in physics?"

"Only too well, brother dear. But I am learning very quickly that aspects of investing are close to a science," offered Machaela.

"I wonder what kind of experiment we'll be conducting tonight," I mused. "I expect Professor Kirzner is about to let us know."

## Class in session ...

There is an interesting phenomenon called *mean reversion*. This theory, which was first introduced in the 19th century, describes a tendency for many variables to fluctuate widely but to eventually return to a central value or mean. This curious observation has been associated with the heights of family members, with a province's economic growth and employment levels, and even with major league batting averages!

It seems that mean reversion is important for stock returns as well. Although stock returns fluctuate widely from year to year, there is a central tendency, just like mean reversion, for them to return to about a 10% level over the long term. In fact, Canadian common shares total returns have averaged a little over 10% per year over the past 50 years. Typically, government Treasury bills and bonds have yielded about 4% and 6% respectively, which means that the anticipated yield on a balanced portfolio is about 8% per annum.

There are exceptions, of course. In the 1980s, bonds and T-bills outperformed stocks as high nominal rates of interest reflected the relatively high inflation levels. Over the past two decades, the average portfolio return has been about 12% to 12.5%.

But, in the long run under normal conditions, it is stocks that yield the highest return of the investment asset classes. What this underscores is the need to always have equities—or stocks—in your portfolio.

## The Politics of Investing: The Conservatives and the Liberals

There are two very distinct schools of thought on how you should go about building your equity portfolio. These two schools reflect the very essence of stock selection philosophy—beliefs about the pricing and informational structure of stocks.

One group of analysts—call it the conservative school—believes that security prices fully reflect all available information at any time and that the analysis of security and market information will not yield anything more than the normal returns you would get by randomly selecting a portfolio by throwing darts at a list of stocks.

Another group of analysts—call it the liberal school—believes that stocks can deviate from their intrinsic values and that by using fundamental and technical information (more about this shortly) you can find undervalued stocks—in other words, stocks that will be a good investment.

If you are a follower of the conservative school (you believe that stocks are in fact properly priced and that earning the average equity return is satisfactory), then you adopt what is called an *indexing strategy*. Your target will be the long-term equity rate of return—the 10% central tendency. We refer to this as *passive investing*.

On the other hand, if you are a follower of the liberal school, and you believe that stocks can deviate substantially from their intrinsic values, you either select individual stocks yourself using analytic techniques or you pay someone to do it for you. This is called *active investing*.

Of course, if your tastes run to the center and you see the merits of both approaches, you will adopt a combination strategy, and include both passively and actively selected stocks (or equity mutual funds) in your portfolio.

## Active versus Passive Investing—Which One?

Proponents of passive investing point out that an investment policy of randomly selecting common shares securities and buying and holding them has returned about 10% to 11% per year over the past 50 years. This observation raises the question of whether there is any value in active security selection—a question that leads right to the core of the efficient markets theory.

### Efficient Markets Theory

Until about the mid-point of this century, it was generally believed that those who spent their time analyzing securities and security prices would always end up with superior returns. Or more specifically, the notion existed that fundamental and technical analysis were worthwhile techniques. (I'll explain these two types of analysis in a moment.)

Some 1950s studies, however, reported that stock price patterns may not be distinguishable from randomly generated patterns. It's also important to note that, unlike many other scientific developments, the results predated the theory. Tests were conducted and some interesting findings were obtained. Theories were eventually fashioned to explain the results. First came the random walk theory and then the theory of efficient markets.

Essentially, the random walk theory proposes that stock price changes occur in a random fashion and, as such, cannot be predicted.

These studies of how security prices change and behave formed the foundation for what eventually became known as the efficient markets theory, which cast doubt on the notion that past information, public information, and monopolistic information could be used to generate excess investment returns. The question is, does the market price of a security represent its true investment (intrinsic) value?

**FIGURE 8.1: MARKET PRICE VERSUS INTRINSIC VALUE**

An efficient market implies that securities are properly priced and do not have positive expected risk-adjusted excess returns. What we mean by that may be best explained by illustrating the three forms of market efficiency theory, described as weak, semi-strong, and strong.

The weak form states that security prices fully reflect past information (such as past security price movements and trading volume).

The weak form of the hypothesis—if it holds—is incompatible with technical analysis.

The semi-strong form states that security prices fully reflect publicly available information (such as financial statements and economic forecasts). The semi-strong form—if it holds—is incompatible with fundamental analysis. It means that there would be no way to improve your expected returns by using financial information about a company to select stocks.

The strong form states that security prices reflect all information, including monopolistically controlled and specialized information. The strong form—if it holds—would be incompatible with insider trading profits and excess returns by fund managers.

In an efficient market, the investor's expected return simply matches the risk. In other words, higher return comes at the expense of higher risk, and not necessarily because you were able to predict stock price movement better than the next person.

You can see, then, that for those who believe in efficient markets, the logical approach is the conservative method of passively investing and not allocating resources to fundamental or technical analysis. In a passive strategy, you also attempt to keep your trading and other transaction and maintenance costs as low as possible.

---

### EFFICIENT MARKETS AND INFORMATION

An efficient market is categorized by:
1. The availability of information at no cost to all participants at the same time
2. Trades have no impact on market prices

---

## Passive Investing: The Conservative Approach

Passive investing is conservative. If you like the comfort of knowing that you will stay closely attuned to how the market performs and have little faith in your own (or your fund manager's) ability to "beat the market" by selecting undervalued securities, passive investing is the way to go.

Passive investing means simply searching for the returns associated with an index, similar to the ones we described in last week's lesson. There are two financial products that are ideal for this—index participation units and index mutual funds. These products are designed to replicate the performance of bellwether market indexes such as the Canadian-based TSE 300 Composite Index or the U.S.-based Standard & Poor's 500 Composite Index.

A product that tracks Canadian indexes very closely is the Toronto 35 Index Participation Units (symbol TIPs, traded on the Toronto Stock Exchange). Essentially, TIPs are based on the Toronto 35 Index, a modified capitalization-weighted index of 35 of Canada's largest public corporations representing most of the major Canadian industries and economic sectors. This product is so closely aligned to the Toronto 35 Index that its market value rises and falls in almost exact proportion to changes in the index itself.

TIPs are traded just like shares of stock. The value of each TIPs unit is ¹⁄₁₀th of the value of the Toronto 35 Index. If, for example, the Toronto 35 Index is quoted at 277.50, the TIPs core asset share value is $27.75. You will notice a small deviation between the TIPs price and the index value, due primarily to accumulated dividends. However, TIPs have tracked the index very closely since their inception in 1990. A TSE Index committee is responsible for ensuring that the product continuously tracks the Toronto 35, even as the composition of the index changes.

You receive quarterly dividends paid by the 35 companies that comprise the Toronto 35 Index. No expenses or fees are charged, as the trust covers its operating costs through the deferred payment of the dividends and from some miscellaneous fee income.

TIPs are actively traded on the Toronto Stock Exchange and have excellent liquidity—you can buy or sell reasonable amounts of stock instantly at market prices.

Another product called HIPs (the hundred index participation units) represents the TSE 100 Index, and also trades on the Toronto

Stock Exchange. The TSE 100 Index is comprised of 100 of the top-ranking companies in the TSE 300 Composite Index. It has identical features to TIPs with respect to trading rules, redemption, quarterly dividends, and dilution protection. HIPs are set at 1/10th of the value of the index and are traded in a similar manner to TIPs.

The TSE 100 index is a broader based index than the 35 and is normally more volatile. As a result, it will generally outperform the TSE 35 in a good year and underperform the TSE 35 in a bad period.

## The U.S. Index Version—SPDRs

If you want to track a U.S. index, the U.S. index participation unit version of TIPs is Standard & Poor's Depository Receipts or SPDRs. These units are traded in minimum increments of 64ths of a dollar, or $.015625.

Like TIPs, SPDRs are quoted and traded in $1/10$th the value of the S&P 500 Composite Index. For example, if the S&P 500 Index is at 698.73, the core value of an SPDR will be $69.87.

The SPDR Trust expires in 2018. The dividends and other distributions of the 500 companies represented in the S&P 500 Composite Index are collected and invested by the trust and then distributed on a quarterly basis to the unit holders. You can buy and sell SPDRs in a similar manner to TIPs through your stockbroker.

## The Foreign Index Version—WEBs

The Morgan Stanley World Equity Benchmark shares (WEBs) were launched in May 1996. Like TIPs and SPDRs, these products represent a basket of securities that replicates the total return performance of the Morgan Stanley Capital International (MSCI) indexes.

The WEBs are traded on the American Stock Exchange. The fund is advised by BZW Barclays Global Fund Advisor. There are 17 different series of WEBs, each one tied to a specific MSCI. The MSCI World Composite Index, launched in 1969, is the most widely used world performance index. All Morgan Stanley composite indexes are total return indexes with net dividends (after withholding taxes) deemed to be reinvested.

The dividends are paid annually, based on the dividends paid on the underlying index. A drawback is that there are no dividend reinvestment plans. Table 8.1 lists the various WEBs, as well as the index they are linked to.

**TABLE 8.1: WEBS**

| Ticker | Index Companies | No. of |
|--------|------------------|--------|
| EWA | MSCI | 49 |
| EWO | MSCI | 24 |
| EWK | MSCI | 20 |
| EWC | MSCI | 84 |
| EWQ | MSCI | 74 |
| EWG | MSCI | 69 |
| EWH | MSCI | 38 |
| EWI | MSCI | 55 |
| EWJ | MSCI | 317 |
| EWM | MSCI | 76 |
| EWW | MSCI (free) | 41 |
| EWN | MSCI | 22 |
| EWS | MSCI | 32 |
| EWP | MSCI | 31 |
| EWD | MSCI | 30 |
| EWL | MSCI | 43 |
| EWU | MSCI | 144 |

## Index Mutual Funds

Passive investing caught on much faster in the United States than in Canada. As a result, since the first index mutual fund was created by

Wells Fargo in the 1970s, there are now scores available in the United States, but only a handful in Canada.

Index mutual funds, like other equity mutual funds, invest in a portfolio of common shares. However, the objective of an index fund is to track, as closely as possible, an underlying market index. No time or effort is devoted to security selection; the objective is to keep the security acquisition and maintenance costs as low as possible.

Canadian index funds have underperformed the TSE Total Return Index (which measures both capital appreciation as well as dividends) by about 1% per annum over the past five years. This underperformance is partially explained by the typical 1% to 1.25% management expense ratio of index funds. Canadian index mutual funds that track the Standard & Poor's 500 index are also available in Canada.

## Active Investing: The Liberal Approach

What would you do if you perfected a foolproof method of picking stocks—publish it or keep it to yourself? Unless you are looking for a Nobel Prize in finance, you may as well keep it to yourself. And if most people act this way, it probably means that superior stock selection methods are not published. This in turn implies that studies examining analysts' performance may be focusing on inferior models. This so-called selection bias may account, at least in part, for how surprisingly strong the support for the random walk theory is.

In 1981, Yale University economist Robert J. Shiller published a startling paper. In an exhaustive examination of security prices and dividend payments spanning the period 1871 through 1979, he found a strong divergence between the market price of the S&P 500 and Dow Jones Industrial Average and the present value of the two indexes.

He found the NYSE alternated between bullish—that is, vastly over-priced for a few years—and bearish—that is, significantly underpriced for a while—relative to the present value of the stock market's cash dividend income. Since a security is supposed to equal the discounted present value of future dividends, he concluded that stock prices did not fully reflect information. This may sound like some arcane academic theory, but it is very important. It means that stocks don't always fully reflect all information and that the search for undervalued stocks might be a fruitful one.

## Liberal Approaches: Fundamental and Technical Versions

If you are a follower of the active investment philosophy, the liberal approach is for you. Active security analysis is the search to identify mispriced securities with the objective of outperforming the market index.

The two traditional approaches to active security valuation are called fundamental and technical analysis.

Fundamental analysis presupposes that the information contained in financial statements, economic forecasts, and other publicly available information provides valuable clues in assessing the intrinsic value of a security. The financial analyst derives estimates of a firm's earnings and dividends and looks to see if the estimate differs from the market consensus, or whether those estimates have been fully incorporated into the current market price of the security.

Technical analysis, on the other hand, assumes that the analysis of past prices and other such data will prove valuable in forecasting future price directions and levels. The technical analyst attempts to predict future stock price directions and makes recommendations on the timing of purchases and sales of specific stocks or market indexes.

Recommendations are based on analysis of patterns and configurations in stock charts; on relative strength charts; and on sentiment, confidence, and contrarian indexes. The technical analyst attempts to determine on the basis of prices and volumes when stocks or indexes should be purchased and when stocks or the market are either overpriced or underpriced. More about that in our next lesson.

Both approaches—fundamental and technical—are aimed at finding undervalued and overvalued securities.

## Fundamental Analysis

The fundamental approach involves the use of financial and economic data to assess the firm's liquidity, solvency and efficiency, and to project the firm's earnings and dividend potential.

The fundamental analyst's kitbag includes corporate financial reports, industry data, macroeconomic data, and comments from corporate officers, all of which are used to determine whether specific company stocks are under- or overvalued. There are different starting points with fundamental analysis and scores of different techniques and measures used. Our objective here is to simply highlight the more important ones.

The key to fundamental analysis is recognizing that the search is for the security's intrinsic value relative to what it is selling for. An appropriate valuation model that will incorporate traditional dividend or earnings growth measures is normally used to estimate intrinsic value. Valuation models range from the simple, such as a one-year forecast of earnings accompanied by a one-year forecast of the price/earnings ratio, to the complex multistage growth models.

---

**THE SEARCH FOR FUNDAMENTAL VALUE**

The key principle of fundamental analysis is that you are searching for mispriced securities. An attempt is made to determine the true or intrinsic value of a security. Then, the intrinsic value is compared with the security's current market price. If the market price exceeds intrinsic value, the security is overpriced. If the intrinsic price exceeds market price, the security is underpriced and a bargain.

---

## Stock Valuation

The return on a stock comes from two sources—dividends and capital growth. You can calculate your expected total return from holding a common share through the following equation:

$$K = \frac{D_1}{P} + G$$

where:

K = expected return
P = value of a share
$D_1$ = dividend over the next 12 months
G = expected growth rate of stock or dividends

For example, a $20 stock which is expected to pay a $1 a share dividend and to grow at a rate of 7% will have an expected return of 12%, as follows:

$$K = \frac{1}{20} + .07 = .12$$

Note there are different ways you can get a 12% return.
For example, a $20 stock that is not expected to pay a dividend but is expected to grow at a rate of 12%:

$$K = \frac{0}{20} + .12 = .12$$

Or a $20 stock that is expected to pay a $2 dividend but only to grow at a rate of 2%:

$$K = \frac{2}{20} + .02 = .12$$

As you can see, there is a logical trade-off between dividends and growth. If the company pays out a high percentage of earnings as dividends, there will be less money available to plow back into new investment projects and the rate of growth will decline. On the other hand, a low payout means that more funds are available for investment and thus greater growth prospects.

If you rearrange the formula ever so slightly, you get the famous Gordon model, the constant growth dividend discount model named after its designer, Professor Myron Gordon.

$$P = \frac{D_1}{K - G}$$

This formula estimates the value of a share as the dividend divided by the difference between expected return and growth. Valuation growth models normally are some variation on this constant or variable growth assumption. This formula serves as the base for most valuation formulas and is the most widely used by security analysts when trying to ascertain whether a stock is overvalued or undervalued.

This simple model also provides great insight into how securities are valued. But you have to be careful and avoid superficial analysis. For example, the higher the share price, the higher the dividend ($D_1$), the lower the discount rate (K), or the greater the growth rate (G).

But as you will soon see, these factors are interrelated. For example, if you increase the dividend, the growth rate may fall (since there is less available for reinvestment).

### The Price/Earnings Ratio

The most important aspect of security valuation is the focus on what is called the price/earnings multiple (P/E) and how it is related to the expected return (K) in the basic valuation equation. The price/earnings multiple is calculated by taking the market price and dividing by the company's earnings per share (earnings per share is the net income of the company divided by the number of common shares outstanding).

Theoretically, the earnings per share should be the expected earnings per share over the next year. As a practical matter, what is published in the financial press is the price/earnings multiple based on the latest reported earnings (see Figure 8.2). So keep in mind that unless you are actually forecasting earnings, what you are dealing with may be a crude estimate only of the real P/E multiple.

## FIGURE 8.2: SAMPLE STOCK PAGE

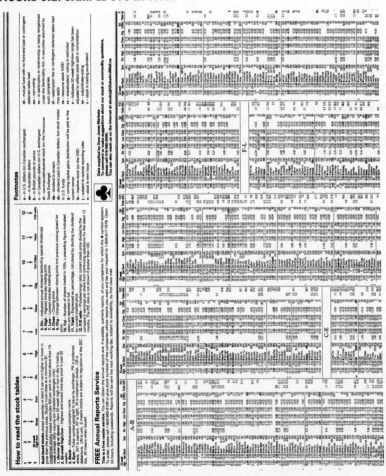

In order to project the future stock price performance, the analyst estimates the firm's growth rate of earnings and dividends, and how the market will value these earnings and dividends through a required rate of return.

Alternatively, and more simplistically, the analyst will estimate the market price/earnings multiple to attach to the latest earnings per share. It is essential to recognize here that the analyst's task is to forecast the *market discount rate*. The key to successful fundamental investment analysis is the ability to project future corporate earnings and how the market is likely to capitalize them, which brings us to some P/E arithmetic.

If a firm's earnings per share is $2.50, and the share price is $20.00, the shares are trading at what P/E? The answer:

Price/earnings multiple = Share price divided by earnings per share
P/E = 20.00 / 2.50 = 8

The P/E is related to the expected return; it is simply the reciprocal of the expected return (see Table 8.2).

**TABLE 8.2: RELATIONSHIP OF EXPECTED RETURN TO P/E MULTIPLE**

| Expected Return | Reciprocal | P/E Multiple |
|---|---|---|
| 25% | 1/4 | 4.0 |
| 20% | 1/5 | 5.0 |
| 14% | 1/7 | 7.0 |
| 8% | 1/12.5 | 12.5 |
| 5% | 1/20 | 20.0 |

## Value and Growth

The P/E multiple is the most important fundamental yardstick and is the distinguishing point between the two broad approaches to security selection: value stocks and growth stocks. Value and growth investing have long represented two basic approaches to stock selection.

Investors who employ a value approach will focus on low P/E stocks, often small-cap ones as well, while investors looking for growth focus on high multiple stocks. These two styles represent interesting extremes. Value stocks are often neglected or disliked companies that have had recent financial problems, while growth stocks are generally stocks of admired companies with strong track records.

## The Value Approach

Although definitions vary, the price/book value (P/B) and the price/earnings ratios (P/E) are often used to distinguish the two approaches.

Value investors focus on the nether part of the universe, searching for undervalued stocks trading at low P/E multiples. Sometimes the market/book ratio (which measures the market value of the firm's traded stock against the shareholder's equity value as reported in the company's financial statements) and the price/dividend ratio (which measures the price of a share relative to its dividend per share) are used as well. The focus would be on companies with low market/book ratios and/or low price/dividend .

Value investing has proven to be the more intriguing and the more rewarding of the two styles in the past. A recent study reported a 3% per annum excess return of value stocks over growth stocks over a lengthy holding period, with the excess return a decreasing function of firm size (that is, the small-cap value stocks had the largest excess returns).

The best way to describe value investing is to say you are buying assets, earnings and dividends at a price below their perceived value. Call it bargain hunting, value searching, or what you will, an under-valued stock is trading for less than it's really worth.

Academic researchers ascribe the basic premises underlying value investing to quirks (one study called these "mental demons") in investor behavior rather than to fundamental factors. Behavioral studies have shown that the value world is one in which investors don't like to be! Stocks often become undervalued because they have poor track records.

The pattern of creating losses for investors has placed those stocks in the "fallen angel" category—a long history of losses creates distrust and distaste among investors. In other words, the stock has disappointed them enough times that they no longer trust it—and so they shun it.

Add to the "fallen angel" notion the observation that many "value" companies are small-capitalization ones with little public exposure and are accordingly ignored by institutional investors. As a result, this lack of mainstream retail and institutional investor demand means that the stock becomes undervalued, trades at a low P/E, low P/B, or a low P/D (a high-dividend yield). This behavioral theory provides a plausible explanation for the finding that value stocks have tended to earn higher returns than growth stocks over the past two decades.

For the record, value investing is associated with a number of investment legends—namely Benjamin Graham, Warren Buffett, Peter Lynch, and Sir John Templeton.

Templeton has been quoted as saying, "If you are building a house, developing a golf course, or running a doctor's office, you're not in a contest with anyone. But you can't buy a stock unless there's somebody willing to sell it. And because you can't buy unless somebody sells, it's likely that a year later, or five years later, one of you will wish you hadn't done it."

He went on to say, "Because it is a contest, and is therefore different from almost every other business activity on earth, you must not go with the majority. You can gain opportunities in investing only by doing something that the majority are against doing or something they don't know about." This parallels his oft-quoted admonition to "buy when others are despondently selling and then sell when others are actively buying."

### The Low P/E Multiple (Small Capitalization) Approach

Studies indicate that stocks trading at with low price/earnings multiples have tended to yield higher returns than those trading at high P/E multiples. The normal definition of low P/E includes stocks in the bottom third of the P/E list.

The P/E effect has been closely linked with buying low-priced and small-firm (capitalized) shares. In fact, buying stocks with low P/Es may be identical to buying small-firms shares (size is measured by the market value of a firm's outstanding stock).

This low P/E multiple may be due to the fact that small firms are neglected by analysts and institutions. They may lack popularity with large institutions and investors or are not widely followed (some institutional investors are not allowed to invest in smaller-cap stocks).

## The Price/Book Approach

Benjamin Graham was one of the founders of modern fundamental analysis and a strong proponent of value investing. His recommended yardsticks for value investing included a screen where he would only buy stocks that were trading at least 33% below their tangible book value per share and 33% below net current asset value per share.

A well-known study by two prominent University of Chicago researchers published in 1992 supports this approach. Analyzing stock returns over a 27-year period, they found that, on average, stocks trading in the lowest price/book (P/B) group yielded returns over twice that of those grouped in the high price/book zone.

## The Price/Dividend Approach

Some value investors focus on high-dividend-yielding stocks (low price/dividend shares). A number of studies have documented the observation that investing in high-dividend-paying stocks has provided substantially higher total returns to investors than investing in a passive selection of stocks as measured by a market index. One definition of high-dividend-paying stocks is those with yields of about 67% or more of that on AAA-rated long-term bonds, as shown in Table 8.3.

**TABLE 8.3: AAA BOND YIELDS VERSUS HIGH-DIVIDEND YIELDS**

| 10-Year AAA Bond Yield | High-Dividend Yield |
|---|---|
| 8% | 5.33% |
| 9% | 6.00% |
| 10% | 6.67% |
| 11% | 7.33% |
| 12% | 8.00% |

The low price/earnings, low price/book, and low price/dividend approaches are by no means foolproof—investing isn't that easy. But if you are value oriented, that's where you start.

---

**THE SMALL-STOCK VALUE APPROACH**

One mammoth study of returns, spanning 60 years, found that small stocks outperformed the S&P 500 Composite Index by just under 6.0% per annum. Part of the phenomenon is explained by risk—smaller firms are more volatile than their larger counterparts. But volatility alone is not enough to explain a difference of this magnitude.

---

One study pointed out something else of great importance—that stocks of small companies may contain more company-specific risk than those of large firms. This implies that small-stock portfolios must be adequately diversified to eliminate the company-specific risks. The bottom line is, if you hold small-cap stocks, hold them as part of a portfolio.

## The Growth Approach

Growth stocks represent the upper end of the valuation spectrum. Although value stocks have outperformed growth stocks, growth stocks have typically been less volatile than value stocks and have shorter periods when they produce negative returns. Growth stocks can be identified as ranking in the top third of stocks according to their respective P/Es.

Recall the Gordon model we looked at earlier in this chapter:

$$P = \frac{D_1}{K-G}$$

For growth stocks, the important fundamental focus is on the firm's return on investment relative to the expected return (K) component of the model. One way to think of expected return is as the return that you—the investor—could realize on an alternative investment of similar risk.

Suppose a firm earns $10 per share, pays out $6 in dividends, and retains the remaining $4 per share for investment. If the firm earns a high rate of return (say, by investing in new projects) on the $4 it retained to reinvest, the firm's value will increase. If it earns a low return, the value will drop.

For example, if the firm's return on investment is 15%, it will earn $0.60 per share on the $4 retained. You can see that this $0.60 represents the growth in earnings and is equal to the percentage of earnings retained multiplied by the return on investment.

In this example, the dividend payout rate is .60 ($6 dividend/$10 in earnings) and the amount retained for reinvestment in the firm (this is called the retention or plowback rate) is .40 ($4 retained earnings/$10 in earnings). The key analytic issue is whether its return on investment exceeds the expected return.

## Tactical Trading—Predicting the Market

We've outlined the two broad approaches to fundamental security selection—value and growth. Some fundamental analysts also apply their tools to assessing the outlook for the market. Be forewarned that trying to predict market cycles and switching from stocks to bonds and vice versa is dangerous. If you guess wrong and miss a few key months of a bull market, you can blow all of the rewards of equity investing. Timing the market is a difficult task.

Sellers are constantly playing the "second-guessing game." Should I sell? Have I held too long? Did I sell too quickly? Did I give someone else too good of a deal? The Sir John Templeton philosophy that I spoke of earlier comes to play in the seller's mind, too, and often painfully.

Clearly, all of us want to sell at the right time, but the right time is something that few professionals have ever really been able to determine with any accuracy. The idea of selling a highflier just before it comes crashing down is more fantasy than reality. Which leads me to restate the obvious: while selling at the right moment is a stimulating concept, it is not usually the right tactic, because over the long term, stocks tend to go up, which is no doubt the reason you purchased the stock in the first place. Think about that for a moment. *If all sales were the right decision, then virtually every stock in history has been bad.*

That being said, if you are convinced that selling is the right thing to do, then do so with blinders on. Don't try to find the top, be content with the price you receive, and move on. And therein lies the most important concept driving a stock sale. The fact you made a sale implies, by definition, that you have some other investment that shows more potential.

So with that in mind, I have three principles that you can use to at least make you a better seller, or at least to help you feel like a better seller.

1. Establish a systematic approach to selling and stick with it. Try to establish a target price when you are buying and, if that price is reached, then take your profits and don't look back. Remember that a sales system must be exact. That it provides you with no options when the time comes is a good thing. Even if it means a system as simple as listing the reasons why you bought the stock, and then selling that stock because those same reasons no longer apply.

2. When reacting to bad news, which usually brings home the fear element, remember to follow your instincts. That highflier that stumbles raises the question, quite rightly, of what to do? The key is to not panic. Stand back and examine whether you are seeing a temporary correction or a fundamental change in the company's business. If the former, then you may want to buy more shares; if the latter, then one of your reasons for buying the stock may no longer exist.

3. Finally, don't think about the stock as a stand-alone investment. Think about it in terms of your entire portfolio. In other words, don't view any specific sale in isolation, but rather in terms of how it affects your overall portfolio, which may lead you to look at the possibility of selling only part of your position. After all, no one said you have to sell an entire position.

So much for sale tactics. Back to the fundamental issues of security selection. The most popular and logical approach is to select important fundamental yardsticks and to measure current values against these yardsticks. The idea is to determine whether the market is "high" or "low" relative to these values. Usually, the analyst starts with economic projections or forecasts of the performance of the economy for the next 12 to 24 months, and this in turn yields a forecast for stock market performance. Certain economic variables (for example, home construction), called leading indicators, normally provide signals of important turning points in equity markets and are particularly important at this initial projections stage. (Recall our discussions about the Canadian business cycle in lesson 4).

## One Yardstick—
## The Price/Earnings Multiplier Approach

The price/earnings multiplier approach consists of estimating an appropriate price/earnings multiple for the entire market. The usual range over the years has been somewhere between 7 and 23, with a median of about 14.

One approach is to take the long-term Government of Canada bond yield and subtract 100 basis points to get the earnings/multiplier ratio (E/P), which is the per share earnings divided by the current price. For example, the recent long-term Canada bond yield was about 8%. The equivalent E/P multiple would be 7%.

Based on these numbers, an appropriate P/E would be $\frac{1}{.07} = 14.2$.

Having ascertained a reasonable P/E number, you then obtain a forecast of estimated earnings for an appropriate index such as the TSE 300 Composite. For example, if all the stocks in the TSE 300 Composite Index combined to earn $300 per share, an appropriate value for the TSE 300, assuming a P/E of 14.2, would be 4260.

Other indicators used for assessing the market outlook are:

| Yardstick | Usual Range | Median |
|---|---|---|
| Price/dividend | 15.4 to 32.9 | 23.9 |
| Price/book | 1.0 to 2.5 | 1.5 |
| Market value of stocks as % of nominal GDP | 60% to 80% | 70% |

## Industry Ratio Analysis

The specific company and the industry in which it operates are usually examined as well, typically using financial ratios which measure the relationship between two or more corporate variables. Various financial measures are identified from the firm's financial statements and then assessed. For example, the "times-interest-earned" ratio, calculated as the firm's operating profit before interest on long-term debt, divided by long-term debt, is a measure of the firm's ability to meet interest payments and hence provides a ratio of solvency.

Most analysts use a dual approach to evaluate a firm: a cross-sectional approach where the firm's performance is compared to other firms of similar size in the same industry and/or to industry averages, and longitudinal analysis where the trend or direction of the firm's ratios, earnings, and growth rates are examined.

The financial ratios used are calculated from the firm's financial statements and include ratios of liquidity, solvency, efficiency, and profitability.

## At the coffee shop ...

"Talk about an informative session!" You could see the enthusiasm on Machaela's face. "It was the first time I had an understanding of what drives stock prices. Of course I knew a company's profits—as in earnings—was important, but I had no idea how to determine the relationship between a stock's current price and its prospects for earnings. The price/earnings ratio, the P/E that was so prominently discussed, is one of the foundations on which to judge the value of a stock. It concisely and clearly defines the relationship between a stock's price and the company's earnings—or profits—per share of stock."

"Obviously, earnings are important in the big picture, Machaela, but why do we need to know the earnings per share. Why can't we just use the earnings?"

"Well, for one thing, Chris, I'm not sure that tells us anything. After all, we are not attempting to value the entire company, just the stock price," replied Machaela. "In that light, the earnings per share number is critical, because it provides us with an apples-to-apples comparison relative to the price of the stock."

"That makes sense, and the bottom line is that the price/earnings ratio is easy to calculate." I wanted to address this issue, because I had brought the local business paper with me, and alongside each stock was the earnings per share for the last 52 weeks. "Let's see now, the Penny's Loafer Company stock price is $25 per share, and according to the paper, the company earned $1 last year. Okay, that works out to a P/E of 25."

"On the surface that looks like an expensive stock," Chris observed.

"What I got from this lesson is that you should never buy a stock with a high P/E. So for me, the first rule of investing is never buy a stock whose price is more than 15 times last year's earnings."

"But," Machaela said, "that may not be true. We cannot fall into the trap of viewing earnings in a vacuum. We cannot say a company is bad simply because it has a P/E over 10, or a P/E of 15. That's like saying Denny's is a nice restaurant because it rains a lot in Vancouver. One has nothing to do with the other."

"Or," I joined in, "it's like saying the Toronto Maple Leafs have scored 50 goals." I wanted to bring in a hockey metaphor to stretch the point. "Without knowing how many games have been played, without knowing how other teams had fared over the same period, without knowing how many goals the Maple Leafs let in, I have no basis on which to make any comparison. Looking at the P/E in a vacuum, without some points of reference, could eliminate some opportunities."

"The fact is, growth stocks have high P/Es. They should have higher than average P/Es assuming they can sustain an above-average growth rate. Who would suggest Microsoft is a bad investment simply because it has a P/E of 35?"

"So what do we use as a benchmark?" asked Chris. "What distinguishes a company that is overvalued because it has a high P/E from a company whose P/E is justified by its growth rate?"

For this I had an answer. "For one thing, you can use the formulas we learned in this lesson. Professor Kirzner introduced a model that factors growth into the stock's price. But what I think we can draw from this lesson, particularly as it relates to growth stocks, is that there has to be a relationship between the rate of growth of the company and the company's P/E."

"How about this?" came the quick response from Machaela. "If a growth stock is fully valued, then the P/E should equal the rate of growth in the company's earnings. If Microsoft can grow its earnings at 35%, then a P/E of 35 is warranted. Put another way, we need to make some assumptions about future growth in order to put the P/E into perspective. Obviously, it is important to understand what the company has accomplished in the past—what were its earnings per share—but we need to also be aware of what the future promises—the future being defined as an expected growth rate."

# Analyzing Securities— The Technical Way

"I think charts are kind of neat. I'm noticing them more these days, as we work our way through this course. In the business press, I see a giant chart of the TSE 300 Composite Index and another showing what the Dow Jones Industrial Average has been doing over the last six months."

"Looks nice, but what does it tell us?" asked Machaela.

"Well, I'm not really sure," came the answer off the top of my head. A mistake really, because I am sure that Machaela was thinking about how I constantly see the creative aspects of any visual presentation, without really being able to interpret its meaning. I needed to add something to my response. "Although, you can certainly see a trend in the market. Each new line plots successive new highs, and that has to be good."

"Better than the alternative, I suppose," Machaela replied.

"In any event, I am looking forward to some insightful comments from today's class. A chance to learn some technical jargon—something more than this is the X axis and this is the Y axis—and perhaps, at the end of the day, I'll be able to interpret a chart's meaning," I said, wanting to get the last word in—just once. But I was going to leave that to Mr. Croft.

---

## Class in session ...

The notion that a picture is worth a thousand words supports the role technicians play in security analysis. The technical approach involves the use of past price volume and other such external data to assess the "crowd's" attitude toward the market and specific stocks. Instead of examining the fundamentals related to a company and its industry, the technical analyst searches for the truth that is found in the chart patterns.

A technician doesn't normally care much about what the underlying company does. Whether it's a department store chain like Wal-Mart or a telephone giant like Bell Canada is not the issue. The pure technician believes that all relevant fundamental information about the market or a company is already incorporated in the index level or share price, and the technician believes (as does the efficient markets proponent) that no direct manipulation of that information can result in superior stock selection.

The real question, from the perspective of the technical analyst, is what do investors think about the company? In search of that information, technical analysts assess trading data to ascertain the ebb and flow and momentum of the market. The technician believes that by studying the past, one can make judgments about the future. This differs from the efficient markets proponent. Technicians believe that past data can help them define a trend, and that once a trend is defined, the trend will persist for an extended period. Efficient market types believe that trends are identifiable only when they are over!

To assess investor sentiment, the technical analyst—by the way, terms like technical analyst, technician, and chartist are all interchangeable—reviews the stock's past performance by charting past price and volume trends. The question is, can someone who studies charts forecast future stock prices?

Well, the evidence is mixed. Louis Ruckeyers of "Wall Street Week," the most popular financial show on PBS, tracks ten well-known technical analysts in the U.S. Each analyst provides "Wall Street Week" with their current view on the market, be it bullish, bearish, or neutral. The scores are added up each week, in what Ruckeyers affectionately refers to as his Elves Index.

Attaching the Elves label to a battery of technical analysts is probably an apt description because, in more than five years, there has never been a week when all ten could agree on the direction of the stock market, let alone the direction of any specific company. More to the point, the index usually falls somewhere along the line of five bulls, three bears, and two neutral, or three bulls, five bears, and two neutral, and so on. And one assumes that they are all reading the same charts.

Probably the best known of the modern-day technicians is Joseph Granville, famous as much for his flamboyant public presentations, replete with pianos and dancing girls, as for his extravagant recommendations that are either dead right or dead wrong!

One story that is particularly relevant took place in the early 1980s, at a time when Granville shared center stage with technician Robert Prechtor. Granville, in the 1980s, was already a veteran analyst, while Prechtor, the new kid on the block, was gaining notoriety for his rather brash pronouncements and pinpoint predictions about the stock market. Both had large followings.

Particularly interesting was the strong position both took in the early 1980s. Granville was an outright bear on the stock market, believing that stocks would tumble into the abyss in a chaotic fashion and remain there for a protracted period of time.

Prechtor, on the other hand, was an outright bull on the market, believing that 1981 was the beginning of one of the great bull markets in history. The point of the story is not to blame Granville for a bad call or to applaud Prechtor for the correct call (of note is the fact that Prechtor later failed to foresee the stock market crash in October 1987). The real issue is that two prominent leaders in this community of chart watchers, presumably both looking at the same graphs, could end up with such diametrically opposed views of the market.

## Defining Chart Patterns

Many of the present technical theories and approaches are simply variations or extensions of the work of Charles Dow, the creator of the Dow Jones Stock Indices. Dow theory holds that stock prices move together in three basic trends—primary, secondary, and tertiary—and, moreover, that it is possible to determine these trends from a careful scrutiny of price and index changes.

The primary trend is an extensive and basic movement underway (that is, a bull or bear market) that has a duration of three months to three years. The secondary trend sets in at some point during the primary trend and retraces anywhere from 33% to 50% of the movement in the most recent primary move.

For example, suppose XYZ stock increases from $10 per share to $15 per share over a six-month period. If the stock peaks at $15 and then falls back to, say, $12.50 per share, it would have retraced $2.50 of the initial (that is, primary) $5 move to the upside. The $2.50 retracement represents 50% of the initial move to the upside and, assuming the stock is able to hold support at the $12.50 level, this move would be considered a secondary trend.

On the other hand, if the stock continued to decline below the $12.50 per share price, which is more than a 50% retracement, then the technical analyst might see this as a reversal of the primary trend and thus the beginning of a new trend. So, in the very preliminary stages of this discussion, a retracement of more than 50% of the initial move to the upside is a dangerous signal, whereas a retracement of anywhere from

33% to 50% is actually healthy and, presumably, lays the foundation to move to even higher prices.

In Figure 9.1, the rise from point A to point B over a period of six months represents the primary trend. The decline from point B to point C over, say, a period of three months, represents the secondary trend. Assuming XYZ stock can hold support at point C, then the stock will begin another primary trend from point C to point D. And so the cycle continues.

## FIGURE 9.1: CONTINUATION OF PRIMARY TREND

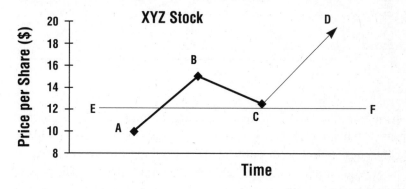

At this point we should define support and resistance. When technical analysts talk about *support* and *resistance,* they are referring to price points at which the security or index changes direction. Support defines a point at which the price of the stock or index stops declining and resumes its upward trend. In this case, there are more buyers than sellers.

Resistance defines the point at which the security or index stops rising and begins to fall. In this case, there are more sellers than buyers. Technicians put a lot of emphasis on the point at which a security or index breaks through upside resistance or fails to hold downside support. Generally, when that happens, it signals a change in direction for the security or index.

Again, in the case of XYZ stock, suppose that it falls below $12.50, which represents more than a 50% retracement from the previous high. Technical analysts would see that as breaking support (defined as the line from E to F), which could lead to a trend reversal, ultimately leading to still lower prices (see Figure 9.2)

## FIGURE 9.2: REVERSAL OF PRIMARY TREND

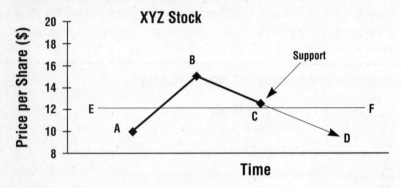

Note that the secondary trend continues beyond point C, a point at which the stock should have received buying support, and the price continues to decline to point D. After breaking through point C, at what point would XYZ now be expected to find support? The answer is that the next logical support would be at $10 per share, the point at which the primary trend began.

The third basic element of technical analysis is the tertiary trend, defined as the day-to-day movement in the price of the stock. Most technicians see that as noise in the market and don't attach much value to those moves in determining the current trend or changes to the current trend.

## The Trend Is Your Friend

Clearly, Figure 9.2 does not illustrate *why* a share price of $12.50, in our example, would be the support level. In this case, we simply used the 33% to 50% guideline to provide us with a support point. In the real world of technical analysis (a statement that some fundamental analysts might define as an oxymoron), the technician draws lines on the chart that actually depict what the current trend is. These so-called *trendlines* connect the high and low price points along the trend, and an upward-moving chart implies support levels. In cases where each successive low price is higher than the previous low price, we have what amounts to an upward sloping chart pattern. The line that connects each successive low price point is referred to as the trendline. Trendlines can also be used as support and resistance points. For example, the line connecting points A and point C in figure 9.3 can be extended upwards and under point D. To a technician, that extended trendline represents support below point D.

## FIGURE 9.3: DRAWING A TRENDLINE

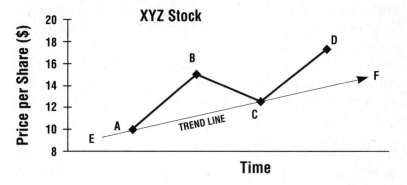

Similarly, a trendline can be used to connect the high points of the security's price pattern. This trendline will basically reflect points of resistance or, perhaps from another perspective, objective price points where the technical analyst thinks the stock may run into resistance. Figure 9.4 shows us an example of a trendline (the line connecting points B and D) that defines resistance points for XYZ stock.

**FIGURE 9.4: DRAWING A RESISTANCE LINE**

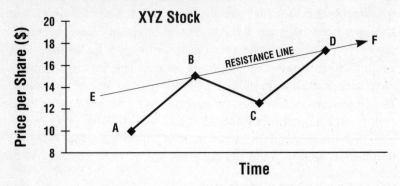

The objective is to look for price points that present an opportunity to move into or out of a stock. If a stock, for example, breaks through upside resistance, then the stock price may move substantially higher before it meets any further resistance. You could say that when a stock breaks through a resistance point, it presents a buying opportunity. Similarly, a sell signal is registered if a stock breaks through a support level.

## The Possibilities and the Pitfalls

As with any aspect of security analysis, you can find chart patterns that have followed the script to the letter when breaking either support or resistance. You can also find just as many charts where the stock price has not done what you might have expected given this or that pattern.

Here are some points to consider. If you buy a stock that rises in price and then changes direction, the trendline can provide a snapshot as to where you should expect to find some buying support. That can add a measure of comfort to your stock position, since you at least have some idea of what to look for.

The trendline that defines the stock's resistance can also be useful as a tool to establish a price at which you might consider selling the stock, assuming you purchased it at much lower prices. For example, if you buy XYZ at $10 and you believe the stock will meet significant resistance at

$15 per share, you might use that point to define your objective.

On the other side of the coin, you have to understand that the premise of technical analysis is to define points at which you can buy or sell the underlying security. And that presumes that you should be involved in buying and selling, a point we are not altogether convinced is the best approach.

Look at a list of the richest men in the world and you won't find a market timer among them. But there at the top of the list is Warren Buffett, an individual who believes passionately in the concept of buying and holding investments. You will also find Bill Gates near the top of the list, and his wealth is tied to the performance of Microsoft, the company he owns. You won't see Mr. Gates buying and selling his shares based on some chart pattern.

The point is, when you decide to sell a stock for whatever reason, you have to make another decision: where to invest the proceeds from the sale. For every decision to sell, there must also be a decision to buy, and presumably, if you are selling at a profit, there should be another stock with the same or better potential than the one you sold.

## There Is More to Price Than Meets the Eye

There is another issue when referring to trendlines that we should talk about. Returning once again to XYZ stock, let's expand the price pattern from figure 9.1. I think most of us would agree that the primary trend for XYZ is up, but in Figure 9.1 we defined that trend with only four price points (A, B, C, and D).

In Figure 9.5, we have simply changed the previous chart to a daily price chart, going back, say, over the last six months. Note that we are using a *high-low-close* chart to define the daily price moves, which is the tertiary trend we talked about earlier.

## FIGURE 9.5: HIGH-LOW-CLOSE CHART

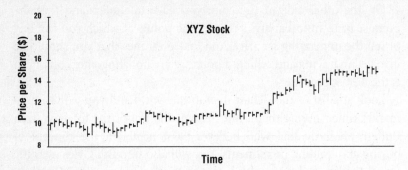

A high-low-close chart is the most common chart used by technical analysts, and simply defines the range of price movement for XYZ during the course of trading on any given day. The top of the line represents the highest price XYZ traded on a given day, the bottom of the line represents the lowest point for the day, and the tick mark on the high-low line represents the price at which the stock closed.

If we draw a trendline to define support, it might look something like Figure 9.6. The trendline clearly emphasizes that the primary trend is up, and the drawing of the trendline is relatively easy to do.

## FIGURE 9.6: HIGH-LOW-CLOSE CHART WITH SUPPORT

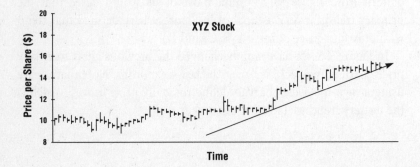

But let's bring another issue into the discussion. Remember, the stock started at $10.00 per share. When the stock advanced from $10.00 to $12.50, it was up 25%. If the stock continues to rise from $12.50 to $15.00 (another $2.50 per share price increase), the increase represents a 20% return, yet it is accorded the same movement on the price chart used to track XYZ stock.

One way around this issue is to use logarithms. Without fogging up this discussion with the intricacies of logarithms, suffice it to say that a logarithmic chart accounts for percentage changes and thus provides a better snapshot of what is happening with a stock's price. A move from $10.00 to $12.50, then, is accorded the same degree of space as is a movement from $12.50 to $15.625, because both represent a 25% price change. Given that, let's recast Figures 9.5 and 9.6 into a logarithmic chart, as seen in Figure 9.7.

### FIGURE 9.7: HIGH-LOW-CLOSE CHART IN LOG SCALE

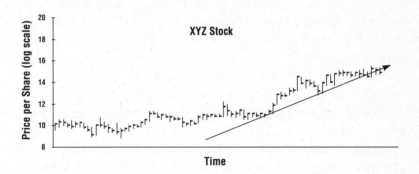

Note that in Figure 9.7 support appears to have broken at the extreme right of the chart, something that did not appear in Figure 9.5 or 9.6. Two technicians looking at the same stock, but calculating the prices using a different methodology, might get different signals. This is why technical analysts can have differing opinions while presumably looking at the same information. With the introduction of a logarithmic chart, we are not promoting one type over another; we simply want to make the point that technical analysis is more art than science.

## The Moving Average

Another way of defining a trendline, and presumably an approach that addresses the problems associated with percentage return skewing, is the so-called moving average. The moving average is, as the name suggests, an average of a stock's price over a period of time. The notion that the average moves simply reflects the fact the stock's price changes on a daily basis. These changes are indicated in the financial sections of *The Globe and Mail* and *Financial Post*.

If we were calculating a 10-day moving average for XYZ stock, we would begin with the closing prices of the previous 10 days, add them together and divide by 10. On day 10, as seen in Table 9.1, the average of the previous 10 days' closing prices was $10.49. On day 11, the 10-day moving average rises to $10.61. That's because in the calculation of the average we added the closing price from day 11 (i.e., $11.25) and dropped the closing price from day 1 ($10.00). And hence the name moving average.

The moving average is another tool used to gauge the current trend. Rather than drawing the trendlines on the chart, the moving average becomes the trendline. The 200-day moving average is the most common one used by technical analysts, because it is thought to define the long-term trend in the underlying stock. The moving average, then, defines the support and resistance points for the underlying stock.

If a declining stock begins to rally and breaks through the 200-day moving average, it is said to have broken through upside resistance, and similarly, if a stock is declining and falls below the 200-day moving average, it has broken support.

## TABLE 9.1: CALCULATING THE MOVING AVERAGE

| Day | Daily Price | Moving Average |
|-----|-------------|----------------|
| 1 | $10.00 | |
| 2 | 9.50 | |
| 3 | 9.75 | |
| 4 | 10.00 | |
| 5 | 10.50 | |
| 6 | 10.75 | |
| 7 | 11.00 | |
| 8 | 11.25 | |
| 9 | 11.00 | |
| 10 | 11.13 | $10.49 |
| 11 | 11.25 | 10.61 |
| 12 | 11.38 | 10.80 |
| 13 | 11.50 | 10.98 |
| 14 | 11.25 | 11.10 |
| 15 | 11.50 | 11.20 |

For short-term trendlines, technical analysts will simply use shorter moving averages, such as a 50-day moving average or a 90-day moving average. All are designed to accomplish the same goal, which is to find points where you could buy or sell the underlying security.

Because the moving average trails the actual daily price changes in the stock, shorter-term moving averages will tend to be more volatile, presumably providing the technician with more frequent signals. That being said, it is more meaningful if the stock breaks through a longer-term moving average. Indeed, the longer the moving average, the more significant the breakthrough becomes.

It is generally felt that when you buy a stock trading below its 200-day moving average, you will usually be disappointed. Buy a stock that is trading above its 200-day moving average, and the results are generally positive. A study published in the *Journal of Finance* in 1992 focused on the performance of the Dow Jones Industrial Average from 1897 to 1986. The results of the study were interesting. When the Dow Jones Industrial Average crossed above its 200-day moving average, it returned about 12% a year, when it broke below the 200-day moving average, it lost 7%.

## Odd Lot Trading

Other techniques in addition to chart reading are used by technical analysts. These include the use of external indicators such as odd lot trading indexes, confidence indexes, and the like. Recall from our discussion of stock price quoting in lesson 7 that most stocks are usually traded in minimum round lots, defined as 100 shares. Some investors, however, will buy stock in smaller lots. For example, a small investor might only be able to afford, say, 50 shares of XYZ, an amount which is defined as an odd lot. There is an index that tracks the number of shares purchased in odd lots, which is of interest to technical analysts because it tells them how much of the volume is attributable to smaller investors. The larger the percentage of trades attributable to small investors, the greater the chance that the market will change direction.

Historically, small investors are buyers at the top of the market and sellers at the bottom. The odd lot index, then, is considered a "contrarian indicator." By contrarian we simply mean that analysts attempt to do the opposite of what the index is telling them. When there are a lot of small investors buying, that is the time to sell, and conversely, when small investors are selling, that is the time to buy.

## The Short Interest Number

The short interest number is another technique and a long-standing contrarian indicator. To explain this indicator, we need to understand one of the more interesting aspects of the stock market, the fact investors can sell something they don't own.

For example, assume that XYZ was trading at $15 per share, and you thought the stock would fall in price over the next three to six months (we are assuming that you do not already own the stock). If you wanted to take advantage of your view on the stock, you could sell 100 shares of XYZ at $15 per share, a trade that is defined as shorting the stock.

The idea with a short sale is that the investor will buy the shares back at some point in the future to close out the transaction. Assuming that you were right about XYZ and the stock indeed falls to $10 per share, you could simply go into the market at that point, buy the shares back, and deliver them against the original short sale.

A question often asked is, how can you sell something you don't own?

To answer that question, we have to go back to lesson 3, on the banking industry. Remember that banks are able to create money because not everyone wants their cash at the same time. If everyone wanted to withdraw their money from the bank at the same time, we would have a crisis in the banking industry.

The brokerage industry works on much the same premise, in that most investors don't really want to hold stock certificates. It is simply too inconvenient. In most cases, the stock certificates are kept at the brokerage firm in segregated accounts. By segregated, we simply mean that the stock certificates are registered in the name of the brokerage firm and held by the brokerage firm for safekeeping.

Stock certificates that are registered in the name of the brokerage firm are said to be registered in street name. The name on the stock certificate provides the company, XYZ in this case, with an address to deliver annual reports and any other pertinent information about the company that would be of interest to shareholders. When registered in street name, the brokerage firm is able to collect that information and forward it to you, the account holder. That's assuming, of course, that you want to receive that information. As the client and account holder, you are the actual owner of the stock certificate, and the brokerage firm is registered as the mailing address for any corporate information.

So, the stock certificates are merely kept at the brokerage firm for safekeeping, and those stock and bond certificates are not part of the brokerage firm's capital structure. In other words, unlike a bank, the brokerage firm cannot use your stock certificates as collateral for a business loan. In effect, then, a brokerage firm could go bankrupt, and that would have no impact on any stocks or bonds or mutual funds that you held in your brokerage account. That's what we mean by segregated.

That being said, the brokerage firm can borrow stock and bond certificates that are held in street name, and can deliver those shares to the buyer in the short sale transaction. In other words, as long as some other client in the brokerage firm has 100 shares of XYZ, you can sell them without actually owning them, and those shares could be delivered to the buyer to complete the original short sale transaction. When you buy the shares back at the lower price, you simply deliver those shares back to your broker, who will then put them back in the client's account from which they were borrowed.

Now, this is a long-winded description of a short sale, designed to bring us full circle and back to the short interest number. The fact that stocks are sold short means that, at some point in the future, those shares will have to be bought back. That, to a technician, means pent-up demand for the stock, or put another way, buying support at some point in the future. The short interest number is simply the percentage of shares sold short versus the total number of shares outstanding. If XYZ had 100 shares sold short, and there were 10,000 shares of XYZ outstanding, then the short interest number would be 1% ($100 \div 10,000 = 0.01$).

The higher the short interest number, the more buying power that will have to come in at some point in the future. According to the theory, as the price of the stock begins to rise, these short sellers will start to buy the stock back in order to cut their losses. As such, the short interest number is another contrarian indicator, where technicians tend to do the opposite of what the index is telling them.

However, that being said, the short interest numbers have lost some of their appeal in recent years, because investors can hedge their short sales with options and other derivative securities. In short—pardon the pun—the hedge provides protection to the short sellers, which means they don't necessarily have to buy the shares back in a panic to protect a profit or cut losses.

Because of this interaction between stocks and options, the short interest numbers can become distorted and, as such, they have not been as effective a contrarian indicator as many technicians would like.

## The Put-to-Call Ratio

A better gauge of short-term market sentiment is the so-called put-to-call ratio. This statistic is relatively straightforward, in that the technician simply divides the number of puts (options to sell an underlying security at a specified price by a certain date) by the number of calls (options to buy an asset at a specified price by a certain date).

Because the investor who buys a put is betting that the underlying security will decline in price, it is similar to a short sale. Similarly, the buyer of a call option is betting the price of the underlying stock will rise, and therefore represents a bullish view on the underlying security. If the put-to-call is low—more calls being purchased than puts—it generally means that the consensus opinion is optimistic. Because this is a contrarian indicator, the technician would view that as a bearish signal. On the other hand, a high put-to-call ratio—more puts being purchased than calls—indicates a negative mood among investors, which to a technician is a signal to start buying.

Overall, the mood of investors is usually bullish, so that in most cases, more calls are being traded than puts. Because the volume of calls is typically greater than the volume of puts traded, the average put-to-call ratio is below 1.00, and in fact usually averages about 0.80. Most technicians are not interested in small variations from the average. Only when the ratio exhibits an extreme divergence is the technician likely to take action—"extremely" being defined as (1) a ratio below 0.70, a very strong bullish reading, which means this is the time to sell, or (2) above 0.90, a very strong bearish sentiment, which technicians interpret as a buy signal.

The sentiment, or as they are sometimes called, the confidence indexes, simply provide technicians with a snapshot of what other investors are thinking. Another index along the same line measures the percentage of investment managers who are bullish versus the number who are bearish at a point in time. Presumably, when there are many more bulls than bears, it is time to sell. The reasoning goes something like this. Presumably, the bullish money managers have already taken positions and, therefore, will be less likely to add to their positions over the near term, and conversely when there are more bears than bulls, these same money managers have probably already sold their positions and are flush with cash waiting for an opportunity to reinvest.

## Types of Charts

When you think about technical analysis, it really is designed to provide a snapshot of potential investments, and then to address the very basic question of when to buy and when to sell. Technicians will admit that chart watching is far from being a perfected science. They will also tell you that it is nonetheless a worthwhile exercise, because you can still make money, even if you don't pick the absolute top or bottom in the current trend.

There have been a number of books written about technical analysis, the most noteworthy being *Technical Analysis of Stock Trends*, now in its fourth edition, written by Robert D. Edwards and John Magee. This work is considered the "bible" of technical analysis.

Edwards and Magee have a very basic three-part premise: (1) that market values of shares are determined by supply and demand, (2) that the factors underlying supply and demand are complex, can influence the market, and are reflected in the market value of shares, and (3) that trends in share prices tend to persist for some time. Any changes in these trends are the result of changes in the basic supply/demand relationship. Thus the role of the technician is to spot trends and to do so by gauging market and stock momentum as revealed in chart patterns.

The most common chart patterns are the line chart (Figures 9.1 through 9.4), the high-low-close chart (Figures 9.6 and 9.7), and something called the point-and-figure chart. The line chart uses one number—usually the closing price—to reflect the day's price movement, while the high-low-close chart uses three numbers for each data point. In many cases, you will also see a volume chart along the bottom of the high-low-close chart.

The volume numbers are another important technical tool, in that they assist in determining the integrity of a particular move. For example, if XYZ rises by $1 on a particular day, that move is given greater weight if the volume on that day was much higher than normal. Similarly, on down days, technicians pay particular attention to volume, as larger volume moves may be an early warning sign of a trend reversal.

It can be the case where the volume increases but the stock price doesn't move. Here, volume can still tell you a great deal. For example, suppose the price of XYZ stock was unchanged from the previous day's closing price, yet the volume today was twice as much as you would normally see in XYZ stock. That could signal a major announcement from the company within the next couple of days, and those with so-called inside information, or thinking they have inside information, may be buying or selling the stock in advance of the announcement. Remember, technicians are keenly interested in the mood of the investor, and any information that can give them advance warning of price changes can be very useful.

Both the line and the high-low-close chart plot the daily (sometimes the plots are weekly or monthly) prices of the underlying stock, whether or not the price has changed. If the stock closes at $10 today, and that was the same close as yesterday, then you would have two data points, each showing a close of $10.

The point-and-figure chart looks at things a little differently. In this case, the technician only records a price if it fluctuates by some fixed amount. For example, if the technician has set minimum price movements at $1 per share, then the price of XYZ would have to move by at least $1 from the previous day's close in order for the move to be recorded on a point-and-figure chart.

Generally speaking, when the price moves by the predetermined amount, the technician plots the event using the letter X. If the price declines by the predetermined amount, the movement is recorded with the letter O (see Figure 9.8 which represents the point-and-figure display of approximately the same XYZ prices used in Figure 9.6).

Here's how it works. Each point-and-figure chart starts with O. The X represents a specific upward move in the price of the stock (usually representing a $1/8$ or $1/4$ point move to the upside), while the O represents a specified downward move (again, usually representing $1/8$ to $1/4$ point).

In fairness, point-and-figure charts are an excellent source of information about price momentum. They don't, however, incorporate volume into the discussion. Most professional technicians believe that, for the average investor, line and high-low-close charts with volume are more useful than the point-and-figure chart.

## The General and the Army

Recall at the beginning of this lesson that we talked about the price action of most stocks. We noted, for example, that a stock in an uptrend could experience a 33% to 50% retracement (see Figure 9.1), which would actually be healthy. In fact, the retracement provides the foundation for the stock to move even higher.

We also suggested that if the stock were to decline more than 50%—what we call breaking support—it could also signal a trend reversal (see Figure 9.2). I trust you see the problem. The stock must decline anywhere from 33% to 50% before you can ascertain whether or not the trend is reversing. If you sell at that point, you are selling at a price that is probably 50% below the recent highs. This is not a very appealing strategy for most investors. And therein lies one of the fundamental flaws with technical analysis.

## FIGURE 9.8: POINT-AND-FIGURE CHART

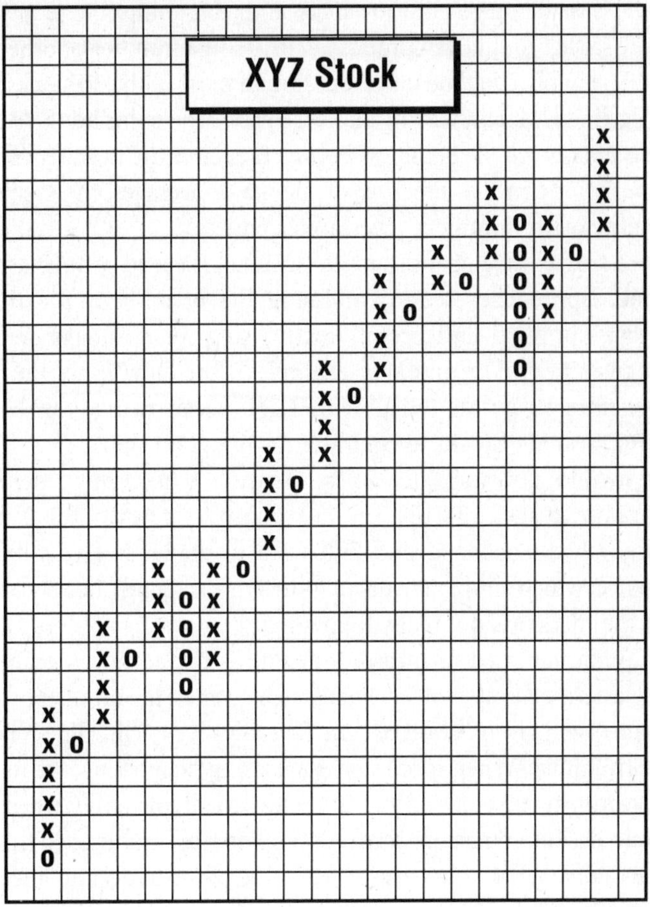

**XYZ Stock**

Fortunately, this flaw is well recognized by technicians. And to address that issue, many technicians tune their analysis with the use of secondary indicators to confirm the validity of a price move.

One approach, for example, is market breadth. Remember when we talked about the flaws in a price-weighted index. Those flaws can cause mixed signals for a technician. The Dow Jones Industrial Average, for instance, is made up of only 30 stocks, and a big jump in one or two of the Dow stocks could overcome small losses in a number of other Dow stocks. The index could be flat, even though most of the 30 stocks in the index declined. Martin J. Pring addressed the issue in his book *Technical Analysis Explained*: "Generally speaking, the fewer the number of issues that are moving in the direction of the major averages, the greater the probability of an imminent reversal in trend."

There are a couple of approaches technicians use to confirm a trend, and both approaches seek to measure the breadth of the market. Breadth is simply a measure of stocks rising versus stocks declining over a given period of time. For example, if the Dow Jones Industrial Average rises 10 points today, with 1,250 issues rising, 1,000 stocks declining, and 500 stocks unchanged, that's a good sign.

You would not want to see a situation where the Dow Jones Industrial Average was up, say, 20 points, yet only 1,000 stocks advanced, 1,250 declined and 500 were unchanged. That's called a divergence, which simply means that the Dow is going one way and the rest of the market is not really following.

One indicator used to measure breadth is the advance/decline line, which tracks the number of stocks advancing versus the number of stocks declining over a given period of time. The advance/decline line is really a cumulative index. When more stocks are rising than falling, the number of stocks moving up is added to the previous total; conversely, when more stocks are declining than are rising, that difference is subtracted from the previous total. What you want to see is the advance/decline line rising when the Dow Jones Industrial Average is rising.

That's important because, as we said, the stocks that make up the Dow Jones Industrial Average are the largest and most blue-chip stocks on the New York Stock Exchange. Technicians often refer to the Dow as the "general" of the market. The rest of the market represents the troops. The key is to make sure the army—the overall stock market—stays in step with the general—the Dow Jones Industrial Average. When both are moving in the same direction, this confirms the current trend.

On the other hand, if there is divergence between the Dow and the advance/decline line, then in effect the general is moving but the troops are not following. In this situation, you should be concerned about the validity of the trend.

Another way to measure breadth is to track the number of stocks making new 52-week highs versus the number of stocks making new 52-week lows. When, say, the Dow Jones Industrial Average hits a low (in this case we mean a low within the context of the most recent move, not an all-time low), while the number of individual stocks making new lows stays the same, a turnaround may be imminent.

Conversely, when a market index like the Dow Jones Industrial Average is rising without a corresponding rise in the number of new highs, a correction is likely. For the record, technicians believe that the measure of new 52-week highs to new 52-week lows must not be viewed in a vacuum, but on a relative basis. Relative in this case, to recent levels.

What we are really saying, then, is never ignore a divergence, and it is particularly important when timing buys and sells. Recall the problems cited with our previous discussion about retracement.

## The Trading Range

One of the real keys when trying to pinpoint buy-and-sell decisions is to determine a stock's trading range. In that pursuit, technical analysis can be quite useful. Essentially, the trading range is defined as the range of trading between the support and resistance points.

In many cases, stocks will go through periods when they seem to be stuck in a range between a high and low price. These stocks will experience huge selling pressure at the top of the range and significant buying support at the bottom of the range. In such instances, you should take notice when a stock regularly moves, say, between $20 and $30. In that case, you might consider buying at $20 and selling at $30, or more likely buying in the low $20s and selling in the high $20s.

In these types of situations, stocks tend to remain in a trading range for some time—and this can be quite healthy. The longer the stock remains in a trading range, the stronger will be the price move when it breaks free of that trading range. When a stock breaks through to the upside—which would be $30 in our example—then that resistance point now becomes the support price.

For example, if the stock breaks above $30, and then rallies to, say, $35, the new support would be at $30. You would be concerned if the stock began to fall and broke through the $30 support level. Breaking support in this type of pattern would be considered a serious setback.

## Relative Strength

One final technical tool—and this is by no means an exhaustive discussion on the subject—is relative strength, which simply measures how an individual stock is performing relative to the overall market. Technicians believe that changes in a stock's relative strength tend to precede changes in the stock's trend.

Relative strength is easy to calculate, in that it is simply the price of the stock divided by the price of a market index. If, for example, you wanted to compare the performance of XYZ to the Dow Jones Industrial Average, you would simply divide the closing price of XYZ by the closing value for the Dow. The technician tracks the stock's relative strength over a period of time, and again is looking for a divergence between the current stock price and its relative strength rating.

If relative strength is rising, it shows that the stock is outperforming the market over time. When relative strength is declining, it means the stock is underperforming the market index. Most technicians believe that a stock is most attractive when its relative strength has improved for four months or longer. However, that being said, you have to be careful, as with any technical indicator, not to view results in a vacuum. You should not, for example, necessarily buy the stock with the highest relative strength. Stocks that reach the relative strength pinnacle may already have gone too far too fast.

Relative strength also works in a down market. A stock may be declining, yet its relative strength is rising. That is simply evidence that the individual stock is declining less than the market index.

Technicians also use relative-strength to identify attractive industry sectors. The idea here is to measure the performance of a specific industry relative to the overall market. In this case, the technician seeks out strong industry sectors, and then proceeds to select individual stocks.

## Summary

Research studies have not been kind to the art of technical analysis, as little support for the method, at least as applied to stock selection, has been found. Still, technical analysis remains one of the best tools to assess buy-and-sell points. If you believe in the buy-and-hold philosophy, then technical analysis may not provide much help. On the other hand, there are valuable lessons to be learned from charts, and in some cases, being able to read a chart can help you steer clear of potential problems.

## At the coffee shop ...

"Another investment tool is always helpful," I reflected, "but technical analysis is not something I would use as a stand-alone guide to buying or selling stocks. It really should be used along with other information that you can get from the company's financial statements."

"Well, Loa, I'm not sure it helps me at all, since I believe in the buy-and-hold approach."

"But, Chris, even knowing that, charts can help you discover price points at which you might want to add to your position," responded Machaela. "And what about a down market? I would like to have some idea where I can expect to find buying support, or where I am likely to experience selling resistance."

"For myself," I said, "it's easier to buy a stock if I can have a snapshot of what it has done in the past. It works for me, I suppose, because I am really a visual person."

"I found the information about relative strength particularly interesting, as I did the sentiment indexes," said Chris. "Who would have thought that an index that measures the opinions of professional money managers would be a good contrarian indicator?"

"Right there with the rest of us novice investors!"

"Well I don't know about you, but I am starting to gain confidence with investing in stocks. The more tools I have at my disposal, and the more understanding I gain, the more comfortable I feel about investment decisions."

"You might say, then," observed Chris, "that an educated investor is the broker's best client!"

"Speaking of being an educated investor," Machaela pitched in, "does anyone understand what Mr. Croft was talking about when he mentioned options?"

"Well, I'm no expert, Sis, but what I do understand is that there are two types of options—calls and puts. A call option gives you the right to buy the underlying stock at a preset price for a predetermined period of time. Really, it's not that much different than during my first year in business, when I had an option to buy my store at a set price for one year. That would have been a call option. When I exercised the option to buy the store, I simply paid the former owner the agreed-upon price and the place was mine."

Chris said, "I understand an option to buy a business, but you didn't pay anything for that, did you?"

"Not in my case. But, in reality, that option had value. From the perspective of the former owner, the fact he granted me that option enticed me to lease the business for a year to get to understand how it worked, and then with that confidence, I could make a decision whether or not to exercise the option."

"But with stock options you do pay a price?" asked Machaela.

"Absolutely! The price is set by the market but, in essence, a call option allows you to profit should the underlying stock rise substantially. In my business, for example, if it went up in value during the first year, I would be entitled to any of that capital gain. To capture that capital gain, I would only need to exercise my option, buy the business, and then presumably sell it at the higher price. It works much the same way in the stock market, only I understand you don't have to exercise the option to make money—you can simply sell the option to another investor. If the price of the underlying stock rises, so too will the price of your option. To make your capital gain, you simply need to sell your option."

Machaela asked, "But what about the put option?"

"Well, the put option grants you the right to sell the underlying stock at a set price over a specified period of time. So, if the value of the stock declines, you, as the holder of a put option, have the right to sell the stock at the higher price. In that sense, it is much the same as a short sale, only with a short sale the stock could rise indefinitely and you would be on the hook for all the losses. With an option, you can only lose the cost of the option—no more, no less."

"Sounds a lot like gambling to me!" commented Chris.

"Well, it is true there is more leverage with options. A few dollars can control many. However, there are also some conservative strategies that can actually reduce the risk of holding the underlying stock. I'm just not that familiar how all of them work. The point is, many small investors trade options looking for the big score, and the fact so many small investors play this game explains the fascination with the put-to-call ratio as a gauge of the short-term mood of the market."

# How to Invest Around the World

"This should be an interesting session tonight," offered Chris.

Chris was doing most of the talking on our way to class. The three of us were car pooling together, and he was driving. More to the point, he had had the day off, while my day had been grueling. The Christmas season was just around the corner, and Christmas is a great time for chocolate giving. I expected this to be my best year yet. Machaela, on the other hand, was in the midst of getting report cards out to parents, and she then had to set time aside to conduct parent/teacher meetings. This was a time of year that always took a lot out of her. So by process of elimination, Chris became the leader of our discussion group, and since he was the one driving, he had a captive audience.

"There has been a lot of talk about the world getting smaller.

Globalization, I think, is the current catchphrase. And I believe it's true, at least from an economic perspective."

"And from an investment perspective, too," I added. "Just the other day, I read an article about the Canadian stock market, and how over the past 20 years investments outside Canada earned—what was the figure, now—something like 5% more per year on average. Just by investing some of your portfolio outside Canada, you could have beaten a 'Made in Canada' investment theme hands down."

"And I think I know why!" said Chris. "Even today, the former Soviet Union is still in disarray as its economy struggles to survive the great communist experiment. And while Soviet citizens struggle for survival, we are enjoying a renaissance in our own economy. What with declining deficits, lower interest rates, lower tax rates, and, from what I read, more trade with more countries, we are reaping the rewards of globalization."

"And your point is …" I think he lost his concentration while weaving in and out of downtown traffic.

"The point is," he snapped back, "world economies are at different stages of development, and even for those countries that are developed, there is opportunity because each country is usually at a different stage of the business cycle."

"So what you are saying is, there is an opportunity for diversification," offered Machaela, trying to put the risk-reduction spin on the discussion. "Putting a little money in the U.S. and a little overseas means that we are less likely to have all of our investments fall out of bed at the same time. Presumably knowing that makes the transition from GICs into equity investments more palatable."

Chris pulled into the school parking lot. "Let's move it, guys. Mustn't keep Professor Kirzner waiting for his star pupil." I decided that I'd drive next week.

## Class in session ...

Some people look at foreign investing as a complex and daunting task. Too many eggs in too many baskets makes keeping track of foreign investments an overwhelming task. Mr. Croft and I, on the other hand, see global investing as a major opportunity—one of the most important in the investment world. But we understand the concerns and think that the best way to discover new opportunities is to follow a well-developed road map that can help you put global investing into action.

We see this as a 12-step process or, if you prefer, we offer 12 rules to making global investing a part of your portfolio. And no, this is not in keeping with the 12 Days of Christmas theme, although if it helps to drive the point home, do what you gotta do!

## Rule #1: Diversification Is Good

Most investors like to avoid risk, like consistency of performance, like to make the right decisions, and like to sleep well at night. Portfolio diversification is the logical outgrowth of these fundamental principles of human behavior.

Diversifying means spreading the risks so you are protected against unexpected shocks such as sudden spikes in interest rates, market crashes, currency collapses, or unexpected inflation.

Diversification means setting an appropriate asset mix of safety, income, and growth securities for your portfolio. Since we all have different tastes and financial needs, our asset mixes range from very security conscious (a high proportion of cash and fixed-income securities) to aggressive, growth-oriented portfolios (high levels of stock or equity investments).

We call this *strategic asset allocation.* It is the key to financial success, and you'll learn more about it in the final lesson next week. For it to work, you have to keep your asset mix intact, which leads us to rule #2.

## Rule #2: Stay Diversified

Keeping with this structured approach to investing, rule #2 should always follow rule #1. Stay diversified by periodically adjusting your current asset mix back to your target asset mix.

Suppose you decided last year that an ideal investment asset mix was 40% stocks, 40% bonds, and 20% cash. That would be your target asset mix. Now, over the last year, I think you will agree that stocks have earned much better returns than both bonds and cash.

If you were to sit down and look at that same portfolio today, your current asset mix might look something like 50% stocks, 35% bonds, and 15% cash. In other words, because stocks did so much better than bonds and cash, you now have a larger percentage of stocks in your portfolio than you intended when you set up your target asset mix. That's what I mean when I talk about monitoring your portfolio. It makes sense to periodically rebalance the portfolio, bringing it back into line with your target asset mix.

For example, if you are contributing to an RRSP, you could simply rebalance the portfolio by using your contribution to purchase more bonds and cash, while keeping your stock position intact. By using new money to rebalance the portfolio, you also bring another discipline to the table—getting into the habit of making regular RRSP contributions.

If you sell some stocks and use the money to buy bonds and cash, you end up, by definition, following one of the most common investment truisms: buy low and sell high.

The goal, no matter how you accomplish it, is to bring the asset mix back into line with your target mix; that is, 40% stocks, 40% bonds, and 20% cash. This process is called dynamic asset allocation or, if you prefer, dynamic rebalancing.

The goal is to keep the target mix in place. Good investment planning doesn't stop at the strategic asset allocation decision. It is important that you evaluate your asset mix regularly every six months. It is one thing to pick your portfolio structure, but it is quite another to maintain it!

This discussion leads to rule #3, and the focus of this lesson—how to diversify your portfolio with foreign securities.

## Rule #3: Asset Allocation Includes Global Diversification

Question: Over the past 30 years, which of the following portfolios do you suppose was more volatile: (1) a $100,000 portfolio consisting of a large number of Canadian stocks from many different industries, or (2) a portfolio consisting of an $80,000 portfolio of Canadian stocks from many different industries, plus a $20,000 portfolio of foreign stocks from many different countries?

Answer: The first portfolio, consisting entirely of Canadian stocks, was much more volatile.

Question: Which portfolio earned the highest return?

Answer: Since we have been talking about how higher-risk portfolios should deliver higher returns, it would make sense to presume that the first portfolio did better than the second portfolio over the long term. In this case, however, the second portfolio outperformed the first. The lower-risk portfolio delivered a higher return, which begins to illustrate how investment management works. At the end of the day, you should strive to earn the most dollars with the least amount of risk for your investment portfolio. And the best way of doing that is to add some global securities to your portfolio.

The massive surge of technological advances is making the world smaller and blurring communication barriers. The Internet has created an information explosion that was absolutely unforeseen two decades ago. If you are skilled at using the Net, you indeed have the world at your fingertips.

You can participate in a global discussion group, pick up information about the best restaurants in Vienna, and get quotes on Hong Kong stocks with a single keyboard stroke. There is little doubt that in the future there will be direct trading access to virtually all world markets from your home video screen (or whatever replaces a screen) and through the next generation of Internet-type networks.

Yet, despite the explosion of telecommunications and information, and the increased mobility of capital, we still live in a fragmented real world. Economic and political systems vary widely, and geographical barriers are still visible. The sun rises on events in Auckland, New Zealand, that are very different from those in Nome, Alaska.

Furthermore, financial markets are organized quite differently. While the Toronto Stock Exchange is primarily an order-driven auction market where participants interact with each other, the London Stock Exchange is primarily a quote-driven market where investors trade with dealers rather than with each other. Markets such as Paris are fully automated, while Amsterdam is still a floor-based manual market.

Segmented countries and markets create wonderful investment opportunities. Since there are different forces at play, markets are moving differently. At any time, there will typically be some financial markets that are particularly strong and some that are weak. Foreign investing means that at any time there will be countervailing forces at work that will smooth out price fluctuations and reduce the overall volatility of your portfolio. If country A is rising when country B is falling, a portfolio that owns securities in both countries will remain virtually unchanged.

That balancing effect can be considered as both good and bad news. The good news is that the portfolio didn't lose anything. But the bad news is, it didn't gain anything either. The trick, of course, is to make sure that, over time, both countries produce positive returns, which allows the portfolio to add value. It stands to reason that if countries are experiencing different growth patterns and are at different economic and political stages, then global diversification will capture these effects. In fact, studies show that a globally diversified portfolio, in addition to supporting portfolio diversification, will provide superior returns, reduce risk, and enrich investment opportunities.

## Rule #4: Foreign Investing Means Opportunity

Canada may be one of the world's major industrialized countries and possess well-developed capital markets—including the seventh-largest stock exchange in the world, the Toronto Stock Exchange—but its record in the investment world is far from stellar.

Although the Toronto Stock Exchange recorded one of the highest returns in the world in 1996, over the past three decades the Canadian market has been one of the most disappointing, ranking near the bottom many years, often ahead of only a handful of markets.

Over that period, the TSE was beaten by the New York Stock Exchange at a rate of about 5% per annum. With the Tokyo Stock Exchange, the differential was about 3% per year in Tokyo's favor. And when we examine the performance of the leading index of world market performance—the Morgan Stanley Capital International's World Index—it beat the Toronto Stock Exchange by 6% per year!

The globalization process of the past two decades has meant a vast array of new and valuable opportunities for investors. The sheer size and limitless opportunities have meant that knowledgeable investors can come increasingly closer to the goal of efficient diversification. Canadian stocks are subject to domestic economic, political, and social factors that can't be diversified away inside Canada, no matter how large the Canadian stock portfolio.

The bottom line is that a well-diversified portfolio will outperform a strictly Canadian one in the long run, based on both return and volatility. That means more return with less risk.

The question now is, how do we go about selecting foreign investments? As you might have guessed, that is the subject of rule #5.

## Rule #5: Diversify by Country, or Top Down

When it comes to buying a global portfolio, you can choose between two approaches: top down and bottom up. By top down, I simply mean that you make your investment based on which country you think is poised to do well in the foreseeable future. Once you pick the country you want to invest in, the next step is to assess which industry makes the most sense, and then choose those companies within that industry that are best suited for your portfolio.

The other approach—bottom up—means that you seek out a good company with great prospects. The geographic location of the company, and the nature of its industry, become secondary, although important, issues.

Even with this course, you may find it difficult to select a good company in a foreign market. Not to mention the time and effort required when deciding which country offers the most potential over the next few years. Evaluating where to invest in a foreign market requires experience, and you may not even be sure where to find information about a foreign country or foreign industry, let alone a foreign company.

And I don't expect you to. In this lesson, I'll show you ways that you can gain exposure to foreign markets without having to select specific stocks. And for those who don't want to study economic trends in different countries—and who can blame you?—we'll talk about international equity mutual funds, where a professional manager will invest in foreign countries on your behalf.

In fact, trying to find the right company in the right country may not be worth the effort for the average individual investor. For the vast majority of individual investors, the choice of which country to invest in is the most important factor when going global. Diversifying by country or region is easier than picking individual country stocks, and studies tell us that about 85% total global returns are the result of the overall market performance within a specific country. Currency and individual stock movements have only a small effect on performance.

So, with the top-down approach, the idea is to first set your overall country mix and then, if that is something you want to spend time on, seek out individual investments to fill the desired allocations.

Most of the rewards of global investing come from striking a good balance within the foreign content segment of your portfolio. A sample allocation might be 40% in Europe, 30% in the United States, and 30% in the Far East.

Tables 10.1 and 10.2 show examples of two suitable asset mixes that include some global investments.

## TABLE 10.1: CONSERVATIVE PORTFOLIO WITH GLOBAL INVESTMENTS

| | | |
|---|---|---|
| Canada | 15.00% | |
| United States | 10.00% | |
| **North America** | | **25.00%** |
| Japan | 2.50% | |
| Rest of Asia | 2.50% | |
| **Far East** | | **5.00%** |
| Europe | 8.00% | |
| **Total Europe** | | **8.00%** |
| Latin America | 1.00% | |
| Other emerging countries | 1.00% | |
| **Total Emerging Markets** | | **2.00%** |
| | | |
| **Total Equity Assets** | | **40.00%** |
| | | |
| Fixed Income | 40.00% | |
| **Total Fixed Income Assets** | | **40.00%** |
| | | |
| Cash | 20.00% | |
| **Total Cash Assets** | | **20.00%** |

## TABLE 10.2: AGGRESSIVE PORTFOLIO WITH GLOBAL INVESTMENTS

| | | |
|---|---|---|
| Canada | 18.00% | |
| United States | 10.00% | |
| **North America** | | **28.00%** |
| Japan | 10.00% | |
| Rest of Asia | 7.00% | |
| **Far East** | | **17.00%** |
| Europe | 15.00% | |
| **Total Europe** | | **15.00%** |
| Latin America | 3.00% | |
| Other emerging countries | 7.00% | |
| **Total Emerging Markets** | | **10.00%** |
| | | |
| **Total Equity Assets** | | **70.00%** |
| | | |
| Fixed Income | 20.00% | |
| **Total Fixed Income Assets** | | **20.00%** |
| | | |
| Cash | 10.00% | |
| **Total Cash Assets** | | **10.00%** |

These are just samples of potential asset mixes. But picking the mix isn't enough. You have to give the mix enough time for all of the issues related to each country to play out, which is the subject of rule #6.

# Rule #6: Global Means Long Term—
## Time Is Not Only on Your Side, It's Essential

Diversification is based on diverse events. For example, two stocks that tend to respond differently to the same event or that are affected by entirely different factors will show different price behavior. We can measure how likely it is—based on past performance data—that one stock will move inversely to another. The statistical tool of choice is correlation. Stocks, or countries, that have low correlation with each other should tend to move in opposite directions at different points along the business cycle (see figures 10.1 and 10.2). If you can buy assets that have exhibited a low correlation, you can reduce the volatility of a portfolio, because like the two-country example I cited before, when one is going down, another will be going up.

Don't worry about trying to calculate correlation. The real issue is to understand how this push-and-pull relationship among assets that have historically had a low correlation can ultimately reduce risk and, if structured properly, can enhance return. Think of this as the "diversification effect." Incidentally, the U.S. market has a high correlation with Canada's. This means that U.S. investment is not a valuable diversification target.

So, because foreign securities have low correlations with Canadian securities, and because foreign securities have, historically at least, had a better performance record than Canadian securities, combining them in a portfolio means higher returns with less risk.

## FIGURE 10.1: TWO MARKETS WITH LOW CORRELATION

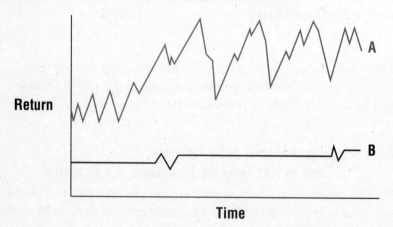

**FIGURE 10.2: TWO MARKETS WITH HIGH CORRELATION**

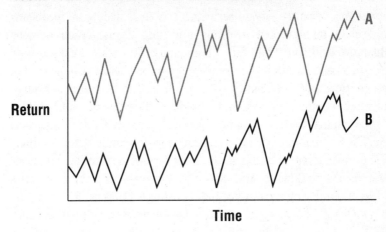

Foreign securities should represent about 10% to 30% of your holdings, and your strategy should be long term. The biggest danger is what is called "Gambler's Ruin," which is being right in the long term but losing out by selling in the short term because you were scared away. Diversification needs time to work. Your portfolio might suffer in the short term because Latin America or Europe is undergoing a weak period. But, as the various regions rotate through the business cycle, the long-run results will smooth all of this out.

Markets tend to move together during economic or political shocks (such as the 1987 global market crash or the 1990 invasion of Kuwait by Iraq). It seems that when the volatility of global markets rises, the correlation between markets increases. So very short-term diversification effects may be limited. However, the good news is that, in general, given differing political and social policies, the longer-run correlations remain low. Overall, the diversification benefits long extolled for global investing remain intact.

Global diversification make sense, but there are barriers that make implementing a global strategy more difficult, which is the subject of rule #7.

## Rule #7: Respect the Barriers

Buying and selecting foreign securities is a challenge. Some problems with direct international investment include thinly traded markets (Milan, Madrid, and Frankfurt are illiquid by our standards); custody (in some countries a custodian must be appointed before you can trade); and political and sovereignty risk, which is the danger of a foreign government taking some action that reduces the value of your holdings or your ability to trade. Some countries such as Chile, India, and Thailand still maintain direct prohibitions on foreign investor trading.

The most severe challenges are in the area of accounting standards and policies. The quality and quantity of available information varies widely, and differing accounting and reporting standards make comparisons difficult. For example, some foreign corporations do not consolidate their financial statements, while many others do not capitalize long-term financial leases. In some European countries, the emphasis of financial reporting is on understating earnings, while in the Far East emphasis is on cash flow rather than earnings.

These point to the lack of international standards for financial reporting. On the auditing side, there are interesting issues as well. For example, in some countries, auditors are required by law to be members of the corporate governing board. This practice is contrary to standards we have set in North America, where auditors must be independent. The quality of the audit, sampling techniques, and general education standards in many places are well below those employed in Canada.

Liquidity, or the ability of an investor to dispose of his or her holdings quickly at market at a reasonable cost, can be a particular problem of investing abroad. The spread between the bid and asked price can at times, be significant. Latin American markets, for example, are notorious for their poor liquidity.

Many foreign markets are also highly inefficient. For example, many banks refuse to handle investment in overseas markets. Prudent lending standards, industry practice, and other such considerations exclude many institutions from participating in specific foreign markets.

Without institutional investors buying and selling, the price you will pay to buy or receive when selling often does not reflect the true value of your assets. Add to that the often rudimentary market structure, weak regulatory environment, and lack of local participants, and you can see why some foreign markets are highly inefficient—which in some cases, may not be that bad. This takes us directly to rule #8.

## Rule #8: Emerging Markets Are a Key Investment Area

Just as countries are often at different stages along the business cycle, so too are countries at various stages along the life cycle. Some are experiencing rapid economic growth while others are in severe decline; some are reengineering and some are rebuilding.

Some of the world's most underdeveloped countries are beginning to secure the attention of global investors. These are emerging states in terms of economic and political growth. Emerging or developing countries have the demographic and economic characteristics that North America had in its supernormal growth period of the 1950s and 1960s. They are typically marked by movement toward free-market economies, more democratic systems, and above-average economic growth. Many are limiting population growth and are increasing their spending on education.

The capital markets of emerging countries in general are under-developed and inefficient. There are numerous barriers to trading. These barriers mean increased search, analytic, and monitoring costs for the investor. They also suggest the existence of market inefficiencies that can provide abnormal returns. The more barriers and problems, the more inefficient the market and the greater the opportunities for the skilled stock or fund picker!

In the 1970s and early 1980s, when we talked about emerging or developing countries, it was usually in the context of poor central planning and concomitant debt escalation, inefficient banking systems, and debt and currency crises. Now, many emerging countries are concentrating on building and improving their equity markets.

They want to provide a foundation for up-and-coming companies to finance their growth through new stock issues rather than through new bond issues. Argentina, Brazil, Chile, China, Mexico, Taiwan, and Thailand are examples of countries focusing on economic growth through equity issues.

The market capitalization of some of the smaller markets has skyrocketed—in some cases by factors in excess of 20 times! For example, the markets of Argentina, Indonesia, and Malaysia have grown by factors of 3 to 10 times in the last five years.

The emerging country phenomenon is a two-edged sword. The huge rush of liquidity into small, emerging country financial markets has helped underwrite world economic growth through the expansion of emerging country economies. But it also has pushed security prices too high in the past and has caused an enormous rundown of liquidity in the United States. This is indeed the Achilles' heel of global security market capital flows.

In selecting emerging markets, you should look for countries that:

- are moving toward democracy
- are experiencing rapid population advance
- have signs of rising incomes, which means there will be increased consumer spending and interest in Western-style products, resulting in industry growth to supply consumer needs
- are upgrading their economies

There are different approaches to foreign investing, although for most individual investors, the best approach is to invest in a mutual fund that specializes in foreign markets. Rule #9 talks about this.

## Rule #9: International Mutual Funds Are Normally the Best Avenue

Global investing isn't simple, but there are so many convenient avenues open that the process is available to anyone willing to invest the time and effort. If you wish to trade directly, you can, through full-service Canadian brokerage firms, some foreign brokerage firms, and in some cases, through domestic branches of foreign banks. All can handle security transactions for you, including initial foreign-currency conversions, delivery and custody arrangements, and currency conversion at the time of sale. You can either trade directly in securities on foreign markets, buy foreign stocks that are listed on North American stock markets—that is, Sony is listed on the New York Stock Exchange—or indirectly through American Depository Receipts (ADRs).

Another efficient approach to foreign investing is to simply buy passive index products. These include the Morgan Stanley WEB index products that we discussed.

If you like the prospects for a country and want to avoid the unique risk of selecting the right country but the wrong investment vehicle, these are ideal.

Still, you have to make a decision about which country is the best place to invest. Because of that, most individual investors buy global and international mutual funds, of which there are now literally hundreds domiciled in Canada with varying objectives, track records, load options, and portfolios.

## Types of International Mutual Funds

In the global framework, there are a number of fixed-income funds, including money market and bond funds, with a wide array of objectives and target portfolios.

In the equity category, there are four types of funds:

1. *Global* funds invest their assets in equities of various countries, including Canada
2. *International* funds invest in securities of different countries (sometimes limited to a few specific regions), not including Canada

3. *Regional* funds invest in stocks from specific regions of the world
4. *Specific country* funds invest in securities of a single foreign country

The general geographic categories include Canada and the United States; Japan and the Pacific Rim; Europe; and Latin America and other emerging countries.

In addition to geographical orientation, funds are often described by investment objectives categories (safety, income, growth, aggressive growth); investment philosophy (active versus passive); and investment style (value versus growth, bottom up versus top down, portfolio structure, small versus medium versus large-capitalization stocks).

International and global funds include both open-end funds and closed-end funds. The open-end variety are the more familiar and are commonly called mutual funds. They are called open-end because the fund can sell additional shares to the public at virtually any time with little or no restriction. The proceeds from the sale of shares are then used to buy additional securities for the portfolio. The shares or units of open-end funds are bought from and sold to the mutual fund corporation itself; there is no secondary market for the shares.

Closed-end investment funds, on the other hand, have a fixed capital structure in that shares are initially sold to the public and the proceeds invested in a portfolio of securities according to a set of objectives. Like the open-end fund, the management of the closed-end fund is paid a fee to manage the portfolio, which may be subject to constant revisions. However, unlike the open-end fund, new shares in the closed-end fund are only issued in specific cases (such as a new investment opportunity or a takeover) and then only with the approval of the appropriate regulatory bodies. The shares of closed-end funds are traded on stock exchanges in the same manner as shares of public companies.

You usually have a large choice of open-ends to choose from and you can ignore the closed-end variety. But there is one case where it matters; see rule #10.

## Rule #10: Watch Out for New Money

Open-end mutual funds are required to redeem units from investors, on demand, at the net asset value per share. There is no secondary market. This redemption right can be a problem if the fund has to sell portfolio assets to meet redemptions. For typically illiquid markets (such as those of emerging markets), selling shares into a falling market can be a disaster, resulting in further erosion to net asset values per share.

There is a problem on the buy side as well. The fund manager has to place new money in what may be an already overheated market. These purchases could have a market impact that results in the manager paying too high a price to the detriment of new and old fund holders. As a result, open-end investment funds are often poor investment vehicles for restricted or illiquid markets.

The shares of closed-end investment funds, on the other hand, are traded in the secondary market (stock exchange or over-the-counter). Shares are not redeemed by the issuer, so the fund is faced with neither the "redemption" nor the "new money" effect. Consider the closed-end version for illiquid markets.

## Rule #11: There Is No "Free Lunch" in Global Investing

You notice that Argentinean government bonds are yielding 18% at a time when Canadian government bonds are yielding 8%—the line forms to the right.

But before you jump into the line, does this really mean you will earn an extra 10% by investing in Argentinean bonds? Of course not! You should know by this stage of the course that investing is not that simple. Otherwise, why would anyone buy a Canadian government bond when higher rates are available elsewhere?

It is a fact that, at any time, interest rates are high in some countries and low in others. However, through the mechanism of something called *interest rate parity* it is not possible to earn higher returns except by chance in the country where bonds are yielding more. The great equalizer is the combination of expected exchange rates and interest rates. If the Argentinean currency loses value relative to the Canadian dollar, that 18% return can quickly turn into a loss. Foreign exchange rate movements usually offset interest rate differentials.

The exchange rate represents the number of units of a given currency that can be purchased with one unit of another currency. The spot rate is the rate paid for a currency "on the spot." For example, when you go to the bank and pay $1.35 in Canadian currency to buy $1 in U.S. currency, that is referred to as the spot rate. Contracts to buy or sell a foreign currency at an agreed-upon future date are called forward contracts, and the rates are called forward exchange rates.

Interest rate parity means that the rate of interest, covered for exchange risk, is equal to the domestic rate of interest. In essence, a foreign currency will depreciate at a percentage rate approximately equal to the amount by which the country's interest rate exceeds the domestic rate. In a literal sense, it means that there are no bargains in foreign exchange markets.

So, if you want to buy a foreign bond, do so for the right reason. The right reason is presented in rule #12.

## Rule #12: Foreign Bonds Are for Currency Exposure— Not Higher Yields

The reason to hold foreign currency bonds is to gain exposure to another currency—not to earn a higher rate of return. Investors who hold all of their wealth in Canadian dollars have discovered that, as the dollar weakens, the cost of a trip to New York and of importing goods from Tokyo have correspondingly risen. If you want to guard against adverse currency fluctuations, you have to hold some of your wealth in something other than Canadian dollars.

Global bond yields are linked by interest rate parity theory. This "no free lunch" model means that the expected yields on foreign bonds are equal to the expected yields on domestic bonds when measured in the same currency. In light of interest rate parity, correlation factors for bond markets don't have the same effect as they do for stock markets. You may not get portfolio diversification by investing in global bond funds—you may get additional costs and increased risk!

This means that if you want foreign currency exposure, you have to get it directly through products denominated in foreign currencies. For example, some mutual fund families have U.S.-dollar denominated versions of the Canadian dollar global bond funds. But if you are looking for European currency exposure (deutsche marks, Swiss francs, or British pounds), or Far Eastern (Japanese yen, Australian dollar, New Zealand dollar), your best investment vehicle is an AAA issuer (such as the World Bank) foreign bond or Eurobond denominated in your desired currency.

A foreign currency bond is simply a bond that has been issued by a foreign government, a supranational institution such as the World Bank, a foreign bank, or a foreign corporation. In general, it is a bond that is sold outside the country of the borrower. If it is sold in a different country than the currency denomination, it is called a Eurobond (that is, for example, a Danish krone bond issued by the Swiss government and sold in Germany). If it is sold in the same country as the currency denomination, it is called a foreign bond (for example, a Danish krone bond issued by the Swiss government and sold in Denmark).

Like all bonds, they pay periodic interest and mature at their par or face value. Eurobonds normally offer higher yields than term deposits, bank deposits, and similar instruments. The yields on foreign and Eurobonds are sometimes higher than available on domestic bond issues as well, although interest rate parity means that the foreign currency is expected to depreciate at a rate that offsets the differential.

An important feature about Eurobonds is that the interest income is not subject to withholding tax at source. You simply include the annual receipts as interest income in the equivalent Canadian dollars in your Canadian tax return. If you sell the bonds before maturity, you will trigger a capital gain (or loss) which is subject to the 75% capital gain inclusion rule.

Finally, Eurobonds issued by a Canadian government, a Canadian corporation, and certain international organizations such as the World Bank are RRSP eligible.

## Global Investing: A Summary

1. Diversify your global portfolio.
2. Invest in countries whose markets have relatively low correlations with that of Canada.
3. The U.S. is the least valuable diversification candidate for a Canadian investor.
4. Direct global investing is hazardous to your health. Buy global or international mutual funds.
5. Timing probably won't work. Don't be constantly switching from country to country in the search for undervalued securities. The danger is that you will miss out on the correlation effects and the advantages of diversification.
6. Select global investment funds whose managers build portfolios that really match the stated objectives.
7. Select global investment funds whose performance generally remains within a specific risk category.
8. Hold some securities denominated in foreign currency.
9. Always negotiate loads for load funds. Back-end loads are often *not* the best choice.

## At the coffee shop ...

"The real question for me," began Chris, "is whether global investing is worth the effort. I like the idea of reducing risk with, what did he say, low correlation assets. It's nice in theory, but I sure don't have the time to analyze each foreign country, let alone try to discover some great companies in solid industries in Germany, Japan, or Australia that might add value and diversification to my portfolio. I can't even keep up with Canadian companies."

"I have to agree with you." You have no idea how hard that was for me to say. But in this case, Chris was right. This is not something any of us had time to commit to. "What I got from this session is why global diversification is good. Any approach that can increase your return and reduce your risk has to be considered."

"So we agree that global diversification is good. How do we go about it?" asked Chris, while pouring some cream into his coffee.

"Since none of us has the time to study foreign markets," came the reply from Machaela, "and since we all agree that global diversification is good, we need to find a good international mutual fund that invests in foreign equity."

"You mean a global equity mutual fund?" I asked, half in a tone meant to correct what I thought was a mistake. How wrong I was.

"Not this time, Loa," Machaela replied. "Remember what Professor Kirzner told us. Global equity funds also invest in the country of origin. Which for us means that a global equity fund can also invest in Canada. The manager of a global fund might decide that Canada is the best place to invest and put most of the portfolio into Canadian stocks. And while the manager might be right at a point in time, a global fund with most of its money in Canada does not give us any diversification in our overall portfolio."

"You mean because our portfolio would presumably already have in it a Canadian mutual fund or a couple of Canadian stocks," said Chris.

"Exactly," Machaela replied. "In fact, even if the global equity fund has most of its portfolio invested in U.S. stocks, it doesn't do much for us in terms of diversification. Remember that Professor Kirzner pointed out that U.S. stocks generally have a high correlation with Canadian stocks. So I really don't want to buy a global equity fund that invests anywhere in North America."

"So what do we buy?" I wanted to know, because I couldn't remember this part of the lesson.

"Well, according to Professor Kirzner, we would have to buy, as I started to say earlier, an international equity mutual fund," offered Machaela, while putting on her I-told-you-so face. "International equity funds only invest in countries outside the country of origin. And many international equity funds will only invest outside North America. And if we are looking for global diversification, I suggest we all look for an international equity mutual fund that only invests outside North America. My question, however, is what about holding some of our portfolio in a foreign currency?"

It was time to redeem some of my self-respect. "I think I have an answer to that. Presumably, if we buy the international equity mutual fund, we already gain some exposure to foreign currencies. If you want that, then simply buy an international equity mutual fund that does not try to hedge against foreign currency risk?"

Machaela said, "But why not simply invest in a global or international bond fund, and gain currency exposure that way?"

"Well," I began, "the problem with that, if I got the correct message from tonight's lesson, is this issue of interest rate parity. I understood Professor Kirzner to say that any potential gain from buying a foreign bond would presumably be lost in the currency translation, making a global bond fund a difficult investment to justify. What he did say, for those of us looking to gain some exposure to a foreign currency, was to buy foreign currency bonds directly. By doing that, at least you would know exactly what rate of interest you would earn and, presumably, exactly what foreign currency you would have exposure to. And remember, don't buy the foreign bond because you expect to earn a higher rate of return; buy it because you want to gain some foreign currency exposure."

# Building Your Portfolio, Step by Step

"Okay," Machaela said, "now it's time for everything to come together. Tonight we find out how to take all the information we've been given and put it in a plan."

"'Portfolio building' is the term, Machaela," said Chris. "It's like making a model building or jet or space station with Lego. What's going to be interesting is seeing how the pieces fit together."

"Not only that," I ventured, "but we're very different people. Look at our class. Some of us are risk takers and others aren't. So one plan isn't going to work for all of us."

"Absolutely right, Sis," said Chris. "I'll remember to pop the question if you don't."

It didn't take long for Mr. Croft to start putting the pieces in place.

## *Class in session ...*

In lesson 2 we defined household assets and investment assets. You may also recall that we classified our investment assets into equities, fixed income, cash, and real estate. And, finally, we introduced asset allocation, where we looked at how different investors can structure their asset mix—that is, what percentage of their money is invested in stocks versus bonds, versus cash, versus real estate—based on their own investment philosophy and long-term goals. In this lesson we will expand on the asset allocation theme and provide you with a foundation to build your own investment portfolio.

I believe asset allocation is the cornerstone of successful long-term investing. If you have an asset allocation program, it means you have a suitable mix of safety securities (liquid assets such as savings accounts and money market funds), income-producing securities (such as term deposits or bond mutual funds), and growth assets (such as equity mutual funds and common shares) in your combined personal and RRSP portfolio. By allocating your investment assets among a number of different securities, you are diversified.

Harry Markowitz is the founder of modern asset allocation principles. In fact, he was awarded a Nobel Prize for his work on modern portfolio theory that was first published in 1952. His work set out the mathematics of diversification. Given our encapsulated format, the bottom line is this: those who diversify will have superior returns to those who don't!

How should you build your own suitably diversified portfolio? Do you do it yourself or do you buy it? Should you structure your own portfolio by hand selecting each of the securities? Or do you buy diversification directly through asset allocation mutual funds or balanced mutual funds? These are simply funds whose managers always keep a percentage of the fund's portfolio in stocks and a percentage in bonds. Asset allocation and balanced fund managers alter the percentage of their money in stocks and bonds based on their outlook for the economy, and whether stocks or bonds are likely to do better given that viewpoint.

## Step 1: Review Your Financial Objectives

We suggest a step-by-step approach that begins with a review of your financial objectives. Make sure that you have articulated your goals and objectives correctly, whether using a financial advisor or looking in the mirror. It really helps if you can qualify and quantify what you are trying to accomplish.

Some people will set portfolio achievement goals based on improving their purchasing power. The goal might be: (1) earning on average a portfolio return of 4% above the inflation rate, or (2) beating a North American inflation index by 2% per annum.

Others will set goals based on outperforming a market index, such as: (1) earning a risk-adjusted rate of return above the TSE 300 Composite Index, or (2) outperforming the TSE 100 by 2% per year.

Still others might articulate their strategy in terms of a benchmark, such as: (1) earning a return equal to a weighted average portfolio consisting of 20% T-bills, 30% bonds, and 50% stocks, as measured by T-bill yields, the Midland Walwyn Canadian Bond Fund Index, and the TSE 300 Composite Index, or (2) earning a return equal to that of the Morgan Stanley World Composite Index.

By setting realistic and quantifiable goals, you not only create discipline for your investment process, but you create standards for measuring your portfolio's progress over time.

## Step 2: Set Your Investment Strategy

The second step in this process is to set your investment strategy—for example, deciding whether you are going to use an active, passive, or mixed approach to investing.

You may recall in lesson 8 that we talked about the efficient markets theory. We showed how the cumulative results of hypothesizing and testing from the turn of the century to the early 1960s resulted in a theory of how securities are priced, and that the general thrust of the large number of studies was that current stock prices reflect historical information and publicly available information. The theory means that you cannot expect to earn excess profits by employing conventional analytic techniques using information available to all. The implication is that financial statements are not expected to provide "news," but only "confirmation" information. If you believe in efficient markets, passive investing is the right approach for you.

But then, as we also saw in lesson 8 and again in lesson 9, not everyone believes in efficient markets. Researchers have uncovered a number of trading surprises and seasonal patterns, including higher than expected returns for stocks with low price/earnings ratios, neglected stocks, small-capitalization stocks, and low-price stocks. There are also studies that show unusual returns at the turn of the year (the January effect), on Monday mornings, and even at certain hours of the day! There are now some 35 of these trading and pricing anomalies that have been documented.

Some market followers believe that chaos theory may in fact be the key to successful stock picking. Chaotic systems are those in which the behavior of things appears random but in fact—at least partially—follows a set of rules.

For example, long-term weather forecasts are never accurate, even if you start with perfect initial formula, because insignificant variations in preliminary measurements become exaggerated over time and change the long-term simulation results through self-reinforcing chain reactions or looping. This looping or buildup behavior is the root of chaos theory.

Chaotic systems have been illustrated in terms of audience applause, which starts as a random clapping process but then synthesizes quickly into a rhythmic pattern. The recent behavior of stock prices, including the crash of 1987, has led some researchers to believe that stock price patterns may be chaotic rather than random, and that forecasts of future stock prices, including the large, abrupt changes during panics and bubbles, are possible. If you accept the pricing anomalies or chaotic view of the world, then an active investment strategy is appropriate.

A lot of investors adopt a mixed approach to their strategic asset allocation by apportioning part of their portfolio to active investing strategies and a part to passive investing strategies.

## Step 3: Set Your Strategic Asset Allocation

The third step in our systematic approach to building a portfolio requires that you set your strategic asset allocation. The cardinal rule of investing is to diversify your portfolio by establishing a target mix of investment assets. Finding the right combination is the most important step in this process—so important that you will want to devote most of your effort to deciding what percentage of your money goes into equities, what percentage into bonds, and what percentage into cash. It is the mix that is important, rather than trying to buy this or that security.

When we talk about strategic asset allocation, we are really talking about the structure of your portfolio. Think of your portfolio as a three-legged stool, with each leg representing one of the three basic investment features: safety, income, and growth. Like the stool, the portfolio cannot stand on its own if one of the components is missing. At the end of the day, then, a well-balanced portfolio should include some safety assets, some income assets, and some growth assets.

When you think about safety investments, think in terms of highly liquid investments that carry little or no risk. For example, a CSB has no default risk in that you can always get back your entire principal investment. A CSB has no market value risk, in that you can always get back your investment dollar for dollar at any time. And finally, CSBs have no interest rate risk since they can be cashed in at any time. A money market mutual fund falls into the same category, because there is virtually no default or market risk.

Safety investments, then, are designed to preserve capital and to earn a rate of return equal to the short-term interest rate. Safety securities include domestic money market mutual funds, global money market funds, Treasury Bills, GICs, commercial paper (short-term IOUs, usually with terms of 90 to 180 days, from large corporations), and short-term government bonds.

Income investments, on the other hand, are designed to generate periodic income for spending or reinvestment. These securities generate the semi-annual interest payments that we talked about in lesson 6. The price of income investments can fluctuate with changes in the level of interest rates, and so there is a price risk if you sell your income investment before it matures.

Now, income securities include government bonds, high-quality corporate bonds, medium-quality corporate bonds, and speculative quality corporate bonds. Also falling into this category are mortgages, mortgage-backed securities (which is simply a pool of mortgages backed by Canada Mortgage and Housing Corporation, which in turn is guaranteed by the federal government), mortgage mutual funds, bond mutual funds, income mutual funds, global bond funds, and preferred shares.

Clearly, safety and income investments are critical components of a well-balanced portfolio. But they are not enough to ensure investment success. Suppose you earn a portfolio return of 6% in interest income during a period in which the inflation rate is 2%. After paying taxes, your real (inflation-adjusted) rate of return is a mere 1% to 1.5%. If your expenses are rising, you need capital growth just to preserve your purchasing power, and that is the reason why all portfolios should have some growth investments.

Growth securities are usually subdivided into domestic and foreign and further subdivided into growth and aggressive growth. High-growth-potential investments typically offer little or no income and generally are riskier investments.

Growth securities include common shares (blue chip, speculative, growth, value, industrial stocks, utility stocks, resource stocks), convertible bonds (an investment that is part bond, part common share), Real Estate Investment Trusts (REITs), equity mutual funds (categorized as growth, aggressive growth, and global), and index products (TIPs, HIPs, SPDRs, and WEBs).

A well-diversified portfolio contains securities within all three purpose categories. Portfolios are often defined in terms of, say, 40% safety, 50% income, and 10% growth for the ultraconservative investor or 10% safety,

20% income, and 70% growth for the very aggressive investor.

Your actual target mix will reflect your financial plans, your family objectives, your life-cycle stage, and your tastes, but unless your situation is really unusual, it should lie somewhere between 30% combined safety and income and 70% growth, to 70% combined safety and income and 30% growth. The mix you select will reflect your tolerance for risk.

If you dislike risk (defined as volatility), you will likely opt for a conservative combination, such as 30% safety, 50% income, and 20% growth. A more traditional portfolio weighting would be 20% safety, 30% income, and 50% growth or, more precisely, 20% safety, 30% income, 30% growth, and 20% aggressive growth.

For people who are about to retire, or who have retired, there has been a lot of discussion about protecting their portfolio from sizable risk. Some of the more recent studies suggest that retirees not only keep a larger portion of their assets in equity investments, but that they hold their investments for a longer period of time. The fact is, people are just plain living longer, and the notion of switching 100% of your portfolio into Treasury Bills and term deposits at retirement is no longer considered sound financial planning.(See Figure 11.1.)

## FIGURE 11.1: FOUR TYPES OF ASSET ALLOCATION

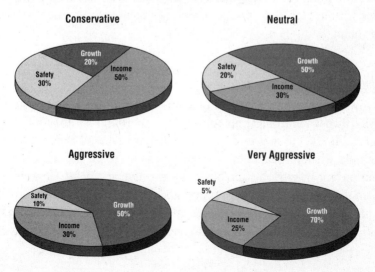

## Step 4: Pick Your Products

The fourth step is to pick your products. Once your asset mix is established, you then start selecting the securities or mutual funds to slot into the safety/income/growth sections of your portfolio. The investment process includes finding investments that are suitable for the circumstances.

Once you have set the structure, investment style becomes critical. Style is a function of what you believe about investment finance. If you believe that markets aren't entirely efficient and that it is possible to find undervalued securities through skill and effort, then you should pursue an active stock-selection strategy, searching for undervalued securities.

If you believe in efficient markets where security prices reflect all information and are properly priced, and that economic cycles cannot be accurately forecast, you won't spend time searching for undervalued securities or looking for changing economic cycles. Instead, your approach will be a passive one where you attempt to add value by constructing and maintaining the portfolio in the most cost-efficient manner.

The key is to choose the style you are most comfortable with and to stick with it. It is impossible to refine a craft if you are always changing your focus, particularly if you change to a style that doesn't work for you. So, assess yourself honestly, go with your strength, and stick with it. Don't adopt someone else's system just because it works for them!

### Adjusting Your Portfolio Mix

If you also believe in market timing and that you can identify market cycles, then you might attempt to adjust your portfolio mix to profit from changes in the business cycle. This is called tactical asset allocation. For example, when interest rates have bottomed out, you could sell some of your income investments and buy more growth investments. Conversely, when the economy is heating up, and stock prices have gone higher than is justified by current earnings, you might want to sell stocks and put more money into safety investments such as Treasury bills. Tactical asset allocation simply refers to the approach you use to change the asset mix. "Tactical" means shifting the asset mix so as to profit from market timing, whereas setting your investment "strategy" means structuring an asset mix based on your personal objectives and risk tolerances.

But we should point out that studies thus far have indicated that market timing is extremely difficult. Mind you, the rewards of correctly timing the market are high, but as Nobel Prize-winner Paul Samuelson has pointed out, timing can be hazardous to your health and, we might add, to your pocketbook.

What are the odds that you will always be able to time your asset shifting correctly? Frankly, we think the odds are against you. Studies indicate that there are few money managers who can time the market consistently, so what are the odds that a small investor can perfectly (or even imperfectly) predict changes in fixed-income and equity market cycles? John Templeton, one of the gurus of mutual fund management, has stated repeatedly that he does not and cannot time the market. Instead, he searches for bargains and lets value investing do the timing for him.

Market timing also has a cost, and in some cases, those costs are substantial. There are commission costs associated with switching from stocks to bonds and back again, mutual funds charge loads and possibly transfer fees, not to mention the "nuisance costs" of signing documents and negotiating instruments (see Table 11.1)

The cost of acquiring and disposing of the investments should be carefully monitored. These costs range from zero for term deposits, GICs, and CSBs, to 10% or more for speculative stocks and bonds. Commissions and loads alone do not capture all costs—many securities are subject to an auction where you may end up buying at the asked price or selling at the bid price. That adds to the cost.

## TABLE 11.1: ACQUISITION AND DISPOSITION COSTS

The following is a representative table of trading costs:

| Securities | Commission | Bid/Ask Spread |
|---|---|---|
| Money market funds | 0%–2% | |
| Government bonds | | 1%–3% |
| Corporate bonds | | 1%–5% |
| Convertible bonds | | 2%–10% |
| Bond mutual funds | 1%–6% | |
| Mortgage-backed securities | 1%–3% | 2%–5% |
| Common shares | 1%–4% | 2%–10% |
| Equity mutual funds | 1%–6% | |

# Step 5: Review Your Portfolio's Performance

The fifth step is to review your portfolio's performance on a regular basis. Having established the asset mix, you need to have some way of measuring whether your portfolio is in fact doing what it was supposed to do. Have you got the right components?

If you want an answer, check the numbers. You can review your progress by constantly checking to make certain your asset allocation mix is still appropriate. Your financial checkup should take place at least once a year and preferably more frequently. You should check that your asset allocation still reflects your needs and tastes. Are your weights assigned to safety, income, and growth still suitable, or has your personal situation changed so that you have to alter your mix?

You also want to calculate your returns. Ultimately, you want to ascertain your total return, which is the measure of investment performance. It reflects all three sources of investment return, namely income, dividends, and capital gains.

It's one thing to know what your portfolio returned, but it is quite another to know whether or not the return was good under the circumstances. For example, we all know that Wayne Gretzky is a great hockey player, but that fact becomes most evident in a game situation, when we are able to compare his ability to that of other professional hockey players. We would not be able to make as clear a judgment about his ability if he were on the ice practicing by himself. We might recognize that he looks pretty good while skating around an empty rink, but until we see him perform in a game situation, we really don't have a full grasp of his talent.

Our portfolios work much the same way. We know that a 17.5% return is pretty good. What we don't know is how that return stacks up against similar portfolios in the current economic environment. If similar portfolios returned 22%, then our portfolio underperformed. Conversely, if similar portfolios returned, say, 10%, then you did pretty well over the last year. The best way to gauge the performance of your portfolio is to measure its return against the return on some passive benchmark index. More on that in a moment. First, we need to learn how to measure the return on our portfolio.

And, it's easy … really! All you have to do is take the closing value of your portfolio, subtract any contributions and add any withdrawals you've made over the period, and finally subtract the opening value. This gives you the gain on the portfolio. You then measure the gain against your opening value to calculate your return on investment. It's a simple A minus B plus C minus D calculation!

For example, if want to know how your portfolio has performed in the twelve months ended December 31, 1997:

|  |  |  |  |
|---|---|---|---|
|  | A | Portfolio value as at December 31, 1997 | $106,000 |
| *minus* | B | Portfolio contributions (RRSP, monthly investments, etc.) | 11,500 |
| *plus* | C | Portfolio withdrawals | 2,000 |
| *minus* | D | Portfolio value as at January 1, 1997 | 85,000 |
|  |  | Increase in value | $11,500 |
|  |  | Rate of return on portfolio ($11,500 / $85,000 $\times$ 100) = 13.53% | |

Incidentally, you can use this same formula for calculating the return on an individual security or mutual fund or bond. This doesn't take into consideration the timing of the contributions and withdrawals, but it does represent how much your wealth has increased. Calculating a time-weighted rate of return is a relatively complex exercise.

## Benchmark Your Returns

After calculating your portfolio's return, you need to measure that return against a suitable yardstick—just as we need to see Wayne Gretzky playing in a real game against other professionals. The yardstick most commonly used in the financial world is a passive benchmark index. Some accepted benchmarks are listed below.

| Portfolio Components | Benchmark |
|---|---|
| Safety | Six-month Treasury bill yields |
| Income | Midland Walwyn Cdn. Bond Fund Index |
| Growth (Canadian equity) | TSE 300 Composite Total Return Index |
| Growth (global equity) | Morgan Stanley World Capital Index |

Fortunately, these numbers are easy to find, as they are published in the financial press on the respective monthly mutual fund performance surveys.

So ... how did you do?

To assess your portfolio's return, let's go back to your target asset mix. If your overall balance is, for example, 20% safety, 30% income, 40% growth (Canadian), and 10% growth (global), just multiply each of those factors by the respective benchmark return.

If we assume, for instance, that over the last 12 months the benchmark returns were as follows:

| Portfolio Components | Benchmarks | Returns |
|---|---|---|
| Safety | Six-month Treasury bill yields | 5.6% |
| Income | Midland Walwyn Cdn. Bond Fund Index | 8.6% |
| Growth (Canadian) | TSE 300 Composite Total Return Index | 13.9% |
| Growth (global) | Morgan Stanley World Capital Index | 16.6% |

then you can calculate your own benchmark return as follows:

| Portfolio Components | Weight | Benchmark Return | Weight x Return |
|---|---|---|---|
| Safety | .20 | .0560 | .0112 |
| Income | .30 | .0860 | .0258 |
| Growth (Canadian) | .40 | .1390 | .0556 |
| Growth (global) | .10 | .1660 | .0166 |
| **Total** | | | **.1092 or 10.92%** |

If you earned more than 10.92% with your portfolio, then you have outperformed your benchmark. Suppose, however, your portfolio only returned 9.15%?

If you underperform your benchmark, is this a cause for concern? Not necessarily. The key is to recognize that long-term results are what matters and that there will be random differences in performance between your portfolio and a benchmark. Returns within a reasonable range of the benchmark imply adequate, and not necessarily poor, performance.

On the other hand, if your portfolio yielded, say, 6.28% (based on the numbers below) over this same period, it may be time for reassessment. It isn't your asset mix, because after all you have weighted the components in your portfolio and the comparable benchmark index the same way. The real problem is that the return of the individual components did not live up to the standards set by the benchmarks. Your benchmark diagnosis will reveal which components let you down, as in the following analysis.

| Portfolio Components | Weight | Benchmark Return | Component Return |
|---|---|---|---|
| Safety | .20 | .0560 | .0570 |
| Income | .30 | .0860 | .0830 |
| Growth (Canadian) | .40 | .1390 | .0230 |
| Growth (global) | .10 | .1660 | .1730 |
| **Total** | | **10.92%** | **6.28%** |

Here the obvious culprit is the Canadian equity component. Investing is a long-term process and you shouldn't normally make decisions based on short time periods. But a severe shortfall such as this relative to a benchmark may be a signal of a problem. You are most likely holding a mutual fund with a rather dismal record over that period, which bears closer watching. This diagnostic approach will help you pinpoint problem areas.

## Step 6: Manage Your Investment Portfolio

The next step in the investment process, after you make your initial investments, is the actual ongoing management of the portfolio.

When it comes to asset allocation, the most overlooked component of the process is what we call *rebalancing*, or what is known in the financial community as the *dynamic* aspect of asset allocation. Please note, we are not talking about the market timing here. Dynamic asset allocation is the process of bringing your portfolio back in line with your target structure when the deviation is caused by fluctuations in market values.

If you were invested in 1996, you had a very good year, particularly if you owned stocks. As a result, your holdings have probably deviated significantly from your target. By that I mean the growth part of your portfolio went up much more than, say, the safety part of your portfolio. Here's how you bring it back into line.

Suppose you started the year with a $10,000 portfolio consisting of $2,000 in money market mutual funds, $3,000 in bonds, and $5,000 in equities. Your target is to maintain this 20%-30%-50% (safety-income-growth) portfolio mix. Here's what your portfolio looked like at the start of the year:

| Component | Dollar Value | Weight |
|---|---|---|
| Safety | $2,000 | 20.0% |
| Income | $3,000 | 30.0% |
| Growth | $5,000 | 50.0% |
| | | |
| Total | $10,000 | 100.0% |

Let's assume, as a result of some exceptional returns produced by your equities (the growth component), that your portfolio has grown by 22.0% and the composition is now $2,100, $3,200 and $6,900. Your portfolio now looks like this:

| Component | Dollar Value | Weight |
|---|---|---|
| Safety | $2,100 | 17.2% |
| Income | $3,200 | 26.2% |
| Growth | $6,900 | 56.6% |
| | | |
| Total | $12,200 | 100.0% |

There are various approaches to adjusting it back to your desired mix. One method is through direct selling and buying of securities. To restore the original weightings in your $12,200 portfolio, you have to change the structure of your portfolio like this:

| Component | Target Weight | Required Value |
|---|---|---|
| Safety | 20.0% | $2,440 |
| Income | 30.0% | $3,660 |
| Growth | 50.0% | $6,100 |
| **Total** | **100.0%** | **$12,200** |

The arithmetic is really quite simple. Multiply each target weight by the total value of your portfolio to get the required value of each component. (For example, the safety value of $2,400 is calculated as 20% of $12,200.)

Finally, to determine the required adjustments, subtract the current value of the portfolio components from the required value to get the difference. As shown below, this means you sell $800 of your equities and buy $340 of money market and $460 of bonds. This is fairly easy to accomplish if you are in a family of mutual funds where there is little or no cost associated with switching from one fund to another.

| Component | Target Weight | Required Value | Current Value | Difference |
|---|---|---|---|---|
| Safety | 20.0% | $2,440 | $2,100 | $340 |
| Income | 30.0% | $3,660 | $3,200 | $460 |
| Growth | 50.0% | $6,100 | $6,900 | -$800 |
| **Total** | **100.0%** | **$12,200** | **$12,200** | **0** |

Another way to rebalance is to use "new money." For example, if you are planning to make an $1,800 contribution to your RRSP, or simply want to add $1,800 to an investment program that is not inside an RRSP, you can go through the same type of calculation.

Based on the new money coming into the program, the total value of your portfolio will be $14,000 ($12,200 original portfolio + $1,800 contribution). You calculate the required values of each component and calculate the difference from the current value. As you can see, the $1,800 would be allocated as $700 to money market funds, $1,000 to bonds, and $100 to equities.

| Component | Target Weight | Required Value | Current Value | Difference |
|---|---|---|---|---|
| Safety | 20.0% | $2,800 | $2,100 | $700 |
| Income | 30.0% | $4,200 | $3,200 | $1,000 |
| Growth | 50.0% | $7,000 | $6,900 | $100 |
| | | | | |
| Total | 100.0% | $14,000 | $12,200 | $1,800 |

The point of this discussion is to understand that rebalancing is an essential adjunct to strategic asset allocation.

### How Often Do You Adjust a Portfolio?

The frequency of the rebalancing is a personal matter. However, there are some general guidelines. One approach is to rebalance based on some specific deviation from the initial weights.

For example, you might choose to adjust every time the portfolio deviates from the target by, say, 5%. Although deviation from weights is theoretically the correct approach, the more practical method is temporal rebalancing, which simply means reviewing your structure and adjusting it periodically, such as semi-annually or annually. Watch the tax and cost implications, however. If you rebalance too often, and have to sell some of your more profitable assets, you will be subject to capital gains tax in the year of the sale. Accordingly, an annual tune-up might be the most practical approach.

Dynamic rebalancing is the passive component of an asset allocation program. The approach assumes that your strategic asset allocation mix is unaffected by changing market conditions. Of course, if you believe the risk structure of the market has changed, or your personal financial circumstances have changed, you might want to alter your target mix.

Regardless of the market's performance, you should give your portfolio a good review at least once a year—including a review of your objectives and your current asset mix. Rebalancing won't necessarily add to your returns every year, but it will keep your portfolio more stable. The real value of rebalancing is ensuring that your portfolio does what it is supposed to do, so that you improve the probability that you will have the funds you were expecting at retirement (or whatever your financial planning horizon is). The key is keeping the costs as low as possible, because if the costs to buy and sell are significant, it won't work.

An important feature of rebalancing is that you are selling securities or funds that have risen and are replacing them with asset classes that have not. It's a good counter approach to cyclical, passive investing.

## Building Your Portfolio: Basic Principles

1. Invest for the long term. Make sure your investment horizon is sufficiently broad to capture a few market cycles and to allow the normal high return on equities to materialize. A market cycle, as we learned in our discussion about the Canadian business cycle, normally lasts from three to eight years. Three years should be your minimum time horizon when considering an investment program.

2. Concentrate on the mix of securities in your portfolio rather than on timing market cycles. The key is giving your portfolio enough time to work. In the long run the unique consequences of abnormally low (as well as unusually high) returns will be washed away. We call it temporal diversification, or as we learned in lesson 8, taking advantage of the principle of mean reversion.

3. Reinvest your dividends. Keep your investment growing with the double-barreled impact of capital growth and

capital reinvestment.

4. Make full use of all tax advantages. Make sure that you can make full use of the tax incentives granted for investing in equity securities. This generally means that you should hold growth funds outside your RRSP and other tax shelters to capture the full benefit of the dividend tax credit and the 25% exclusion for capital gains. In a moment I'll talk about tax.

5. Ignore short-term fluctuations. Selling your securities when the market is falling is the worst thing you can do. Studies show that many investors sell at precisely the wrong time. Don't fall into that trap.

6. Don't watch the markets every day. Be patient and allow the effects of growth and compounding to work their way through. And although you should monitor your portfolio's progress regularly, don't look at it every day.

7. Protect your portfolio against unexpected changes in exchange rates. As the external value of the Canadian dollar falls, your purchasing power in foreign securities falls. Investments denominated in a foreign currency (buying, say, a global mutual fund isn't enough—the investment has to actually be denominated in a foreign currency) are the only way to guard against exchange rate risk.

8. If you are concerned about Canada's financial future or you want foreign currency exposure for simple diversification purposes, there are a number of useful vehicles. If your required currency is the U.S. dollar, then U.S. Treasury Bonds or Treasury Notes (that is, U.S. government debt with terms-to-maturity between one and five years) are ideal. Some mutual fund families have U.S.-dollar-denominated versions of the Canadian dollar global bond funds.

9. Ensure that you have inflation protection. If inflation rates increase, the purchasing power of an investment, everything else being equal, drops. To preserve your portfolio's purchasing power, you want to include investments

that provide protection against unexpected increases in domestic prices. Common shares and real estate are the traditional hedges against moderate 3% to 5% inflation rates. However, high rates of inflation may well be accompanied by high interest rates, sending price/earnings and stocks lower. The ultimate hedge against high rates of inflation is a basket of commodities. A well-diversified commodity mutual fund is the best vehicle. Gold bullion is a crude proxy for this. A small portion of an investment portfolio should be dedicated to permanent (high) inflation rate protection.

10. If you are employing strategic asset allocation (which I recommend), you alter your target mix with your changing life cycle and tastes, not with the changing investment outlook. You rebalance in order to maintain your target mix.

## A Tax Primer

Total return is the measure of investment performance. It reflects all three sources of income from investments, namely, income, dividends, and capital gains. If you buy 1,000 units of a balanced mutual fund for $10 a unit, earn $500 in interest income, and receive a $500 dividend plus a $500 capital gain distribution, you will have realized a total return of $1,500 ($500 + $500 + $500) or 15% before commissions.

Each source of income gives rise to a different tax treatment. For example, interest income is treated in the same manner as ordinary income. If you receive $500 in interest income in a given year and your marginal tax rate (tax paid on an additional dollar of income) is about 50%—reflecting provincial taxes and federal, but not including provincial surtaxes—you will pay $250.00 in tax.

Canada does not have a capital gains tax; instead, capital gains are treated in a particular manner. You include only 75% of a capital gain in income. This amount, called the taxable capital gain, is then taxed as ordinary income. Taxable capital gains can also be offset by allowable capital losses. If you earn a $500 capital gain in a given year and your marginal tax rate is 50%, you will pay $187.50 in tax.

Dividend income, since it is nondeductible at the corporate level, is given preferential tax treatment at the personal level. Dividends received from taxable Canadian corporations are grossed up by 25% and then a dividend tax credit is applied, computed as 16.67% of the dividend. The net effect of this treatment is to reduce the effective tax rate to well below that paid for comparable interest income.

That being said, your investment decisions should reflect your long-term financial plan, your tastes, and your family needs. Tax considerations should be secondary.

In lesson 12, we will review the fundamental elements of investing.

## At the coffee shop ...

"Well, this lesson put it all together for me," Chris announced. "For the first time, I feel comfortable enough to buy investment assets other than GICs."

"Not a moment too soon, what with GICs paying less than 5% per year," replied Machaela. "Actually, Mr. Croft was saying the things that I have always believed when it comes to investing. A portfolio should have a dash of this and a bit of that, seasoned to my personal taste."

"And the concept of dynamically rebalancing the portfolio through all phases of the business cycle is going to be particularly useful. I don't have the time to spend assessing whether this or that move by the Bank of Canada, or a sharp upward or downward move in the stock market, will ruin me financially."

"That is, Chris, it won't as long as you can stick with a long-term plan, can maintain a reasonably balanced approach, and review your situation at least once a year."

I jumped in to add to Machaela's observations. "I think that's probably the most important lesson I could have learned. There is more to investing than simply saying I want to buy this or that stock, double my money, and move to the next big winner. The fact is, whenever I make a decision to sell, I have to replace that investment asset with something else."

"The key is to stay invested!" added Chris.

"So, Chris, what kind of portfolio do you think is right for you?"

"I've been thinking about that for the past few weeks. There is a part of me that would like to own individual stocks. I think of that as my aggressive growth component. Not too much, though—perhaps no more than 5% of my portfolio. The rest of my portfolio …"

"Your serious money?" I interjected

"Yes, my serious money. It would be divided between equity mutual funds, a couple of bonds, with the balance in Treasury Bills."

"I'm the opposite of you," I said, "just as we have been in every other aspect of life. I like the challenge of finding that new investment opportunity. Being in my own business, I know what it is like to find something about a company that other investors have missed. It's exciting, and the rewards are well worth the effort that goes into the research."

"But what about finding some balance in your portfolio?" asked Machaela. "You are, after all, a business owner. How about some diversification? Must you always fly by the seat of your pants at 100 miles per hour?"

"Yeah, you're right," I replied. She had a point, and it was one that I had been thinking about. The fact is, I own my own business, and my business is subject to the vagaries of the business cycle just like any other business. When things are slow in my business, it is quite likely that things will also be slow in my investment portfolio. More to the point, my business has to take priority over my investment portfolio. If my business was slow, and needed an infusion of cash, that money would come from my portfolio. And such is the rationale for having the balanced approach that Machaela was quite correctly pointing out to me.

"What about you, Machaela?" asked Chris. "What do you want in your investment portfolio?"

"In my case, nothing much has changed. I find myself, as I always have, between the two of you. I have a streak in me that likes to be aggressive, and because I am still young, I have lots of time to recover from a loss."

That's Machaela, as with everything else, weighing the pros and cons of an investment strategy, not wanting to make a decision unless she can justify it as a prudent investment for the long term.

"I would probably have 25% of my portfolio in aggressive investment assets, another 40% in equity mutual funds, perhaps 25% in bonds, and the balance in Treasury bills."

It had now come full circle. After spending this much time together, we decided to start the Nordal Family Investment Club. We would meet once a month, something that we had never been able to do before this. But now we made a commitment, that no matter how busy we were, no matter how tired we were, investing in our future was important. And to do it right, we needed each other's input. In the investment game, we all agreed, our different personalities were our strength. The investment club would become our sounding board, a place to state our case for an investment and to hear each other's opinion about what the potential and the pitfalls were.

And we wanted ground rules. You couldn't just stand up and say this was a good investment. Before you could pitch an idea, you had to justify why the investment made sense. Not only in terms of the merits of a particular company, but how it could fit in each of our portfolios. And throughout the meeting, everyone would have their say—good or bad! In the end, we might agree to disagree, but we would have thrashed out our differences and there would be no hard feelings.

# Key Points to Remember About Being an Investor

## From Lesson 1: Who Needs a Financial Plan, Anyway?

### Financial Planning and Your RRSP

- You and your financial advisor should monitor the foreign content in your self-directed plans to ensure that you don't exceed the limit within your overall portfolio. If foreign content is more than 20% of the book value of your self-directed plan, you have a choice: the excess assets can be sold and transferred to, say, a Canadian money market fund, or you could make an RRSP contribution to bring the foreign content into line.
- Self-directed plans offer a cost-effective approach to investment management, flexibility of investments, and the chance to earn superior returns over the long term.

## From Lesson 2: Understanding the Two Asset Classes—Household and Investment

### The Importance of Your Investment Asset Mix

- In terms of building wealth, understanding your investment asset mix is critical because it has an important bearing on your overall return. Just how important? Studies have shown that 85% (some studies have suggested as much as 90%) of your overall return can be pegged to your asset mix decision, while another 5% to 10% comes from market timing (that is, shifting in and out of investments in response to economic changes), and the remaining 5% to 10% from selecting one specific security over another.

### Understanding Mutual Funds

- Mutual funds give you diversification within an asset class. A relatively small amount can be spread around a great deal of investment activity. Funds can also permit you the luxury of being wrong about a single investment or class of investments, because returns are smoothed out over a wider range of possibilities.
- In general, expect specialty funds to be more volatile than broadly based equity funds, which invest in stocks across many different industries.

## From Lesson 3: Time, Money, and Value

### Compounding Your Returns

- There are alternatives to holding money in a savings account. Money market funds, for example, have recently yielded on average about 5% per annum in interest, and that interest is reinvested monthly.

## The Rate of Investing

- Set up a regular savings/contribution program, and most of you will tell me a year from now that it becomes addictive. You need to pay yourself first, and then take care of the incidentals later.

# From Lesson 4: The Business Cycle Roller Coaster

## The Business Cycle

- While there is a lot of theory about the cause-and-effect relationship within the business cycle, economists have at least been able to agree that there are four distinct phases within the business cycle: the trough, the expansion phase, the peak, and finally, the contraction phase.
- We know that stocks and bonds—the two major investment assets—will rise and fall with the tides of the business cycle. The trick is to keep your eyes fixed firmly on the long term, and to buy when there seems to be no hope.

# From Lesson 5: Cash in Hand

## Bank Accounts

- Savings and chequing accounts usually pay relatively low rates of interest, usually pay interest on the minimum monthly balance, and require a minimum balance.
- If interest is paid on the minimum monthly balance, be sure that the funds are transferred to the account at the beginning of each month, and not in the middle.
- No matter how you cut it, bank accounts are not investments. Bank accounts should be a liquid source of funds that can be used to meet your monthly, weekly, and daily obligations.

## Canada Savings Bonds

- If you are considering cashing a CSB, it is best to wait until the beginning of the month. Regular or simple interest on the bond accrues to the holder each month. Therefore, if the bond is cashed in the middle or near the end of the month, you will forfeit all the interest accrued during that month.

## Treasury Bills

- Treasury Bills are liquid, are purchased at a discount, offer competitive short-term interest rates, and offer 91- and 182-day maturities. Sometimes a 365-day maturity is available.

## Term Deposits

- Term deposits are short-term investments, offer competitive rates, and offer maturities ranging from 30, 60, 90, and 180 to 365 days.

## Money Market Funds

- Money market funds are liquid (you can access your money within 24 hours plus any accrued interest), offer competitive rates of interest, offer any term, and the management fee is paid from the earnings.

## Guaranteed Investment Certificates

- GICs have one- to five-year maturities, have possible interest penalties for early withdrawal (if that option is available), and offer competitive rates of interest.
- The rates for GICs are generally better than Treasury Bills, but then your money is tied up for a longer term.

# From Lesson 6: Bonds—What They Are and How they Work

## The Yield-to-Maturity Concept

- The yield-to-maturity is the best estimate of your expected realized yield on the bond.

## Strip Bonds

- With a strip bond, there is only one payment to contend with, and that is the repayment of the principal at the end of the term. The good news is that since there are no interim interest payments to reinvest, there is no reinvestment risk. The yield-to-maturity for a strip bond is not only a theoretical concept, but a real-world principle. The bad news is that your tax return must include an amount in income each year equivalent to the implied interest component of the bond. As a result, strips are only suitable for RRSPs and other tax shelters.

## Mortgage-Backed Securities

- Mortgage-backed securities are safe, in that there is no default risk to the investor, and they provide monthly payments that include both principal and interest.

## Bond Principles

- Principle #1: Bond prices move inversely to interest rates. When rates are rising, bond prices will fall; when rates are falling, bond prices will rise.
- Principle #2: The longer the term-to-maturity, the more volatile the bond's price will be given a change in interest rates. The bottom line is that long-term bonds are riskier than short-term bonds.

- Laddering your bond portfolio is essentially the same thing as investing in GICs with different terms-to-maturity. Buy a short-term bond, a mid-term bond, and a long-term bond so that something is coming due on a regular basis. At least with this approach you don't have to forecast interest rates, and at the end of the day you will probably do as well as most professional money managers.

## Lesson 7: Going to Market—The Stock Market, That Is!

### Dividends

- Because dividends are paid from corporate profits, tax has already been paid on this income. As such, dividends receive preferential tax treatment in Canada.

### Company-Specific Risk

- What is interesting about company-specific risk is that it can be eliminated with a properly diversified portfolio. In fact, studies tell us that as much as 95% of company-specific risk can be eliminated with a portfolio of 30 different stocks representing a number of different industries.

### Market Risk

- The trick to minimizing market risk is to build a diversified portfolio.

## Lesson 8: How to Analyze Your Securities

### The Politics of Investing

- If you are a follower of the conservative school (you believe that stocks are in fact properly priced and that earning the average equity return is satisfactory), then you adopt what is called an *indexing strategy*—that is, searching for returns associated with a market index.

- On the other hand, if you are a follower of the liberal school, and you believe that stocks can deviate substantially from their intrinsic values, you either select individual stocks yourself using analytic techniques or you pay someone to do it for you. This is called active investing.

### The Price/Earnings Ratio

- A high price/earnings (P/E) ratio means low risk and/or high growth potential. A low P/E ratio normally means high risk and low growth potential.

### The Price/Dividend Approach

- Stocks of small companies that are considered high-dividend-yielding may contain more firm-specific risk than those of large companies. This implies that small-stock portfolios must be adequately diversified to eliminate the company-specific risks. The bottom line is, if you hold small-cap stocks, hold them as part of a portfolio.

### Tactical Trading

- Don't think about the stock as a stand-alone investment. Think about it in terms of your entire portfolio. In other words, don't view any specific sale in isolation, but rather in terms of how it affects your overall portfolio, which may lead you to look at the possibility of selling only part of your position. After all, no one said you have to sell an entire position.

# Lesson 9: Analyzing Securities—The Technical Way

## The Technical Analyst

- The real question, from the perspective of the technical analyst, is what do investors think about the company? In search of that information, technical analysts assess trading data to ascertain the ebb and flow and momentum of the market. The technician believes that by studying the past, one can make judgments about the future. Technicians believe that once a trend is defined, the trend will persist for an extended period.

## Support and Resistance

- Support defines a point at which the price of a stock or index stops declining and resumes its upward trend. In this case, there are more buyers than sellers.
- Resistance defines the point at which a security or index stops rising and begins to fall. In this case, there are more sellers than buyers.
- Technicians put a lot of emphasis on the point at which a security or index breaks through upside resistance or fails to hold downside support. Generally, when that happens, it signals a change in direction for the security or index.

## Pros and Cons of Technical Analysis

- Research studies have not been kind to the art of technical analysis, as little support for the method, at least as applied to stock selection, has been found. Still, technical analysis remains one of the best tools to assess buy-and-sell points. If you believe in the buy-and-hold philosophy, then technical analysis may not provide much help. On the other hand, there are valuable lessons to be learned from charts, and in some cases, being able to read a chart can help you steer clear of potential problems.

## Lesson 10: How to Invest Around the World

### Asset Allocation

- At the end of the day, you should strive to earn the most dollars with the least amount of risk in your investment portfolio. The best way of doing that is to add some global securities to your portfolio.

### Foreign Investing

- The bottom line is that a well-diversified portfolio will outperform a strictly Canadian one in the long run, based on both return and volatility.
- Foreign securities should represent about 10% to 30% of your holdings, and your strategy should be for the long term.

### Currency Exposure

- The reason to hold foreign currency bonds is to gain exposure to another currency—not to earn a higher rate of return.

## Lesson 11: Building Your Portfolio—Step by Step

### Market Timing

- The rewards of correctly timing the market are high, but as Nobel Prize-winner Paul Samuelson has pointed out, timing can be hazardous to your health and, we might add, to your pocketbook.

### Portfolio Review

- Regardless of the market's performance, you should give your portfolio a good review at least once a year—including a review of your objectives and your current asset mix.

## Portfolio Principles

- Invest for the long term. Make sure your investment horizon is sufficiently broad to capture a few market cycles and to allow the normal high return on equities to materialize.
- Concentrate on the mix of securities in your portfolio rather than on timing market cycles.
- Reinvest your dividends. Keep your investment growing with the double-barreled impact of capital growth and capital reinvestment.
- Make full use of all tax advantages. Make sure that you can make full use of the tax incentives granted for investing in equity securities. This generally means that you should hold growth funds outside your RRSP and other tax shelters to capture the full benefit of the dividend tax credit and the 25% exclusion for capital gains.
- Ignore short-term fluctuations.
- Don't watch the markets every day.
- Protect your portfolio against unexpected changes in exchange rates.
- Ensure that you have inflation protection.

## The Final Word

- Your choice of investments should reflect your long-term financial plan, your tastes, and your family needs.

# Glossary

**Active Investment:** An investment strategy based on the premise that securities may be under- or overvalued and that active security selection can add value.

**Advances and Declines:** The number of stocks advancing during the trading day, versus the number of stocks declining during the day.

**Advancing Stock:** A stock that is rising in value.

**Asset:** Something of monetary value. A current asset is liquid; a fixed asset is not.

**Asset Allocation:** The process by which an investor allocates financial resources across various financial assets, including cash, fixed income, equity, and real estate.

**Back-end Load:** The commission is paid by the fund company at the time of purchase. Investors pay the commission cost at the time they redeem the fund, unless they remain invested in the fund — or fund family — for a specific period of time; usually six years.

**Bank Rate:** The minimum rate of interest charged by the Bank of Canada when making short-term loans to the chartered banks.

**Banker's Acceptance:** A negotiable, short-term, time-draft used in international markets. Returns are usually higher than the going market price.

**Basis Point:** A financial term used to describe differences in bond yields. A basis point is 1/100th of a percentage point.

**Benchmark:** A passive index designed to gauge the performance of a security or asset class.

**Beta:** A measure of the response of the rate of return on an asset or a portfolio of assets to changes in the rate of return of the entire capital market.

**Blue Chip Companies:** The largest, most well-known companies with long records of solid earnings and regular dividend payments.

**Broker:** One who arranges the purchase and sale of assets; for example, a securities (stock) broker, a mortgage broker, etc. A broker does not buy or sell the asset, but simply brings buyers and sellers together.

**Bull Market:** A strong, positive growth cycle in the stock market.

**Business Cycle:** Short term, recurring fluctuations in the performance of the Canadian economy.

**Call Option:** An option that grants the holder the right to buy an underlying security at a specific price for a predetermined time period. The seller of a call option is obligated to deliver the underlying security – should the call option be exercised — to the call buyer at a set price for a predetermined time period.

**Canada Deposit Insurance Corporation(CDIC):** A government agency that guarantees currency deposits in approved financial institutions up to a maximum of $100,000.

**Canada Pension Plan(CPP):** A federally sponsored (except in Quebec) pension plan that requires mandatory contributions from salary or business income, and that guarantees a minimum monthly income for Canadians when they retire or are disabled.

**Canada Savings Bonds(CSBs):** Debt obligations issued by the federal government where the price is fixed at par, and interest rates are reset annually.

**Capital Gains (Losses):** The difference between the price one pays for a security and the value one receives when selling the security. When the price paid at the time of purchase is less than the value received at the time of sale, the investor has a capital gain. When the price paid at the time of purchase is greater than the value received at the time of sale, the investor has a capital loss.

**Capitalization Weighted Index:** An index whose value is calculated by multiplying the share price for each company by the total outstanding shares for that company. The result is expressed as a percentage of the average value during the base period.

**Cash Assets:** Any asset where there is no risk to the principal investment, and where that asset can be readily turned into cash within a short period of time, usually within 24 hours.

**Cash Flow:** A company's net income for a stated period of time, plus any deductions that are not actually paid out in cash. Such deductions could include depreciation, amortization, and deferred taxes.

**Common Shares:** The ownership shares of a corporation. Common shares have voting rights and share pro rata (proportionately) in the earnings of the corporation after all dividends have been paid to the preferred shareholders.

**Compound Interest:** Interest that is paid or received on interest accumulated from prior periods.

**Consumer Price Index:** A measurement tool used by the federal government. The cost of a specific "basket" of consumer goods is measured over time to determine the average consumer inflation rate from year to year.

**Convertible Bonds:** Bonds that can be converted at the option of the holder into a specified number of common shares of the underlying company.

**Corporate Bonds:** Bonds issued by companies where the interest rate is fixed and terms to maturity range from one to thirty years.

**Coupon:** The interest payment on a bond.

**Coupon Rate:** The interest rate payable as a percentage of the bond's face value.

**Correlation:** The degree of comovement between the price of two securities.

**Current Account Surplus:** The amount that annual government revenue exceeds annual government expenditures before interest expenses (see also Deficit and National Debt).

**Current Ratio:** Current assets divided by current liabilities; a measure of a firm's liquidity.

**Debit Cards:** Bank cards that allow you to pay for goods and services by simply debiting your bank account at the point of purchase.

**Debt-to-Equity Ratio:** Measures the amount of debt a company owes relative to the company's capitalization (see market capitalization).

**Declining Stock:** A stock that is falling in value.

**Deficit:** The annual difference between government revenues and government expenditures, including interest payments. When annual expenditures exceed revenues, the government is running a deficit (see also National Debt and Current Account Surplus).

**Defined Benefit Plan:** A pension plan in which retirement benefits are determined according to a fixed formula.

**Derivatives:** Financial arrangements between two parties whose payments are based on (derived from) the performance of some underlying asset or benchmark.

**Discount or Premium:** The difference between the price paid for an investment and the price received at maturity. An investment is said to be trading at a discount when the price paid is less than the price guaranteed at maturity. An investment whose purchase price is higher than the price guaranteed at maturity is said to be trading at a premium.

**Discount Broker:** A stock brokerage firm that will execute orders to buy and sell securities at a lower commission, but that does not normally provide investment advice.

**Discount Rate:** The rate used to calculate the present value of future cash flows.

**Diversification:** The process of allocating your investment portfolio over many investment classes and types in order to reduce exposure to specific sources of risk.

**Dividend:** A payment to shareholders from the earnings of the corporation. The dividend payout rate is the percentage of earnings paid out as dividends.

**Dividend Funds:** Mutual funds that invest in good quality common and preferred stocks that pay regular dividends.

**Dow Jones Industrial Average(DJIA):** An average of the prices of the shares of 30 blue chip companies traded on the New York Stock Exchange. The DJIA is widely followed as a barometer of the New York Stock Exchange's performance.

**Duration:** The average period required to repay a bond investment; the average life of a bond.

**Equity Mutual Funds:** Mutual funds that invest in stocks.

**Exchange Rate:** The price of one country's currency in terms of another country's currency.

**Financial Planners:** Professionals who design financial plans for individuals and companies, including issues such as tax planning, retirement planning, and estate planning. The Chartered Financial Planner (CFP) is one of the recognized professional designations for financial planners. Financial planners generally work from one of three basic compensation schemes: 1) commissions generated from products the planner sells (i.e., insurance products, mutual funds, etc.), 2) a fee-for-service arrangement, where costs are set as a fixed fee or hourly rate, or 3) a combination of fees and commissions.

**Fixed-income Assets:** Any asset that pays a fixed rate of interest for a specific period of time, and whose value is guaranteed at maturity.

**Front-end Load:** When the investor pays a commission to buy a fund at the time of purchase.

**Fundamental Analysis:** Security research designed to identify undervalued or overvalued securities based on fundamental financial factors such as the firm's liquidity, solvency and efficiency ratios, and its earnings and dividend prospects.

**Futures Contract:** A contract between two parties calling for future delivery of a commodity, cash flow, or other underlying asset at a prearranged rate or amount.

**GST:** Goods and Services Tax.

**Global or International Bond Funds:** Mutual funds that invest in bonds issued by foreign companies and/or foreign governments, denominated in a foreign currency, usually in U.S. dollars.

**Global Equity Funds:** Mutual funds that invest in shares of companies from around the world, including North America.

**Government Bonds:** Bonds issued by federal, provincial, or municipal governments, with a fixed rate of interest, and most with terms to maturity of between one and thirty years.

**Gross Domestic Product:** The total value of all goods and services produced in the Canadian economy over a specific time period.

**Growth Approach:** A fundamental stock valuation approach based on selecting stocks with high price/earnings multiples and strong growth prospects.

**Guaranteed Investment Certificates(GICs):** Interest bearing certificates issued by local financial institutions, that promise to pay a fixed interest payment and guarantee the return of principal at maturity. Average terms (there are exceptions) range from one to five years, and early redemption will usually result in financial penalties.

**HIPs:** HIPs (or Toronto 100 Index Participation Units) are publicly traded units that represent a basket of the shares that comprise the Toronto 100 Index. The units trade at 1/10th the value of the index.

**High-Low-Close:** A chart used by technicians, where each plot defines a stock's high, low, and closing price.

**Index of Coincident Economic Indicators:** Economic indicators that tend to move up or down at the same time as changes in the business cycle.

**Index of Lagging Economic Indicators:** Economic indicators that tend to lag changes in the performance of the Canadian business cycle.

**Index Mutual Funds:** Mutual funds whose portfolio is invested in common shares in proportion to their representation in a market index such as the TSE 300 Composite Index.

**Inflation:** The increase in the costs of goods and services, measured by changes in the consumer price index.

**Initial Public Offering (IPO):** The first time the stock of a formerly private company is sold to the public.

**Interest Income:** Money paid by a borrower to a lender.

**Interest Rate:** The rate of interest charged by the lender and paid by the borrower.

**Interest Rate Parity:** The theory that the differential between forward and spot exchange rates is equal to the differential between foreign and domestic interest rates.

**International Equity Funds:** Mutual funds that invest in shares of companies from around the world, excluding North America.

**Internal Rate of Return (for a bond):** The discount rate, normally expressed on an annual basis, at which a bond has a zero net present value. It is equivalent to the yield-to-maturity.

**Large-Cap Companies:** Companies whose market capitalization is more than $1 billion (see market capitalization).

**Load:** The commission costs of buying a fund (see Front-end and Back-end Load).

**Leveraged Buyout:** Buying the shares of a company by using borrowed funds to acquire the firm's common shares.

**Liquidity:** A measure of how quickly an investor can dispose of a security at close to the market price.

**Margin:** The amount paid by an investor in acquiring a security, usually expressed as a percentage of the security's purchase price.

**Market Capitalization:** The total market value of a company, computed as the price per share multiplied by the number of shares outstanding. A company with 10 million shares outstanding whose price per share is $10 would have a market capitalization of $100 million.

**Market Sentiment Indicators:** Indicators that measure the bullish or bearish sentiment of investors. Examples are odd lot trading indexes (measures the ratio of odd lot purchases to odd lot sales) and advance/decline ratios (measures the number of advancing stocks to declining stocks).

**Market Timing:** An investment strategy where one moves in and out of particular sectors or individual stocks attempting to profit by selling high and buying low.

**Market Value of a Security:** The price of a security based on the consensus opinion of buyers and sellers.

**Maturity Date:** The date at which the borrower repays the principal investment – plus any outstanding interest — to the lender.

**Management Expense Ratio (MER):** The total costs borne by the fund, including management fees and commissions, divided by the total assets.

**Mid-Cap Companies:** Companies whose market capitalization is more than $500 million but less than $1 billion (see market capitalization).

**Money Market Funds:** Mutual funds whose portfolio is invested in money market securities. Money market securities include Treasury Bills, and are short-term highly liquid securities.

**Moving Average:** Calculated by adding the closing values of a stock (or index) over a period of time, and then dividing by the time period. A moving average smooths out the short-term fluctuations in the value of a security helping to establish that security's long-term trend.

**Mutual Fund:** A company that invests in securities using money raised from selling shares to individual investors. The company offers its organizational, managerial and investment skills to the investor for a fixed fee per year.

**National Debt:** The total amount of money owed by the federal government (see Deficit and Current Account Surplus).

**New York Stock Exchange Composite Index:** A capitalization weighted index of the price of all the common shares listed on the New York Stock Exchange (see Capitalization Weighted Index).

**North American Free Trade Agreement (NAFTA):** An agreement between the US, Canada, and Mexico, that generally allows for the duty-free movement of goods and services across borders.

**Net Asset Value Per Share(NAVPS):** The total assets of the fund divided by the outstanding shares that have been issued by the fund. A fund that has $1 million in assets and has issued 100,000 shares would have a net asset value per share of $10.

**Open-End Funds:** Mutual funds that sell shares directly to investors, and redeem shares directly from investors.

**Par Value:** The face value of the bond that is guaranteed at maturity.

**Passive Investing:** An investment strategy based on the premise that markets are efficient.

**Preferred Shares:** Shares in a corporation that pay a fixed or variable dividend. Preferred shares are typically non-voting and do not share in the earnings of the company over and above the stated dividend.

**Premium:** (See Discount Premium.)

**Present Value:** The discounted value of a series of cash flows.

**Price/Book Ratio:** The ratio of a stock's market price to its book value.

**Price/Dividend Ratio:** The ratio of a stock's market price to its dividends per share.

**Price/Earnings (P/E) Ratio or Price/Earnings (P/E) Multiple:** The ratio of a stock's market price to its earnings per share.

**Principal:** The amount of the investor's capital placed at risk, or the face value of a bond at maturity.

**Put Option:** An option that grants the holder the right to sell an underlying security at a specific price for a predetermined time period. The seller of a put option is obligated to buy the underlying security – should the put option be exercised – at a set price for a predetermined time period.

**Put-to-Call Ratio:** The number of put options traded divided by the number of call options traded during a trading day. The daily ratio is usually compared to a moving average, and trades are implemented when extreme readings occur.

**Rate of Return:** The total percentage return from an investment, including income and capital gains.

**Registered Retirement Savings Plan (RRSP):** A tax-sheltered investment plan. The contributions to the plan are tax deductible, and the income, dividends and capital gains realized within the plan, are not taxed until the plan matures.

**Registered Retirement Income Fund (RRIF):** A tax-sheltered plan. An investor can transfer the proceeds of a matured RRSP into a RRIF and avoid paying income taxes on the matured RRSP proceeds. Income taxes are paid as the proceeds from the RRIF are received.

**Rental Income:** Income received from rental properties.

**Reserve Requirement:** The percentage of a bank's assets that must be retained in cash (including Government of Canada Treasury Bills, overnight paper, etc.) at all times. The reserve requirement is set by the Bank of Canada.

**Resistance:** The price at which technicians expect more sellers than buyers to enter the market.

**Risk-adjusted Basis:** Determines the performance of an investment after adjusting for risk.

**Rule of 72:** By dividing an investment's rate of return into 72, investors can determine how long, in years, it will take for their money to double.

**Short Selling:** The sale of shares that an investor does not own. The seller borrows the shares and maintains a cash balance as margin for the short position. At a later date the seller buys back the shares, realizing a gain if the price has dropped since the sale or a loss if the price has risen.

**Simple Interest:** Interest calculated on the principal investment only.

**Small-Cap Companies:** Companies whose market capitalization is less than $500 million (see market capitalization).

**Specialty Mutual Funds:** Mutual funds that invest in specific sectors of the economy, i.e., precious metals funds, resource funds, science and technology funds.

**Standard & Poor's 500 Composite Index:** A capitalization weighted index of the price of the shares of 500 large- and mid-cap U.S. companies (see Capitalization Weighted Index).

**Standard & Poor's Depository Receipts (SPDRs):** Publicly traded units that represent a basket of the shares that comprise the Standard & Poor's 500 Composite Index. The units trade at 1/10th the value of the index.

**Stockbroker:** An individual who is licensed to buy and sell securities for a commission.

**Strip Bond:** A bond that pays no coupons, sells at a discount, and matures at face value.

**Support:** The price at which technicians expect more buyers than sellers to enter the market.

**Tactical Trading:** Trading in securities in an attempt to predict changes in the economic cycle. A tactical trader predicting a recession and stock market slide would switch from stocks into money market securities.

**Technical Analysis:** Security research designed to identify undervalued or overvalued securities based on historic stock price patterns and market sentiment indicators.

**Term Deposits:** Deposits that have a specified term to maturity made at financial institutions.

**TIPs:** TIPs (or Toronto 35 Index Participation Units) are publicly traded units that represent a basket of the shares that comprise the Toronto 35 Index. The units trade at 1/10th the value of the index.

**Toronto 35 Index:** A capitalization weighted index of the price of the shares of the 35 largest companies traded on the Toronto Stock Exchange (see Capitalization Weighted Index).

**TSE 300 Composite Index:** A capitalization weighted index of the price of the shares of 300 companies traded on the Toronto Stock Exchange (see Capitalization Weighted Index).

**Trailer Fee:** An ongoing annual fee paid by the fund company to the financial advisor as compensation for managing the relationship with the client.

**Treasury Bill:** A short-term, highly liquid (maturities are one year or less) government security. It is issued at a discount and matures at face value. The difference between the maturity value and the issue price is treated as interest for tax purposes.

**U.S. Federal Reserve:** The U.S. Central Bank, similar to the Bank of Canada.

**U.S. Treasury Securities:** Bonds issued by the U.S. government. Treasury securities maturing in less than 10 years are conventionally called Treasury Notes; those maturing in 10 years or more are called Treasury Bonds.

**Value Line Composite Index:** An equally weighted index of 1,700 stocks that measures performance in terms of each stock's percentage price change.

**Warrants:** Options that provide the holder with the right to buy a specified number of common shares at a specified price within a specified period of time.

**Yield:** The investor's expected cash flow from an investment. Current yield on a bond is the annual interest paid on a bond divided by the current price of the bond.

**Yield-to-Maturity:** The yield, normally expressed on an annual basis, that the investor expects to realize by holding a bond to maturity.

**Value Approach:** A fundamental stock valuation approach based on selecting stocks with low price/earnings multiples and low price/book values.

**Worldwide Equity Benchmarks (WEBs):** Publicly traded units that represent a basket of the shares that comprise various market indexes.

# Index